PSYCHOANALYTIC PSYCHOTHERAPY

Theory, Technique, Therapeutic Relationship
and Treatability

OTHER BOOKS BY DR. PAOLINO:

PAOLINO, T. J., JR., and McCRADY, B. S. (1977) *The Alcoholic Marriage*: *Alternative Perspectives*. New York: Grune and Stratton.

PAOLINO, T. J., JR. and McCRADY, B. S. (Eds.) (1978) *Marriage and Marital Therapy*: *Psychoanalytic, Behavioral and Systems Theory Perspectives*. New York: Brunner/Mazel.

Psychoanalytic Psychotherapy

Theory, Technique, Therapeutic Relationship and Treatability

by

THOMAS J. PAOLINO, Jr., M.D.

*Director of Clinical Services and Co-director of Psychiatric
Residency Training, Department of Psychiatry,
The Cambridge Hospital, Cambridge, Massachusetts;
Assistant Professor of Psychiatry,
Harvard Medical School;
Advanced Candidate,
Boston Psychoanalytic Society and Institute,
Boston, Massachusetts*

BRUNNER/MAZEL, *Publishers* • New York

Library of Congress Cataloging in Publication Data

Paolino, Thomas J   1940-
  Psychoanalytic psychotherapy.

  Bibliography: p.
  Includes index.
  1. Psychotherapy.   2. Psychoanalysis.   I. Title.
[DNLM: 1. Psychoanalytic therapy.   WM 460.6 P211p]
RC480.5.P296   616.89'17   80-28659
ISBN 0-87630-261-4

Copyright © 1981 by THOMAS J. PAOLINO, JR.

Published by
BRUNNER/MAZEL, INC.
19 Union Square
New York, New York 10003

*This book is dedicated
with deepest love
to ANNE, my wife
and best friend.*

Techniques without theory are blind,
and theory without technique is empty.
—KANT QUOTED BY EKSTEIN, 1956

FOREWORD

Psychoanalysis and psychoanalytic psychotherapy are currently being challenged by new forms of individual and group treatment which seek to shorten the course of therapy, or which introduce new techniques for achieving therapeutic change. Some of these therapies, like psychoanalytic group psychotherapy, draw heavily upon psychoanalytic concepts, while others, such as holistic healing methods, are more closely linked to eastern and western religious traditions. These other treatment approaches are often experienced as more in keeping with the technological and cultural changes of the '70s and '80s, especially the recent emphasis on directness and immediacy of experience, and are attracting many patients or "participants" who might have sought psychoanalytic treatment but a few years ago.

In the light of these changes psychoanalysts and psychoanalytically oriented clinicians, who once were considered pioneers in the treatment of mental and emotional disturbances and in exploring uncharted regions of the mind, are now perceived as conservatives, clinging to traditional and at times outmoded models of the mind and treatment approaches. There are two basic ways that psychoanalysts can respond to these challenges. One way, a "purist" approach, would be to narrow the definition of what are truly psychoanalytic concepts and to distinguish sharply psychoanalysis from other psychotherapies which draw upon its principles. The other response would be to consider psychoanalysis to be an evolving body of knowledge about human mental and emotional processes, with a range of clinical techniques available for their exploration and understanding. Those who follow the second approach would begin with the concepts central to psychoanalysis, such as the operation of a dynamic unconscious and the power of psychic determinism, and build upon these in extending clinical knowledge and/or developing new treatment techniques.

In this work Paolino demonstrates that he belongs in the second group. He distinguishes clinicians who separate sharply psychoanalysis and psychoanalytic psychotherapy from those who regard these treatment techniques on a continuum, both deriving from psychoanalytic concepts and treatment principles. By placing himself in the second group Paolino is able to provide a basic text, both clear and yet sophisticated, for the many clinicians who might not necessarily be formally trained as psychoanalysts but are practicing psychotherapy based on psychoanalytic principles.

Paolino has selected the therapeutic relationship for his central focus. Psychoanalysis and psychoanalytic psychotherapy are not static or mechanistic treatment exercises. Therapeutic change is the outcome of an active, dynamic, often creative, at times idiosyncratic, relationship between two people who make a deep commitment to each other. Before we can understand the process of personal growth that takes place in the context of this relationship, it is necessary to have a much fuller appreciation of its multiple dimensions.

The treatment relationship is not quite like any other human attachment. In an attempt to distinguish its several facets Dr. Paolino has designated four principal components of the therapeutic relationship: the transference, the therapeutic alliance, the narcissistic alliance and the real relationship. Another writer might have made a somewhat different division. What is of special value in Paolino's work is his recognition of the complexity and multivaried nature of the treatment relationship, which has tended at times to be viewed two-dimensionally as "the transference and the therapeutic alliance" or "the transference and the real relationship."

The patient brings a variety of needs and expectations to the treatment relationship. This relationship creates the context for therapeutic change as well as becoming its agent. The patient carries in his mind conscious and unconscious representations of the past and of objects from the past, which he recreates in the present in his experience of the therapist (transference). He requires that the person in whom he is making such a profound investment, one in which he will experience considerable vulnerability, be someone upon whom he can rely, with whom he can feel a bond of trust and confidence (therapeutic alliance). At the same time as this alliance forms, the patient will seek to create the therapist as part of himself, to perform for him coping and defensive functions, to complete his psychological organization or substitute for elements in his personality structure (narcissistic alliance). Lastly, the therapist exists for the patient as a new object, a person with whom he relates "in his own right" (the real relationship).

Therapeutic change can range from small gains in the form of symptom relief, improved self-confidence or better management of one's personal life, to radical transformations of character or of the quality of life. It is extraordinarily difficult to sort out the relative contributions made to the achievement of such change that is the result of the therapeutic work from that which grows out of extra-therapeutic influences. Furthermore, to understand the processes of change, the contributions that are the direct result of the treatment *relationship* need to be distinguished from those in which the therapist functions as an enabler or facilitator of change through insight or other forces which bring about personal growth and emotional freedom. This problem has troubled theorists for several decades. Before it can be meaningfully approached the several dimensions of the therapist's role need better to be delineated. Paolino's book makes an important contribution to our understanding of these processes.

Dr. Paolino's detailed examination of the therapeutic relationship also contributes to our understanding of the nature of therapeutic dependency. As he shows so clearly, especially in the discussion of the concepts of the narcissistic alliance and secondary trust, the dimensions of dependency extend beyond familiar notions of support and trust. They also include the therapist's participation in the basic organization or structure of the patient's personality. This aspect of the therapeutic attachment points to the basic interdependence of all human relationships and to the relativist quality of the idea of ego autonomy, for self-governance always depends to a degree upon the active role played by the internal guidance of the voices of others, not merely left over from the past, but as actively present agencies in the contemporary context of the patient's life.

The long concluding chapter on "treatability" is really far more than that. It is a comprehensive discussion of diagnostic assessment as this relates to treatability and to treatment strategies and techniques. It contains a penetrating examination of the strengths and vulnerabilities, such as the capacity or incapacity to bear painful affects, that will determine treatment goals and, possibly, the therapeutic outcome.

I feel certain that the reader will complete this book feeling rewarded, but also in one sense frustrated. We are left wanting to go on, to see how the parts of the engine for change that is the therapeutic relationship will actually work once the treatment adventure is begun. Perhaps Dr. Paolino will take us on this journey in his future work.

JOHN E. MACK, M.D.
Professor of Psychiatry
Harvard Medical School at
The Cambridge Hospital

ACKNOWLEDGMENTS

I would like to acknowledge my gratitude to the numerous friends, colleagues and teachers on the staffs of The Cambridge Hospital Department of Psychiatry and The Cambridge-Somerville Mental Health and Retardation Center and on the faculties of the Harvard Medical School and the Boston Psychoanalytic Society and Institute, Inc. Many of these people have read and commented on various parts of this manuscript, have encouraged me to continue my work on it, and have created the working and scholarly environment that has made this book possible.

I am especially grateful to Lee Macht, Professor and Chairman, Department of Psychiatry, Harvard Medical School at The Cambridge Hospital, for his friendship, encouragement, visionary leadership and unselfish protection of my time from numerous other duties so that I would have time to work on this manuscript. I am deeply indebted to John Mack, George Vaillant, and the Clinical Chiefs of The Cambridge Hospital Department of Psychiatry for their guidance, friendship, support and representation of clinical and academic excellence and honesty. I am very grateful to Michael Greene for his wise advice and constant support. I am thankful to Robert Mehlman and Suzanne vanAmerongen, the two people who, of all the fine teachers I have had, have taught me the most about sitting with a patient in psychoanalytic psychotherapy.

There are not words to express my gratitude to my own analyst, Rolf Arvidson, the person most responsible for my appreciation of the human dimension in psychoanalytic therapy and the inestimable value of the therapeutic relationship as a vehicle for resolving intrapsychic problems.

I would like to emphasize that, despite my indebtedness, none of the people mentioned above will agree with all of what I have said in this book and should not be held responsible for any part of it.

This manuscript could not have been completed without my being fortunate enough to have outstanding secretarial help represented by Nancy Christopulos, Pearl Levy and Kathy Canessa. I am also thankful to Susan Zuckerman for her thorough reading of an earlier version of the entire manuscript and for her invaluable editorial recommendations, many of which were incorporated.

I would like to acknowledge my wife, Anne, my children, Pia, TJ and Tara, my parents, Thomas and Florence Paolino and my wife's parents, Hans and Ruth Lang. It seems to me that a book representing the work that is so important to me should somewhere contain the names of these people who are much more important to me.

Finally, a special debt is owed to my patients and students who have granted me the privilege of working with them and have inspired me to write this book.

CONTENTS

PSYCHOANALYTIC PSYCHOTHERAPY
Theory, Technique, Therapeutic Relationship and Treatability

CHAPTER 1

INTRODUCTION

1.1 Purpose and Overview of Book

This book is intended to facilitate the observation of relevant clinical material that presents itself among a variety of otherwise disconnective variables. An attempt has been made to put into words what many psychoanalytic therapists have been doing for years, often take for granted and often refer to as self-explanatory.

This volume is directed toward the psychoanalytic therapist who 1) struggles with the clinical problems of an active psychoanalytic psychotherapy practice, 2) relies on current psychoanalytic understanding and working hypotheses, and 3) is willing, in accordance with clinical observations, to undergo reexamination and revision of theory and technique within the psychoanalytic framework. It is written primarily for psychiatrists, Ph.D. and Masters degree clinical psychologists, psychiatric social workers, advanced degree psychiatric nurses and clinical students, such as psychiatric residents, psychology interns, medical students, social work students and advanced degree nursing students, all of whom may be delivering and learning their various forms of psychological therapy in mental and community health agencies, community clinics and private practice offices. Although the target readership is the clinician, nonclinical students of psychology may also benefit from the variety of theoretical concepts described that do not require clinical experience to be understood. Since an attempt has been made to reference the literature comprehensively, the clinical researcher may benefit from this volume, and the liberal referencing may be of use to the reader who wishes to further pursue these concepts in the psychoanalytic literature.

Chapter 1 introduces the volume to the reader by presenting the purpose and overview of the book as well as discussing the need for theory and definitions, and acknowledging the inexactness of psychoanalytic theory as a science. The chapter concludes with a brief discussion of the capacities that are essential in order to be a clinically successful psychoanalytic therapist.

Chapter 2 discusses the differences and similarities between classical psychoanalysis and other forms of psychoanalytically oriented psychotherapy. This subject is presented by comparing and contrasting the "Sharp Difference" and "Blurred Difference" perspectives as they relate to techniques, transference, and goals of therapy. Chapter 2 also includes a definition of the term "psychoanalytic psychotherapy" and a discussion of how the term is used throughout the book. This volume's modified "Blurred Difference" approach is a highly controversial point of view, so many classical psychoanalysts will strongly disagree with the failure to identify psychoanalysis as a distinct treatment modality.

Chapter 3 includes a discussion of some essential principles of psychoanalytic psychotherapy. These principles comprise the working hypotheses and operating assumptions that are presupposed by any therapist employing psychoanalytic psychotherapy. It is necessary to delineate these concepts at the outset of the book since psychoanalytic psychotherapy is the means by which we apply the basic principles. While space limitations make a detailed discussion impossible, a highly selective discussion of a few of the most essential principles that should be solidly understood by any student or practitioner of psychoanalytic psychotherapy is presented.

Chapter 4 discusses the therapeutic relationship, which is conceptualized as consisting of four components: transference, therapeutic alliance, narcissistic alliance and real relationship. Although there is considerable overlap, each of the four components of the therapeutic relationship can be distinguished from the others, and all four components must be fully recognized and utilized by the therapist for the psychoanalytic psychotherapy to be successful.

The discussion of therapeutic relationship does not conceptualize therapeutic alliance and basic trust in the usual psychoanalytic way, as promoted by Elizabeth Zetzel (1956, 1970) and her followers. For example, Zetzel conceptualizes the therapeutic alliance as essentially equivalent to "basic trust." Chapter 4 will promote a different model that distinguishes basic trust from "secondary trust" and includes the concept of "narcissistic alliance" (Mehlman, 1976, 1977) as a necessary component for a successful psychoanalytic psychotherapy and as a phenomenon often confused with "transference cure." Furthermore, the "real relationship" will be presented as a component of equal importance to the other three. The emphasis on the real relationship is in contrast to the writings and teachings of many, but certainly not all, psychoanalysts and psychoanalytically oriented psychotherapists.

Chapter 5 deals with the issue of assessing treatability and its relationship to the basic concepts of psychotherapeutic process. Treatability is discussed by dividing relevant concepts into two major groups: 1) those aspects that can be pre-analytically assessed, and 2) those aspects of treatability that cannot be adequately assessed until treatment has begun. The categorization model presented entails a complete literature review of the subject of treatability for psychoanalytic psychotherapy (as psychoanalytic psychotherapy is defined in Chapter 2). In essence, then, a literature review of treatability comprises a literature review of "analyzability."

Throughout this book clinical examples are used for clarification. All clinical examples come from my own patient work or from cases of therapists whom I have supervised. All clinical examples are, of course, appropriately disguised.

1.2 AUTHOR BIAS

No book can totally avoid author bias, especially when the material involves the subject of psychic functioning and human behavior, a relatively imprecise body of knowledge that is not well tested empirically. I have made no attempt to appear to the reader as nonpartisan since I do, in fact, have some rather strong opinions. My bias is that the hallmark of well-being is awareness of one's psychic and bodily self. Furthermore, I believe that psychoanalytic psychotherapy as defined here is the most potent of psychotherapeutic instruments by which we can elicit a fundamental and relatively permanent and stable alteration of personality structure and eradication or significant reduction of painful psychological processes. The psychoanalytic psychotherapy will not be useful to the patient, however, unless the following three conditions are met: 1) the therapist has the capacities mentioned in Section 1.5 as well as proper training and knowledge of the essential principles (some of which are discussed in Chapter 3); 2) the therapist has the deepest respect for, is fully aware of, and actively utilizes the therapeutic relationship (discussed in Chapter 4); 3) the patient is appropriately selected for this particular treatment modality (see Chapter 5).

My bias by no means represents prejudice toward other responsible treatment modalities. The prejudice that I do have, and that is reflected by the very fact of the writing of this book, is against the delivery of psychotherapeutic techniques of any kind that are not based on a well-thought-out model of psychic functioning and human behavior. The therapist's operational model should be based on knowledge and clinical observations as well as the capacity to be in touch with his or her own psychic and bodily self.

Although this book is on psychoanalytic psychotherapy, I want to emphasize my conviction that a variety of other types of therapy may be more useful to some patients (for example, see Karasu 1977; Paolino and McCrady 1977, 1978). A discussion of the indications for choosing various forms of nonpsychoanalytic psychotherapy are beyond the scope of this volume. The clinician who has a solid knowledge of indications and contraindications of psychoanalytic psychotherapy is on the way to being equipped to determine when the nonpsychoanalytic psychotherapy is indicated. Of course, the clinician will not be completely equipped until familiarized with the indications and contraindications for other legitimate treatment modalities founded on drastically different theoretical frameworks, such as behavior therapy, psychotropic medication, interactional therapy, group therapy, the various nonpsychoanalytic forms of marital and family therapy, the emotive therapies and others. The psychotherapist can no longer feel reassured by the preposterous belief that, whether or not the patient is treatable, psychoanalytic psychotherapy is at least worth a try since no other therapy is better; any clinician who holds this assumption is destined for repeated disappointments. Freud's words are still valid: "There are many ways and means of practicing psychotherapy. All that lead to recovery are good" (1904, p. 259).

1.3 THE NEED FOR THEORY AND DEFINITIONS

The attempt to include some theory associated with the process of psychoanalytic psychotherapy and to define terms before discussing them certainly accounts for much of the length of this book. It is, of course, only through our techniques that ". . . the pure metal of valuable unconscious thoughts . . . can . . . be extracted from the raw material of the patient's associations" (Freud, 1905, p. 112). While not minimizing the

value of technique, we must acknowledge that psychoanalytic psychotherapy is more than merely a technique. The psychoanalytic approach
encompasses a profound psychological theory that attempts a comprehensive explanation of both normal and abnormal human behavior. One of
the greatest strengths of psychoanalytic therapy is that its theory of psychic
functioning and psychotherapeutic process is closely interwoven with the
techniques of the therapist. Technique is implemented to elicit data, the
organization of which is facilitated by the theory (unless, of course, the
theory is invalid, in which case the theory should be discarded). Valid
theory in turn promotes an understanding of the effectiveness of the
techniques.

> One can here speak not of a vicious circle constantly creating new
> difficulties, but rather of a benign circle of a mutual and beneficial
> influence of practice upon the theory and the theory upon the
> practice (Ferenczi & Rank, 1925, p. 47).

When there is a lack of integration between technique and theory,
both suffer. An adherence to faulty technique will inevitably lead to
incorrect theoretical concepts. Furthermore, incorrect theory often results
in costly technical mistakes.

Psychoanalytic theory is encumbered by many concepts that, unfortunately, are capable of many subdivisions, and each subdivision has
been assigned in the literature an inconsistent diversity of definitions,
references, and levels of abstraction. The consequence of this "semantic
jungle of psychoanalytic theory" (Zinberg, 1963, p. 811) is that many
psychoanalytic terms have lost most, if not all, of their original or intended meaning. Frequently, an apparent discrepancy between two
authors, or between author and reader, is merely the consequence of
different definitions and could have been eliminated by a greater pre-
cision in the use or definition of words. Very often, readers cannot fully
understand a psychoanalytic writer unless they are fortunate enough to
be able to infer from the context which usage the author follows. The
need and value of exact definitions were well expressed by Stanley Cobb:

> If terms could be defined before every meeting of psychiatrists [and
> every manuscript] and the definitions adhered to by these speakers
> and discussors [and authors], much waste of time and printing could
> be avoided (Cobb, quoted by Reid & Finesinger, 1952, p. 413).

The many definitions and subsequent discussions and clarifications of the definitions in some ways give this book the characteristics of a dictionary. The definitions are an attempt to facilitate communication between author and reader and to make my reasoning more systematic and precise.

Because of space limitations, the concepts discussed throughout this volume are at times unavoidably abbreviated or simplistic. Those abbreviated presentations result in the psychoanalytic concepts being, at times, removed of their complexities and subtleties while at the same time making it appear that the roles of the body and the external environment are ignored. Nevertheless, the infinite complexities of human life should not discourage us from attempting to cognitively and rationally isolate some of the basic principles that form the foundation from which therapeutic techniques evolve. If not too great a sacrifice of truth is made, it is of value to attempt relatively simple formulations and to minimize the numerous complicated, obscure attempts to explain the underlying principles of psychoanalytic therapy.

1.4 PSYCHOANALYTIC THEORY AS AN INEXACT SCIENCE

Let us keep in mind then what the scientist strives for. Science attempts to find approximations of truth about ourselves and the world in which we live. It depends upon: (a) methods of gathering empirical data; (b) methods of testing the degree to which these data conform to external realities, thus establishing approximate "facts"; (c) methods of interpreting causal relationships between such approximate facts; and finally (d) methods of testing the accuracy of these interpretations by predictions of future events. Ultimately science can accept nothing as valid until it is supported by evidence of this general nature. It would seem to be a logically inescapable deduction from the scientific axioms that psychoanalysis [psychoanalytic psychotherapy] will not become an exact science until some less subjective method than interpretations will be found for making articulate the relationship between conscious and unconscious processes (Kubie, 1952, p. 75).

Psychoanalytic theory as a body of knowledge about human behavior and as a treatment of psychological disorders must be considered an inexact science founded on a literature that is lacking in substantial empirical research. This in turn has resulted in a lack of psychoanalytic parameters that are empirically measurable. Some of the obstacles to empirical research are social and political and thus relatively correctable (Engel, 1968). Others are the result of inherent, perhaps unavoidable, components of the treatment and theory itself (Kubie, 1947, 1952). The psychoanalytic movement's attempt (or should I say lack of attempt?) to do empirical research continues to reflect the inability to solve the perhaps unresolvable problem of applying a scientific method without diluting the clinical aspects of the independent variable. So far, test instruments that attempt to quantify the human factors associated with psychoanalytic psychotherapy are confined to those variables that are conscious, relatively available and easily verbalized. Such instruments fail to measure accurately the involved parameters. In addition, they tend to 1) restrict the resources of the clinical observer; 2) suggest underestimations of the complexities of psychic functioning and human behavior; and 3) minimize the importance of the individual (Schafer, 1958).

1.5 THE CAPACITY TO BE A PSYCHOANALYTIC THERAPIST

The task of psychotherapy as a means to relieve human suffering is a task that, although loaded with emotional hazards, is indeed a great privilege to perform. Sharpe's words about psychoanalysis apply to all psychotherapy:

> . . . I personally find the enrichment of my ego through the experiences of other people not the least of satisfactions. From the limited confines of an individual life, limited in time and space and environment, I experience a rich variety of living through my work. I contact all sorts and kinds of living, all imaginable circumstances, human tragedy and human comedy, humour and dourness, the pathos of the defeated, and the incredible endurances and victories that some souls achieve over human fate. Perhaps what makes me most glad that I chose to be a psychoanalyst is the rich variety of every type of human experience that has become part of me, which never would have been mine either to experience or to understand in a single mortal life, but for my work (Sharpe, 1947, p. 6).

The complete mastery of psychoanalytic psychotherapy is largely unteachable and can only be achieved if the therapist possesses certain fundamental qualifications. No amount of reading can make up for deficiencies in these areas, and all any book can do is provide some useful supplement to these qualifications. I believe that the following seven qualifications, while not sufficient, are absolutely essential: 1) An extensive clinical experience as a psychoanalytic psychotherapist. 2) The subjective experience of being a patient in psychoanalytic therapy. 3)

Integrity, a sincere desire to help people and a respect for the dignity of the patient. 4) A relative freedom from intrapsychic and environmental conflicts that may lead to behavior that is detrimental to the treatment, such as biased judgments about how people should behave. 5) The capacity to listen with "neutrality" (see Section 2.4311), i.e., the therapist must have the attitude that the meaning that the therapist ascribes to a specific mental or environmental event is not necessarily the meaning that the patient ascribes to the same event. 6) The capacity for psychoanalytic empathy. This kind of empathy must not be confused with the usual use of the word. Empathy by the psychoanalytic therapist requires a special capacity that is far more than feeling sad for the person or being pleasant, tolerant and agreeable.

> True sympathy [empathy] enables the therapist to look through the patient's false front. It is easy to recognize the deceptions of a bad actor who tries to express emotions that are not really his own. It is much more difficult to understand unconscious emotional distortions beyond the volition and grasp of the patient who has become the slave of defensive habits. His false front is a powerful protection against a panic that might transiently overthrow his rationalizations and self-control (Weigert, 1961, p. 193).

7) The capacity to liberate oneself from the confines of the intellect and to experience deeply within one's psychological and bodily self the intensity of feelings and excitement generated within the therapeutic relationship. Although the therapeutic relationship does not *behaviorally* extend into a social or sexual realm, the therapist must have the capacity to *psychically* experience the full range of interpersonal emotions and bodily feelings and, in many ways, to be as exposed to the patient as the patient is exposed to the therapist.

> Anything less, and the patient must stop abortively; he cannot move past the limitations of the therapist's vision, the limitations of the therapist's soul (Olsen, 1977, p. 147).

Singer (1970), in a brilliant exposition on this subject, shows how these capacities are seen in normal children. Some examples of such childlike capacities are creative imagination, flexibility, fearlessness of uncertainty, and fearlessness of lack of structure. Singer goes on to say that we must not confuse childlikeness with childishness, and that all therapists must try to achieve for themselves the "maturity of the child" (p. 71). Sometimes this seventh capacity is called "connectedness" or "listening with the third ear" or "intuitive empathy" or "being with the paitent" or similar phrases. Whatever concepts or metaphors we use to describe this capacity, it is the capacity of the therapist to reach down into his most intimate inner self and to listen with his own mental and physical being in order to grasp fully and share the message that the patient is trying to communicate.*

---

* The words "his," "he," "himself," etc. will be used throughout this book for the purposes of linguistic convenience.

CHAPTER 2

SIMILARITIES AND DIFFERENCES BETWEEN PSYCHOANALYSIS AND PSYCHOANALYTIC PSYCHOTHERAPY

2.1 INTRODUCTION

My goal in this Section is to familiarize the reader with some of the conceptual and practical issues surrounding the controversy of similarities and differences between psychoanalysis and psychoanalytic psychotherapy and to establish the definition of "psychoanalytic psychotherapy" to be used here. Once established, the reader is asked to keep this definition and perspective in mind. The definition of psychoanalytic psychotherapy, as the term will be used throughout this book, is very similar to what some people would call "psychoanalysis" except this book's definition does not use technical criteria to identify the treatment. This operational definition allows me to reference, in many instances, both the psychoanalytic and psychotherapy literature in developing discussions.

2.2 SOME BASIC DEFINITIONS

Before proceeding with our discussion of similarities between psychoanalysis and psychoanalytic psychotherapy, some basic definitions may be helpful. Throughout this book terms are often defined before they are related to the concepts of a specific discussion. These definitions are intended to first establish the subject within a broad category and then localize it by the use of relatively explicit differentiating attributes. Whenever possible, definitions have been operationalized by integrating them with the psychoanalytic process itself. *Throughout the book the various terms are used in strict accordance with the definitions presented.* Occa-

12

sionally terms are used in a way that does not follow the definition presented, but in each case the context makes clear the meaning of the term.

2.21 *Psychotherapy*

Psychotherapy is as old as medicine itself and is one of the few endeavors in life where science, art and creativity join together in everyday practice (Greenson, 1966), although it is perhaps the least likely of medical treatments to receive credit for being founded on a rational and scientific basis. Psychotherapy can be broadly defined as a profoundly human caring and mutually trusting relationship between two people, one ("patient" or "client") suffering from a psychical problem and another ("therapist") who has the training, skills and motivation to alleviate that suffering through some conscious verbal and nonverbal interaction with the patient. Psychotherapy is aimed at modifying thoughts and feelings in a way that the patient is relatively aware of as a therapeutic process. The interaction between the therapist and the patient is based on the therapist's systematic knowledge of psychic functioning and human behavior that is the result of the therapist's structural observation and reasoning. Strictly speaking psychotherapy does not cure patients. Instead, psychotherapy (or at least psychodynamic psychotherapy) is founded on the basic principle that the capacity for cure lies within each patient provided the psychotherapy can remove the obstacles to normal psychic growth and mental functioning. The "modifying of thoughts and feelings" distinguishes psychotherapy from other treatments of psychic problems such as educational procedures, which provide information rather than modifying psychic processes. The presence of verbal interventions distinguishes psychotherapy from nonverbal procedures such as electroconvulsive treatment (ECT) or psychotropic medications. Furthermore, environmental manipulations such as occupational therapy, foster homes or school placements, while potentially very therapeutic, are not considered psychotherapy by this definition (Snyder, 1947).

Every responsible therapist has the same ultimate goal for his patient, namely:

> . . . to make the best of him that his inherited capacities will allow and so to make him as efficient and as capable of enjoyment as is possible (Freud, 1923, p. 251).

Psychotherapists request that their patients engage in the *painful* task of abandoning their maladaptive satisfactions. It must not be forgotten, however, that the goal of psychotherapy is a more permanently meaningful and *pleasurable* existence.

While the ultimate goal is the same, therapists differ in their operational models of the mind and human behavior, and their therapeutic approaches differ accordingly, thus leading to different categories of treatment models. Each therapist emphasizes theoretical concepts and techniques with which he feels comfortable and which have worked for him. Most often the dominant psychotherapeutic perspective of a given era is largely influenced by the cultural and sociological attitudes and values of the people at that time and place (Frank, 1971). Some therapists adapt personal techniques and theories, ascribe to them a quality of universality and regard them as fundamental. Therapies called "psychoanalytic," "behavioral," "interactional," "Jungian," "Kleinian," "Rogerian," "Sullivanian," "Reichian," the various emotive therapies, and others less easy to label all have to some degree different rules, techniques and formats. All types of psychotherapies have "cures" and "failures" to their credit, although, with the possible exception of the use of behavior modification in the treatment of certain phobias and addictive behaviors, no empirical research has unequivocally demonstrated the superiority of one type of psychotherapy over another (Luborsky et al., 1975). Clinical experience as well as the empirical research literature support the concept that, regardless of the patient's presenting level of functioning, some clinical improvements result from any reasonable and responsible psychotherapy (Appel et al., 1953; Luborsky et al., 1971).

Despite the differences, all forms of competent psychotherapy have certain elements in common: a situation in which one person needs help and the other person is trained and wishes to give help; a patient desirous of change; a therapist who cares about the patient and accepts and respects the patient as a human being; a sharing between patient and therapist; a therapist with confidence in his method of treatment; a therapeutic ideology provisionally accepted by both patient and therapist; facilitation of abreaction; an enhancement of the patient's feeling of mastery or control over himself and his environment; the preparation for a new knowledge which is transmitted by an increased self-awareness, by example, or by directives; and persuasive powers of the therapist which lead to increased hopefulness that the patient's problems will be alleviated (Frank, 1971, 1974; Karasu, 1977).

2.22 *Psychodynamic (Dynamic)*

In 1952, the American Psychiatric Association held a conference attended by 86 psychiatrists, including 24 psychoanalysts (Fromm-Reichmann, 1954). At that conference, the meaning of the terms "psychodynamic" and "psychoanalytic" was discussed at length. It came as no surprise that agreement on this subject could not be reached. Today, the use of those terms continues to be a confusing issue as reflected by the variety of usage in the literature. Despite these complexities, however, the use of these two terms must be clarified in order to distinguish psychoanalytic psychotherapy from other forms of psychodynamic therapy that are not psychoanalytically oriented.

One of the most ambiguous and often erroneous usages of the terms psychodynamic and psychoanalytic occurs when the two are used interchangeably, such as in the otherwise excellent review by Karasu (1977). If the terms refer to certain theories of pathogenesis, psychosocial development, or treatment techniques, then they may, in certain situations, be used correctly as synonyms. At other times, however, the terms refer to totally different and even opposite ideas. For example, many techniques recommended by some psychodynamic therapists are avoided and even contraindicated by psychoanalytic therapists. It is not at all uncommon to find two authors differing on some aspect of psychodynamic theory or technique, but on closer inspection the difference proves to be semantic rather than theoretical, since each author is discussing different phenomena based on different operational definitions of the term psychodynamic.

Most if not all psychological theory builders and their clinical supporters would agree with the fundamental hypothesis that a person's thoughts, feelings and behavior are based on continuous and complex interactions between the mind, body and external environment. (See Figure 2.1.)

The external environment consists of the physical world external to the body of the person in question, the past and present interpersonal experiences, and the past and present surrounding cultural and social settings. The body consists of all aspects of the internal physiological, chemical, genetic and neurological life of the person, much of which is still to be discovered by future research. The term psychodynamic can be broadly defined as referring to a model that applies various specific *mental* concepts to the fundamental hypothesis represented in

Figure 2.1. A psychodynamicist describes isolated components and experiences of the mind as possessing numerous distinguishing characteristics and functions. Psychodynamic theories conceptualize the mind as consisting of a coherent arrangement of separate hierarchically ordered psychic processes and functions that operate in specific ways and directions. The psychodynamic functional anatomy of the mind always includes identifiable psychological factors that are often in conflict and are powerful, usually unconscious, always influential motivating forces of human behavior.

The mind is, of course, an anthropomorphism and does not concretely exist. Nevertheless, according to the psychodynamic perspective, the mind is a concept of experiential value since it provides some logical explanations of observed thoughts, feelings and behavior. Freud's defense of the psychoanalytic model of the mind can be applied to psychodynamic models in general.

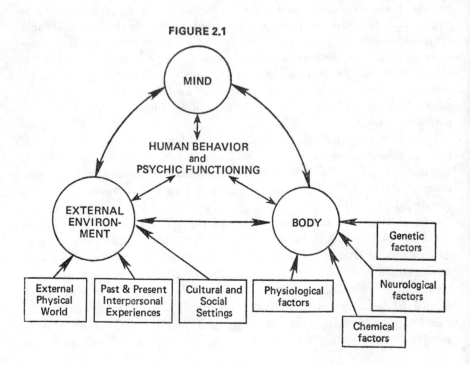

FIGURE 2.1

I see no necessity to apologize for the imperfections of this or of any other similar imagery. Analogies of this kind are only intended to assist us in our attempt to make the complications of mental functioning intelligible by dissecting the functions and assigning its different constituents to different component parts of the apparatus ... we are justified, in my view, in giving free reign to our speculations so long as we retain the coolness of our judgment and do not mistake the scaffolding for the building (Freud, 1900, p. 536).

It should be added that the term psychodynamic refers not only to theories of psychic functioning and human behavior but also to psychotherapeutic *techniques* based on such theories. Furthermore, it can be safely said that all psychodynamic therapists believe that psychopathology is a consequence of repression and a lack and/or avoidance of self-knowledge about how one's mind works, although, of course, the different psychodynamic perspectives may differ on what is repressed or how the mind does or should work. Accordingly, all psychodynamic therapists attempt to help their patients recover and reintegrate those parts of the patient that were lost to the unconscious and attempt to achieve some degree of insight (self-knowledge) into the patient's psychic apparatus. Furthermore, all psychodynamic therapists presuppose that people have the capacity to change if they can achieve meaningful mental insight (Singer, 1970).

2.23 Psychoanalytic

If we use the definition of psychodynamic set forth above, then "psychoanalytic" can be considered a term referring to one specific subcategory of psychodynamic. Psychoanalytic refers specifically to those concepts originated by Sigmund Freud.*

---

* Freud's first psychological publication (1888) was at the age of 32 when he wrote an introduction to his translation into German of Bernheim's (1886) revolutionary book on hypnosis (Macalpine, 1950). Freud wrote consistently and voluminously on a variety of theoretical and technical aspects of psychoanalysis for the next 51 years, shifting emphasis from psychoanalysis as a symptom cure to psychoanalysis as a process of profound psychic growth. Freud's writings are founded on his great courage, frankness and inspiration combined with his genius, artistic writing skills and an unyielding integrity that could not be influenced by political, social or financial pressures. Freud has established himself as one of the first, if not the first scientist to attempt complete understanding of the human being as an intergrated biological and psychological conscious and unconscious functional whole. Of course, like most, if not all, scientific discoveries, Freud's ideas were not all absolutely original but rather were

The psychoanalytic subcategory can be further categorized into three complimentary meanings (Freud, 1923): 1) The first meaning refers to Freudian principles of psychic functioning and human behavior. Actually, to be more precise, the term Freudian refers not only to the ideas of Freud himself but to those ideas of post-Freudian adherents who expanded and added to the basic tenets of Freud's theories without deviating so greatly as to be considered non-Freudian.* These Freudian principles can, as a body of knowledge, be categorized into theories of resistance; the unconscious; repression; narcissism; the developmental importance of the libido, anxiety and aggression and their intrapsychic conflicts; the significance of infancy; the phenomenon of transference being derived from a sexual and aggressive content; the dynamic, genetic, structural, economic and adaptive perspectives of the id, ego and superego; and of course a strict adherence to the concept of psychic determinism. 2) The second meaning refers to a technical instrument of investigation by which one can learn more about the processes of the mind. Of course, the most effective psychoanalytic method of *investigating* the mind is not always the most effective psychoanalytic approach to *treating* a disturbed mind. 3) The third meaning refers to psychoanalytic "technique" as a treatment modality. This usage also refers to the techniques that distinguish psychoanalytic psychotherapy from nonpsychoanalytically oriented therapy such as behaviorism, systems theory, or nonpsychoanalytically oriented psychodynamics.

---

greatly influenced by previous thinkers, writers and teachers. (For a more in-depth look at this subject the reader is referred to Fine [1979] and Sulloway [1979]).

Freud's writings, among other things, demonstrate that mind and brain are not identical and that man has both more *and* less control over his own mind than he dared to realize. Some of Freud's most brilliant writing was done in the last few years of his life when, while in his eighties, he wrote "Analysis Terminable and Interminable" (1937), an "Outline of Psycho-analysis" (1938) and "Moses and Monotheism" (1939) each containing original and enlightening contributions. Even when Freud's ideas were shown to be wrong, many of them have stimulated other great thinkers. No matter how many of Freud's theories and constructs have been, or eventually will be, proven to be unnecessary or invalid, there can be no doubt that Freud was a creative genius whose contributions to man's knowledge of himself and his world have permeated almost every aspect of human existence.

* Although decreasing in number, there are still some analysts who, for the most part, rely totally on Freud's writings, believing that all the therapist has to know can be learned from Freud himself. Greenson (1970) makes the helpful suggestion that these people be considered "orthodox" Freudians, as distinguished from Freudians who make use not only of Freud's writings but also of those by followers who expanded on his ideas.

It should be noted that most psychoanalytic therapists agree with Freud's doubts that the value of the clinical results from psychoanalytic therapy could ever match the value or potential value of psychoanalytic theory as a body of knowledge or as a research instrument (Benedek, 1954).

It is important to remember that not all psychoanalytic techniques are in opposition to some specific aspects of psychodynamic nonpsychoanalytic perspectives. For example, the psychodynamic Sullivanians agree with the Freudians that a successful therapy requires skillful handling of the transference, resistance to the unconscious, dreams and free associations. On the other hand, the Freudians and Sullivanians strongly differ in their conception of the unconscious psychic elements that are transferred or resisted against. The Freudians, with their emphasis on psychosexual development, talk about childhood development in terms of "erotogenic zones" and the Oedipus complex in terms of sexual aims, whereas the Sullivanians, with their focus on interpersonal relationships, speak of "zones of interaction" and an Oedipus complex that focuses on jealousy of the closeness between parents (Fromm-Reichmann, 1954; Rangell, 1954a). Another example is that the Freudians, who tend to conceptualize normal and abnormal behavior in terms of psychosexual development, are more likely to make a vertical interpretation of transference in an attempt to understand the relationship between infantile and childhood conflicts and the compulsion to repeat these conflicts in adult life. The Sullivanians (e.g., Fromm-Reichmann, 1950; Horney, 1939), however, severely criticize the Freudian preoccupation with infantile conflicts and focus on current interpersonal relationships. The Sullivanians, accordingly, tend to make horizontal interpretations of the transference ("parataxic distortions," in Sullivanian terms) so that the patient may become more aware of a distortion within one relationship as it relates to some other current relationship (Orr, 1954).

According to our definitions, all psychoanalytic theories and techniques are psychodynamic, but not all psychodynamic theories and techniques are psychoanalytic, since there are various theories of the psychic apparatus and therapeutic techniques that attempt to change the mental processes but are not founded on Freudian principles. For example, Sullivanians, Kleinians, and Jungians can be considered psychodynamic but not psychoanalytic since their theories and treatments, although not largely operating on Freudian principles, are nevertheless strongly mentalistic. In contrast, the behaviorist and systems theorist are not psychodynamic (and therefore by definition not psychoanalytic) because neither perspective focuses on specific structural concepts of the mind, nor does either perspective attempt to change differentiated components of a postulated psychic apparatus.

A grasp of the concepts discussed above is enough to prepare the reader for the discussions in this book. Any attempt to try further to resolve the issue of how and when these terms are accurately used interchangeably or separately would take the reader beyond the scope and intent of this chapter. For an exhaustive review of the various psychodynamic perspectives, the reader is referred to the comprehensive works of Munroe (1955) and Ellenberger (1970). For a comparison of psychoanalytic, behavioral and systems theory perspectives, see Paolino and McCrady (1978). For a comparison of psychoanalytic, behavioral and "experiential" therapy see Karasu (1977), and for a comparison of behavioral and psychoanalytic therapy and theory see Feather and Rhoads (1972), Wachtel (1976), Ainslie (1975) and Ainslie and Schaefer (1981).

2.24 Psychoanalytic Process and Psychoanalytic Situation

The term "process" of investigative psychoanalytic psychotherapy as I am using it should be clarified. I am *not* using the term in the specific sense that Loewald (1960), Greenson (1967), Zetzel (1970) and others do, distinguishing the "analytic process" from the "analytic situation." These authors consider the "situation" to be a phenomenon where patient and therapist share a common goal and which is characterized by the various manifestations that result from the interactions of patient, therapist and external setting. In contrast, the analytic "process," according to these authors, refers to the intrapsychic changes that are engendered and worked through in treatment.

In this book, the use of the term "psychotherapeutic process" will refer to any aspect of environmental *or* intrapsychic phenomena that is regularly or predictably associated with the proceedings of psychoanalytic psychotherapy and which significantly influences the patient-therapist relationship. Unlike Zetzel, Loewald, Greenson and others, when I use the term "process" here I do not assume that there have to be intrapsychic or structural changes. It is enough to say that the patient-therapist relationship is significantly influenced, based on external observations of thoughts, feelings and behavior. Another way of saying the same thing is that this use of the word "process" will include all aspects of the analytic process *and* analytic situation, and accordingly, will encompass all that both therapist and patient say, think and feel, and all the consequences of these events.

The term "analytic process" or "process" will be used in a way that will encompass the essential elements of the natural flow of constructive psychoanalytic therapy. This flow of events, as noted by Peterfreund (1975), includes, in varying degrees and chronological orders, the following patient experiences: 1) some abreaction and relatively immediate symptomatic relief; 2) new insight into current external situations (see Section 5.2162 for definition of insight); 3) awareness of causal relationships between past and present; 4) memories that occur for the first time and shed new light on the causal relationships between past and present; 5) active participation by the patient; 6) error-correcting feedback by which some hypotheses are strengthened and others dropped; 7) adaptive regression (see Section 5.219 for discussion of adaptive regression); and 8) working through.

2.3 An Unsettled Controversy

With the advent of various forms of psychoanalytically oriented psychotherapy in addition to psychoanalysis, the issue of the similarities and differences between psychoanalysis proper and other forms of psychoanalytic psychotherapy became complicated. As an example of the unsettled controversy, the American Psychoanalytic Association organized an official Committee on Evaluation of Psychoanalytic Therapy. After five years of work, the Committee was never able to agree on criteria by which to distinguish psychoanalysis from psychoanalytic psychotherapy (sometimes called psychoanalytically oriented psychotherapy). The Committee did, however, conclude that the members of the American Psychoanalytic Association as a group displayed a strong resistance to any investigation of this problem (Rangell, 1954a). This situation remains unchanged.

There are at least two reasons for understanding the concepts involved in comparing and contrasting psychoanalysis and psychoanalytic psychotherapy: 1) Much of the literature that has been written specifically for psychoanalysis can be applied to psychoanalytic psychotherapy (and vice versa) provided the reader is familiar with the relevant concepts. It is not uncommon to find one author referring to psychoanalysis while another discusses identical concepts but associates them with psychoanalytic psychotherapy. 2) Many referring clinicians are unsure of the differences and similarities and, in fact, use the terms interchangeably. An understanding of these concepts may be useful in deciding whether or not to recommend psychoanalysis or psychotherapy for a given patient.

In addition to clarifying concepts and facilitating referrals, discussions on this issue may serve the purpose of stimulating a much needed dialogue. It is paradoxical that, despite the importance of the subject of similarities and differences between psychoanalysis and psychoanalytic psychotherapy, the issue is strikingly neglected in psychotherapy and psychoanalytic literature and in the relevant institutes, training programs and seminars, thus giving the false impression that the controversy has been resolved.

Since the psychoanalytic movement began with Freud, it seems appropriate to make some initial comments about Freud's role in these issues. The development of ego psychology and psychoanalytically oriented psychotherapy other than classical analysis developed after Freud's time. In 1914, Freud wrote that anyone who accepts the concepts of transference, resistance and the profound role of the unconscious can consider himself an analyst. In other writings, Freud considers the frequency of at least three sessions per week; the appreciation of sexuality, repression and the Oedipus complex; the therapist's attitude and training; and the utilization of free association as fundamental and inflexible criteria by which a treatment is called psychoanalysis (Freud, 1913, 1923, 1940). Freud never mentions that other legitimate psychoanalytically oriented therapists not implementing classical psychoanalysis may also fit these criteria.

If Freud were alive today and were criticized by a contemporary as being too rigidly committed to the strict format of classical psychoanalysis, he would perhaps remind us of an attitude that he expressed on many occasions:

> I consider it quite justifiable to resort to more [meaning more than psychoanalysis] convenient methods of treatment as long as there is any prospect of achieving anything by their means (Freud, 1905, p. 262).

2.4 THE SHARP DIFFERENCE (SD)/BLURRED DIFFERENCE (BD) APPROACH

The controversy here can be stated as follows: When does technique, although still grounded in Freudian principles, stray so far from that of psychoanalysis that the treatment must be called psychoanalytic psycho-therapy? For example, if a patient and therapist adhere to all of the rules of psychoanalysis except that the patient sits in a chair five times a week rather than lying on a couch, is this to be considered psycho-analysis or is it investigative psychoanalytic psychotherapy? Or, let us take Weigert's (1954) and Alexander's (1954a) discovery that their patients in five times a week classical psychoanalysis viewed the frequency as a relentless invasion of their privacy. The frequency was changed to two or three times per week and the resistance was markedly reduced. If this change in technique results in the patient doing more of the work of psychoanalysis, and if nothing else changes in the treatment format, that is, the patient still lies on the couch, free associates and develops a transference neurosis, and the therapist adheres to all of the other tech-nical guidelines of psychoanalysis, does it make sense to say the patient is no longer in psychoanalysis, when all that is changed is a switch from obligatory to optimal frequency?

Let us begin to explore the issue by dividing the perspectives into two groups represented by the "Sharp Difference" (SD) perspective and the "Blurred Difference" (BD) perspective. The SD proponents attempt to preserve the identity of the psychoanalyst and assert that psychoanalysis is a highly idiosyncratic and necessarily exact procedure that requires maximal amounts of specialized, technical and theoretical knowledge and training and that should be kept distinct for a variety of reasons including the need to compare psychoanalysis to other forms of psycho-analytic psychotherapy. In contrast, BD proponents are not at all con-cerned with establishing criteria as a way to distinguish the psychoanalyst from other psychoanalytic psychotherapists. They assert that the SD polarization of psychotherapy and psychoanalysis has little or no clinical or theoretical value.

Of course, there are important differences within each perspective and many psychoanalytic therapists do not fall sharply into either group. The reader must keep in mind that there is an unavoidable conceptual overlap between and within each group. For example, a psychoanalyst or psychotherapist may take a SD approach to the frequency of sessions but apply a BD perspective to the transference. Some analysts (e.g., Fenichel, 1941; Greenacre, 1959) use a BD approach to the use of the couch but apply a strict SD approach to the conceptualization of treat-ment goals. In the real clinical world the SD/BD distinction is, in fact, artificial. Nevertheless, the establishment of the two groups as major polarities highlights controversial points and allows us to define more sharply the divergent perspectives. The delineation of differences is, in my opinion, more instructive and more clinically useful than the alternative of avoiding discussion of fundamental differences. By polarizing these issues into a SD/BD model, I hope to clarify my use of the term psychoanalytic psychotherapy and thereby facilitate the direction of the reader's attention to the relevant clinical material.*

The SD/BD issue has become a very sensitive and heated subject among many psychoanalysts, especially those on the SD side. The reasons for such emotional fervor are undoubtedly, at least partially, a reflection of the psychoanalytic movement's long and difficult struggle to free itself from the disappointing consciousness-oriented organic and phenomenological psychiatry of the early twentieth century. There were many opponents to psychoanalysis who tried to associate psychoanalysis with suggestion or with phenomena even less scientific. Just as the anatomists were once forbidden to dissect the human body, the psychoanalysts had to overcome much stubborn resistance and angry opposition in their attempt to examine and report on the sacred and untouchable deepest workings of the mind and to establish psychoanalsyis as a science worthy of distinction.

Initially, psychoanalysis was not only not accepted by the general medical and psychiatric establishment, but it was also excluded by the academic medical and psychiatric communities. Thus, psychoanalysis was forced to develop apart from the existing medical, psychiatric and academic fraternities. Perhaps this historical fact plays a significant role in the emotionalism regarding the SD/BD issue and the rivalry, desired isolationalism and distrust that some psychoanalysts have always shown towards other psychiatrists and medical practitioners. The SD isolationalism is reflected in a variety of ways. One example is the refusal of the American Psychoanalytic Association in 1961 to allow psychoanalysis to be established as a subspecialty of psychiatry (Zinberg, 1963).

---

* The discussion of the SD/BD model in terms of technique, transference and goals certainly does not have to be limited to a discussion of psychoanalysis versus psychoanalytic psychotherapy. The same categorization could be used for other discussions. For example, in discussing psychoanalytic psychotherapy versus nonpsychoanalytic psychotherapy, we could polarize the two viewpoints from an SD versus a BD perspective with regard to "nonpsychoanalytic" techniques. The SD proponent in this discussion would strictly limit the techniques to only those that are considered psychoanalytic; the BD proponent would use psychoanalytic techniques but might introduce a variety of other techniques such as social learning or gestalt techniques.

2.41 *A Major Thesis of This Book*

The thesis developed in the following pages is that the SD polarization of psychotherapy and psychoanalysis is invalid. Chapters 3, 4 and 5 are written from a perspective that is consistent with this point of view. Chapter 3 discusses essential principles, Chapter 4 deals with the therapeutic relationship, and Chapter 5 is on treatability *with no attempt to distinguish between psychoanalysis and psychoanalytically oriented psychotherapy since it is assumed that the reader is aware that I am always referring to psychoanalytic psychotherapy as that term is defined in this chapter.* In order for the reader to follow this author bias, however, it is necessary for the reader to first of all be familiar with what is meant by the SD perspective.

2.42 *The Sharp Difference (SD) Perspective*

The SD viewpoint has been expounded in the literature by numerous authors (Bellak, 1961; Benjamin, 1947; Berliner, 1941; Bibring, 1954; Bouvet, 1958; English, 1953; Fenichel, 1945; Fuerst 1938; Gitelson, 1951; Glover, 1931, 1960; Heiman, 1953; Margolin, 1953; Rangell, 1954b; Stone, 1951, 1954; Windholz, 1954). Of course, the SD proponents agree that certain kinds of psychotherapy are on the "borderland" (Rangell, 1954a, p. 737) between psychoanalysis and nonpsychoanalysis, but according to the SD view, to deny the distinction between psychoanalysis and other forms of psychoanalytic psychotherapy would be like denying the difference between black and white just because there is a gray, or denying the distinction between the unconscious and conscious just because certain psychic elements are in the preconscious (Rangell, 1954b).

One way to further describe the SD perspective is to organize the sometimes confusing mass of relevant concepts around a troika of basic themes: 1) technique, 2) transference, and 3) goals. Each of these categories provides a different but complimentary view of the SD perspective.

2.421 TECHNIQUES

For use in this book, "technique" is defined as a form of intervention that is a consciously intentional verbal or nonverbal behavior of the therapist enacted with the motive to change the patient in the direction of the goals of treatment (Bibring, 1954). The discussion of techniques as related to the SD/BD controversy can be approached from two sides:

1) the overall attitude towards technique, and 2) the specific techniques themselves.

Regarding the overall attitude, the SD proponents believe that the *psychoanalyst* observes the patient from the periphery of the patient's mind and only minimally involves himself in interactions with the patient. When the psychoanalyst does interact with the patient or intervenes in some way, it is only to facilitate the transference neurosis or to facilitate the making of the unconscious conscious. In contrast, according to the SD theory, the *psychotherapist* functions within the realm of the patient's psychic apparatus and interacts with the patient by displaying more personal thoughts and feelings (Rangell, 1954b).

Regarding the more specific aspects of the technique issue, the SD theorists assert that there are Freudian techniques and situational factors which can be used in very specific and intricate combinations that clearly distinguish psychoanalysis from other forms of therapy. According to Stone (1951), these techniques and situations can be categorized into the following six groups: 1) regularity of length of sessions, frequency of appointment and length of the treatment process; 2) priority use of free association to the extent that all other means of communication with the therapist are of secondary importance; 3) relatively strictly defined financial agreements that usually prohibit gratuitous or deferred payment; 4) conducting all sessions with patients in an anterior recumbent position on a couch; 5) the avoidance of overt and direct attempts to cure symptoms, focusing instead on free association, resistance and transference, and assuming that eventually the symptoms will be alleviated if the treatment succeeds; and 6) top priority being assigned to interpretation as opposed to other techniques such as suggestion, abreaction, manipulation, confrontation and clarification.

Stone (1954) struggles with the issue of where psychoanalysis leaves off and psychoanalytic psychotherapy begins. He tries to resolve this issue by employing the term "modified psychoanalysis," which entails the psychoanalytic process but does not necessarily include the six criteria noted above. Stone defines modified psychoanalysis as follows:

> If . . . the essential structure and relationship of analysis have been brought about, if a full blown transference neurosis has emerged, if the patient has been able to achieve distance from it, if it has been brought into effective relation with the infantile situation, *if favorable changes in the ego have occurred as the result of interpretation* and working through, if the transference has been reduced to the

maximum possible degree, I would say that the patient has been analyzed (Stone, 1954, p. 576, italics added).

Gill (1954) provides a definition of psychoanalysis that is essentially identical to Stone's definition of modified psychoanalysis. Gill differs only in his insistence on psychoanalytic technique.

> Psychoanalysis is that technique which, employed by a neutral analyst, results in the development of a regressive transference neurosis and the ultimate resolution of this neurosis by techniques of *interpretation alone* (Gill, 1954, p. 775, italics added).

While chairing an American Psychoanalytic Association panel discussion of differences and similarities between psychoanalysis and other forms of psychoanalytically oriented psychotherapy, Rangell, a self-proclaimed SD proponent, offered the following definition:

> Psychoanalysis is a method of therapy *whereby* conditions are brought about favorable for the development of a transference neurosis, in which the past is restored to the present, *in order that* through a systematic interpretive attack on the resistances which oppose it, there occurs a resolution of that neurosis (transference *and* infantile) *to the end* of bringing about structural change in the mental apparatus of the patient to make the latter capable of optimal adaptation to life (Rangell, 1954a, p. 739, italics in the original).

Rangell does admit that the ingredients of his definition can and do, in fact, occur in the "practice of dynamic psychotherapy" (p. 741); however, in agreement with Stone (1954), he says:

> . . . they [ingredients of his definition] do not all exist [in psychoanalytic psychotherapy] systematically and together with the same consistency, degree and long range view, and with the deliberate maintenance of freedom of obscurities which make psychoanalysis rigorously different from ordinary daily human relations [including other forms of psychotherapy] (Rangell, 1954a, p. 741) .

Rangell differs with Stone on the unexpendable technical items in the definition of psychoanalysis and considers his own definition (given above) to possess *all* of the nonexpendable items of psychoanalysis. Rangell then points out that in response to a questionnaire sent out by the American Psychoanalytic Association, many of the analysts responding included in their definition of psychoanalysis what Rangell calls:

> . . . inclusions which can only be considered not as wrong but as tangential, peripheral or fatuous or as a pet emphasis rather than as vital and non-expendable (Rangell, 1954a, p. 740).

Some of these "pet" items include techniques listed by Stone (1951) as the six items that are unexpendable and essential to the definition of psychoanalysis.

Another technical characteristic that distinguishes the SD perspective is the psychoanalyst's attitude as characterized by "analytic anonymity" and "benevolent neutrality." In their view, this attitude is often confused by the uninitiated. The SD proponent does not want the patient to think that the analyst either assumes a specific role or remains uninvolved, cold and aloof (Stone, 1954). Instead, the patient should view the neutrality and anonymity as something the analyst has imposed on himself out of concern for the patient's best interests. The SD analyst (e.g., Greenacre, 1954) continually reminds himself that psychoanalysis is an artificial situation governed by specific techniques. The SD analyst fully realizes that he acts out a role that is far less "human" than his other daily activities. Unlike the BD proponents, the SD adherents propose that a significant fusion of the analyst as a person and as a technician would significantly interfere with a constructive analytic process. For example, if the analyst shows his feelings, the transference will not fully develop. Stone represents this view in his comments on the interaction of giving a cigarette to a patient:

> . . . the giving of the cigarette aside from its obvious susceptibility to unconscious symbolic countertransference interpretation is, in ordinary practice [the practice of psychoanalysis], with non-psychotic patients always unnecessary—never relevant to the treatment [psychoanalysis] as such (Stone, 1954, p. 577).

Not all psychoanalysts adhere totally to the approach represented by Stone's statement. For example, Anna Freud writes:

> With due respect to the necessary strictest handling and interpretation of the transference, I feel still that we should leave room somewhere for the realization that analyst and patient are also two real people of equal adult status, in a real relationship to each other.

I wonder whether our—at times complete—neglect of this side of the matter is not responsible for some of the hostile reactions which we get from our patients and which we are apt to ascribe to "true transference" only (1954, p. 618).

2.422 TRANSFERENCE

According to the SD perspective, only in psychoanalysis can there occur a useful, complete (e.g., Langs, 1974, p. 196) and regressive transference neurosis although, of course, transference phenomena occur in all forms of interpersonal relationships. (For a definition of "transference" and "transference neurosis" see Section 4.1.) The SD adherents propose that the psychoanalyst "analyzes" transference and resistance so that the transference neurosis eventually is fully resolved. Only in psychoanalysis can the therapist effectively use interpretations of the transference.

> Any psychotherapeutic method makes use of transference, but only in psychoanalysis does this use consist in *interpretation* of the transference, that is, in making it conscious. The analyst makes this interpretation effective by not reacting emotionally to any of the patient's emotional wishes, to his love, hatred, or anxiety; he remains the "mirror" that does nothing but show to the patient what he is doing. He refuses to participate in any of the patient's transference actions, because his is another task, incompatible with such participation: to be the patient's doctor [therapist] and to cure him (Fenichel, 1945, p. 571, italics in the original).

In contrast to psychoanalysis, according to the SD view, investigative psychoanalytic therapy recognizes transference phenomenon and resistance and then applies this recognition by using a variety of techniques such as suggestion, manipulation and confrontation. As clearly exemplified by Gill (1954),* the SD view recognizes the continuity between

---

* Merton Gill has made some important and very useful revisions on the SD/BD issue since his 1954 position. The concept of the continuum was supported by Gill in 1954 when he recommended that psychoanalysts try to use more of the nondirective techniques of psychoanalysis with their psychotherapy patients. Gill no longer believes that psychoanalysis and psychotherapy (as practiced by most people) operate on a continuum. He now (1980) notes that most people doing psychotherapy do not analyze transference, because they believe the analysis of transference cannot and should not be done in the lack of optimal conditions present in psychotherapy, as opposed to psychoanalysis, especially regarding frequency and length of treatment, use of the couch, diagnosis and treatment goals. Gill believes that, despite the lack of optimal

psychoanalysis and psychotherapy and even supports the idea that the transference in psychotherapy yields derivative conflicts. Such conflicts can be separated from the transference proper and can, to some degree, be resolved through reality oriented interpretations. These interventions may even include some analyzing and resolution of the transference resistance phenomena themselves but *certainly* never includes mutative interpretations of the transference and other interventions that entail a thorough investigation and resolution of the transference neurosis and resistance.

2.423 GOALS

All therapists have the same ultimate goal for their patients: a meaningful, productive and pleasurable existence. The intermediate goals that must first be achieved, however, differ among therapists of different perspectives. The SD adherents (e.g., Oberndorf, 1950) propose that the intermediate goals of psychoanalysis are far more ambitious than those of "lesser" forms of Freudian therapy. The comparison of the goals of psychoanalytic psychotherapy to those of psychoanalysis is analogous to treating a malignancy with supportive measures when complete surgical removal would be better (Johnson, 1953).

As noted many times (e.g., Wallerstein, 1965) the goals of psycho-

---

conditions, the psychoanalytic therapist should still attempt to thoroughly analyze the transference, especially the transference of the here and now. If the transference is only sporadically analyzed, says Gill, the treatment should be called something other than psychoanalytic psychotherapy.

With regard to the use of the terms, Gill suggests that the term "psychoanalytic therapy" be used in those cases where the analysis of the transference is a central part of the treatment. The term psychoanalytic therapy then can be subdivided into "psychoanalysis," when conditions are optimal, and "psychoanalytic psychotherapy," when the conditions are less than optimal. He also suggests that "psychodynamic psychotherapy" be the term used for any therapy which employs psychodynamic theory (including psychoanalytic theory) but does not make the analysis of the transference a central part of the treatment.

With respect to the criterion of analysis of transference, Gill's newest proposition makes an even sharper distinction between what most people would call the psychotherapist and the psychoanalyst. We could therefore say that Gill is now even a stronger proponent of the SD view. On the other hand, despite his maintenance of the distinction, Gill (1980) seems to represent a BD perspective regarding conditions such as frequency, goals and diagnosis since he recommends that the psychoanalytic technique (thorough investigation of the transference) should not be limited to those patients who meet only the optimal conditions. Gill's current use of the term psychoanalytic psychotherapy is in many ways identical to the term as used in this book.

analysis or any other psychotherapeutic modality are never easily agreed upon nor are they simply a circumscribed spectrum of change or behavior. A full discussion of goals involves such wide ranging issues as technique, the theory of pathogenesis and cure, the assessment of clinical outcome and the definition of mental health. Despite these complexities, however, it is possible to describe the SD perspective on idealized goals of treatment. We can then have a means of contrasting it with the BD perspective on idealized goals.

According to the SD proponents, psychoanalysis is unique in that the goals are strictly set and consist of a progressive uncovering that starts with conscious factors and extends to the deepest layers of the unconscious. Such a probe requires an extensive investigation of resistance, defense mechanisms, the regressive transference neurosis, and the psychic psychogenesis of symptoms (Stone, 1954). All these procedures of psychoanalysis are aimed towards the time-consuming process of working through major structural changes in the mind and personality and complete resolution of the transference neurosis so that there occurs the psychic structural changes that would have occurred had the obstacles to normal psychosexual development never existed. The working through must follow explicit *verbal* interpretations made by the analyst and a meaningful cognitive insight achieved by the patient. Intrapsychic structural change is more than a mere adaptation to a specific situation or interpersonal relationship. The structural change is a major alteration of behavior that has wide-ranging applicability.

The SD theorists propose that, in contrast to psychoanalysis, psychoanalytic psychotherapy cannot produce significant and permanent psychic structural changes. According to the SD proponents, psychoanalytic psychotherapy is aimed at achieving relatively rapid symptomatic relief and has a wide range of intermediate goals that are selected based on ego strengths and involve a variety of behavioral manifestations, all reflective of some shift in defense mechanisms such as repression or intellectualization (Gitelson, 1951). Also, therapeutic goals of psychoanalytic psychotherapy include external adjustments resulting from the suggestive powers of the therapeutic relationship. According to the SD perspective, only through psychoanalysis can the patient and the therapist completely understand the pathogenesis of the symptoms, and only through psychoanalysis can there emerge permanent alterations of the psychic apparatus and the total personality (Wallerstein, 1965).

The SD theorists strongly assert that one of the principal ways that psychoanalysis achieves its goal of psychic structural change, such as re-integration of the ego, is through the breaking down of certain defense mechanisms. In contrast, according to the SD view, psychoanalytic psychotherapy attempts to *strengthen* adaptive defense mechanisms; the therapeutic goal is for the patient to reestablish himself to the point at which his psychic structures and defense mechanisms were operating before he became symptomatic. Even when psychoanalytic psychotherapy attempts some analysis of the defense mechanisms, it is done with a significant assistance of strong supportive techniques such as suggestion and manipulation.

Since only psychoanalysis significantly analyzes resistance and defense mechanisms, the only patients that are analyzable are those who are healthy enough to undergo such breaking down of defense mechanisms. According to this SD logic, an analyzable patient is almost always treatable by lesser forms of therapy whereas a treatable patient is not necessarily analyzable.

2.43 *The Blurred Difference (BD) Perspective*

This book is written from a BD perspective. It is my opinion, as well as the opinion of others (e.g., Alexander, 1944, 1953, 1954a, 1954b; Alexander & French, 1946; Fromm-Reichmann, 1954; McLean, 1948; Oberndorf, 1942, 1946), that there is an unavoidable blurring of differences between psychoanalysis proper and investigative psychoanalytic psychotherapy.

In the BD view, numerous techniques and goals, and the use of transference phenomena are all variations of the standard techniques and goals of classical psychoanalysis. By flexible application of techniques and goals and the use of transference, the psychoanalytic therapy can be broadly classified into two groups called "supportive" and "investigative" (Alexander, 1944, 1953, 1954a, 1954b). Thus, the whole issue of whether psychoanalysis is a more revealing therapeutic modality than psychoanalytically oriented psychotherapy (psychoanalytic psychotherapy; psychoanalytic therapy) is avoided by simply examining each individual patient to determine what clinical material requires supportive or uncovering work. It should be emphasized that both supportive and uncovering therapy require extensive training in and skillful use of both technique and theory (Alexander, 1953, 1954b). Furthermore, a certain amount of uncovering usually occurs in supportive therapy, and uncovering therapy is to some degree supportive. Despite the similarities, the two (investigative and supportive) types of therapies use different techniques and therapeutic goals and perhaps even different formats. In an attempt to clarify the comparison between the SD and BD perspectives, it is again useful to organize the subject around the three basic themes: technique, transference and goals of therapy.

2.431 TECHNIQUES

Many SD proponents are blinded by a need for tradition, a worship of authority and a fear of emancipation from the creative genius of Freud. The best therapy is one in which the therapist allows himself technical flexibility. According to the BD perspective of this book, one patient in psychoanalytic therapy may come five times a week, another once a week; one may lie on a couch while another sits up; one may free associate and deal primarily with childhood experiences while another may do little free association and deal instead with current conflicts. Furthermore, a given patient in psychoanalytic psychotherapy may, during the course of treatment, experience the full range of such techniques.

The less formal and more flexible BD therapist, by his very lack of rigidity, has to be *more,* not less, self-reflective than the SD psychoanalyst. He must possess more, not less, knowledge, experience, empathy, intuition and technical skills; and be more, not less, aware of his own psyche and body so as not to let countertransference interfere with the therapy (Alexander, 1953; Steele, 1953). The SD format of classical psychoanalysis in some ways protects the therapist from his own interpersonal weaknesses just as many people establish rigid and stereotyped relationships with family members or colleagues as a way to stay distant from them. Freud, himself (1913), mentioned that a major reason for his asking the patient to lie on a couch was that he disliked being stared at for long periods of time. If, for some reason, Freud decided that it was in the patient's best interest to sit up, he would then have had to deal more directly with his own countertransference problems of being stared at.

If a therapist is determined to follow in every detail the strict systematic techniques of so-called classical psychoanalysis, he does not have to be as sensitive to that clinical material which indicates a need for a deviation from the classical approach. If the therapist only adheres to strict psychoanalytic technique, he does not have to learn the variety of other psychoanalytically oriented techniques of therapy. A patient in psychoanalysis with the analyst maintaining the SD perspective is *less* difficult to treat since both patient and therapist have more structured ideas of what to expect than do the patient and therapist who operate within the BD perspective.

In essence then, I am proposing that classical psychoanalysis for the SD therapist is less anxiety-provoking than psychoanalytic therapy utilizing the BD perspective. The adherence to a rigid procedure protects the therapist from having to make specific independent clinical decisions that he might otherwise be forced to make. Let us consider the following clinical examples:

Mr. A is in "psychoanalysis" with therapist X, an SD adherent, and Mr. B is in "psychoanalytic psychotherapy" with therapist Y, a BD proponent. Therapist X never recommends that his patients in psychoanalysis sit up whereas therapist Y occasionally has his psychoanalytic patients sit up. Let us further assume that both patients come five times per week, lie on a couch, free associate and develop a constructive transference neurosis. Now let us suppose that both patients report difficulty in looking at the therapist and let us continue to assume that both therapists want to continue "psychoanalyzing" their patient. Therapist X, inflexibly committed to the couch for all patients in psychoanalysis, does not have to make the difficult decision of whether or not the patient could sit up as a manipulation by which the therapist and patient could better deal with the patient's inability to look at the therapist (unless, of course, therapist X chooses to abandon the "psychoanalysis" of Mr. A). On the other hand, therapist Y has to consider an alternative form of psychoanalytic therapy with the patient sitting up and associating to the feelings and fears that he has while looking at the therapist.

Even some SD adherents agree that psychotherapy can be more difficult than psychoanalysis. Take, for example, the words of Adelaide Johnson:

> Having done both analysis and psychotherapy for some years I certainly feel far less confused when doing classical analysis. When I feel lost in psychoanalysis I just keep quiet waiting to see how the transference neurosis and dreams evolve. It is much easier, far less anxiety producing for me than doing psychotherapy (Johnson, 1953, p. 552).

A natural corollary to the BD perspective is that the false dichotomy between analysis and psychotherapy can lead to serious technical errors when the SD analyst administers psychotherapy. The SD therapist is more likely to fail to realize that important technical rules of classical psychoanalysis and psychoanalytically oriented psychotherapy, is less likely to have his technical guard down and thus might act out countertransference, whereas the BD therapist, making no distinction between psychoanalysis and psychoanalytically oriented psychotherapy, is less likely to be careless.

The techniques by which symptomatic relief is achieved through supportive psychoanalytic therapy are rarely discussed in the literature. However, Alexander (1953, 1954a, 1954b) categorizes them into five groups: 1) the indulgence of dependency needs which in turn reduces anxiety; 2) abreaction; 3) advice (suggestion) which, of course, is facilitated by the dependent position; 4) support of neurotic defenses (Defense mechanisms can be supported through offering encouragement, praise or some other form of narcissistic support to adaptive defense mechanisms and through confronting maladaptive defenses. Supportive therapists refrain from investigating any defense mechanism that maintains psychic equilibrium); and 5) manipulation of the external environment so that the environment is less demanding.

Knight (1948), an SD proponent, also proposes a list of techniques belonging to supportive psychoanalytic therapy as opposed to those techniques associated with investigative psychoanalytic therapy. The fact that Knight's list is essentially identical to Alexander's is another example of the blurring and complex nature of the SD/BD controversy.

The techniques employed in psychoanalytic therapy, as the term is used here, include those of the supportive treatment only to a small degree. Psychoanalytic psychotherapy relies primarily on the technique by which a regressive transference neurosis can develop. Thus, there is little advice, a large amount of silence, and an emphasis placed on free association and interpretation, as well as the use of the other basic therapeutic techniques to facilitate free association and interpretation.

The therapist may employ interpretive work and interacts with the patient in an attempt to elicit abreaction, the breaking down of defense mechanisms, the awareness of previously unconscious or preconscious pathogenic psychic elements, and the removal or at least the alleviation of anxiety and symptoms through meaningful insight. These techniques are very similar in form, if not identical, to those advocated by the SD classical psychoanalyst. *In my opinion, it is not the techniques themselves that separate the SD and BD perspectives; it is the attitude towards the techniques and the emphasis placed on the influence that the interpersonal relationship between the therapist and patient has on the impact of techniques.* For example, the BD therapist, before making a critical interpretation, emphasizes the trust that the patient must have in the therapist before such an interpretation is given. In comparison, the SD therapist, while never minimizing the value of trust, stresses the importance of the ego's resistance to any interpretation that threatens the constellation of defense mechanisms before the patient achieves cognitive and emotional insight into those aspects of his mind.

My overall attitude toward technique in psychoanalytic psychotherapy is that the psychoanalytic therapist does not *only* observe the patient from the periphery of the patient's mind, but also, when clinically indicated, interacts with the patient's psychic apparatus, always making sure that such interaction is done for the good of the patient and not for the therapist. Of course, this empathic flexibility requires that the therapist always be self-reflective and in close touch with his own inner self.

2.4311 *Analytic Anonymity and Neutrality*

Both the SD and BD proponents appreciate the clinical need for abstinence in the therapeutic procedure, and both groups agree that the therapist should be "human." The problem arises, however, in the determination of what it means to be human in the therapeutic situation and how the therapist can reconcile that definition with the rule of abstinence.

We should not cherish the role of benign neutrality and analytic anonymity, especially since the terms are self-contradicting. The psychoanalytic therapist and patient are ". . . real people of adult status in a real relationship to each other" (A. Freud, 1954b, p. 618). It will not necessarily interfere with a constructive relationship for the therapist to show his personal self. The categorical split between the therapist as a person and as a technician is misleading and encourages both patient and therapist to withdraw cathexis from the therapeutic alliance to the ultimate detriment of a constructive alliance and transference. By engaging in a relationship that is significantly lacking the real human side of the therapist, the patient is deprived of a meaningful interpersonal relationship from which he psychically can grow (Singer, 1977).

In essence, the phenomenon of analytic anonymity is a myth. I am not referring to biographical facts. The patient usually has no therapeutic need and usually does not benefit from knowing biographical or idio-syncratic details of the therapist's life. On the other hand, the patient *is* in a position to learn something far more important about the real person, the therapist. If the patient has the courage and the strength to interact in, and observe, the therapeutic relationship, he has almost as much opportunity to learn how the therapist cares for and relates to people in the therapist's personal life as the therapist learns about the patient. Furthermore, close observation by the patient will reveal many aspects of the therapist's psychodynamics and hierarchy of values. What actually happens, however, is that resistance to the psychoanalytic process (a resistance that may be felt by both patient and therapist) often mani-fests itself in the patient consciously and/or unconsciously not observing the person of the therapist.

Dr. A, a 30-year-old clinical psychologist, had been seeing a patient in four-times-a-week psychoanalytic therapy for over two years. The ther-apist's office was a room on the first floor of his home and the waiting room was in the foyer of the therapist's house. During one session the patient complained bitterly that psychoanalytic therapy was a rather impersonal and one-sided experience since all she did was talk about herself with the therapist but the therapist never shared any of his life with her. After she complained for several minutes on this issue, the therapist calmly pointed out that the patient had been waiting in the foyer of his home four times a week for over two years, and the patient had never once made any comment about it. The therapist continued to point out that on occasion the patient had seen the therapist's wife in the garden outside, the therapist's two children coming in and out of the front door through the foyer, the therapist's pets, paintings hanging on the wall of both the foyer and the office, numerous books and other personal items, all of which reflected some aspects of the therapist's per-sonality, and yet the patient had never once mentioned observing them.

This interchange was a major turning point in the therapy of this patient. It became rather suddenly clear to the patient that her com-plaint was more of a wish. The patient was, in fact, very afraid to observe the numerous clues that reflected the real life of her therapist. The patient became acutely aware of the fact that she wished to see the therapist as a professional person and not as a human being who cared for her and was trying to help her. The patient had never been consciously aware of the fact that she was afraid to look at the therapist, the therapist's wife and children, and anything else that reflected the human dimension of the therapist and of the therapeutic relationship.

This fear reflected a more basic fear that the patient had that involved issues of intimacy, sharing and secondary trust (see Section 4.225 for a definition of secondary trust). After the patient became aware of her fear of observing the materialistic items within the home and office, she began to see that there were many ways she could observe the therapist within the therapeutic relationship that revealed personal sides of the therapist. Each time that the patient became aware that the therapeutic relationship offered glimpses into the therapist's personality, the patient would feel the resistance to observe and become more in touch with her own fear of closeness and of secondary trust.

In essence, the patient's resistance to knowing his inner self is reflected in his resistance to knowing his therapist's inner self. The less the patient and therapist observe in the session, the less the patient and the therapist have to confront their own psychic lives.

> . . . the value of self-disclosure by the therapist has become recognized, it has provided me with, among other things, additional opportunities to worry and wonder. It is much easier to avoid all self-disclosure than to have to decide what is or is not desirable to express. But is it more therapeutic? (Basescu, 1977, p. 160).

Of course, no matter how tempting it may be, the therapist must not make any interventions that are made only to satisfy the therapist's needs. Accordingly, the therapist must never engage in self-indulgent talk or self-centered ruminations. This cardinal rule should not, however, be taken to mean that the therapist must remain anonymous. The task of the psychoanalytic therapist is *not* never to reveal his personal side. The task of the therapist is to behave in a manner that does not interfere with the progress of therapy. As noted by the Balints (1939), Freud's often quoted metaphor of the therapist serving as a mirror image to the patient is frequently misunderstood. The mirror image metaphor does not necessarily propose that the therapist lack a personality or should fail to show aspects of his own inner feelings.

> Returning to Freud's metaphor, we see that the analyst must really become like a well polished mirror—not, however, by behaving

passively like an inanimate thing, but by reflecting without distortion the whole of his patient. The more clearly the patient can see himself in the reflection, the better our technique; and if this has been achieved, it does not matter greatly how much of the analyst's personality has been revealed by his activity or passivity, his severity or lenience, his method or interpretation, etc. (Balint & Balint, 1939, p. 229).

The therapist must remain neutral at all times, but in a way that is not divorced from the interpersonal connectedness that is necessary for a successful psychoanalytic therapy. It may seem contradictory that the therapist should always remain neutral and at the same time not fear revelation of his own inner self when it seems to be in the patient's best interest. This is true if we define "neutrality" in the traditional psychoanalytic sense of meaning that the therapist should try not to behave in any way that influences the patient's expression and perception of his (patient's) inner self as it actually exists. This traditional sense of neutrality is, in fact, an impossible task since there are innumerable unavoidable and inadvertent ways that the therapist influences the patient's thoughts, feelings and actions (Gill, 1980). In essence then (although, of course, we make every attempt to keep such suggestive influences at a minimum), there is always some suggestion or influence from therapist onto patient and, in actual clinical practice, there is no such phenomenon as an uncontaminated transference.

Gill (1980) points out that psychoanalytic therapists unfortunately tend to be unaware of the impossibility of neutrality in the traditional sense of the word. The futile attempt to be neutral in the traditional sense is what leads to antitherapeutic interpersonal sterility and artificial noninteraction between patient and therapist. Psychoanalytic psychotherapy is an interpersonal as well as an intrapsychic experience, both of which are necessary for clinical success. If the therapist avoids interaction, thinking that he is displaying the necessary neutrality, then the treatment can never reach its fullest therapeutic heights.

The therapist's revelation of his inner self is not incompatible with neutrality if we follow Gill's (1980) ideas and first assume that whatever the therapist does or doesn't do, the patient will attribute some important meaning to it. *Therefore, instead of defining neutrality as having no influence, we should define neutrality as "never taking for granted that the meaning we intend is the meaning the patient ascribes"* (Gill, 1980).

2.4312 *Additional Comments on Technique*

Although the psychoanalytic therapist should feel relatively unrestrained by technique, I still believe that the verbalization of interpretation ranks at the top of the list as useful tools. I would not, however, consider it nonpsychoanalytic should the therapist make use of techniques such as clarification or confrontation during the course of the treatment, provided the goals of therapy are consistent with what is described in Section 2.433 and provided the mind is conceptualized by the therapist in a way that is consistent with Freudian principles. In essence, then, any interaction by the therapist should indirectly contribute to the achievement of the goals and is contraindicated if it obstructs such goals.

Regarding the more specific aspects, techniques should not be used as criteria by which we identify a treatment modality. It is not the frequency of sessions, the technical instrument of free association, the priority of interpretation, or any other technique or format that labels a specific treatment "psychoanalytic therapy." The techniques are merely ways to achieve specific goals that have been identified as characteristic of a psychoanalytic approach. It is the *goals* and the underlying psychological theories of psychic functioning and human behavior that define the treatment, not the techniques or instruments.

I wish not to be misunderstood. I am not saying that techniques are of secondary importance in the actual implementation of the treatment. In fact, the very writing of this book is a documentation of my conviction of the importance of technique. If the sessions are not held at least once a week, the regressive transference will usually (but not always) not develop and will remain a potential or latent phenomenon. Furthermore, several sessions weekly are often required in order for the therapist to maintain optimal control over the intensity of the transference. Frequently the attempt to explore the unconscious and to develop the intense transference is met with such enormous resistance that daily sessions are required. Free association is usually the most effective instrument in the treatment. The recumbent position on a couch, the therapist's relative disregard of symptoms, the therapist's silence and other forms of absence of reality, and the therapist's constant effort not to gratify resurrected needs all may be employed as useful technical manipulations to decrease resistance and facilitate transference, free association, verbalizations of fantasies and the evocation of repressed memories.

In fact, psychoanalytic therapy will fail unless the therapist skillfully implements techniques and situations such as free association, properly timed interpretations, frequent sessions and social abstinence.

What I am saying, however, is that techniques should be selected on the basis of objective assessment as to whether or not they will facilitate the achievement of the goals of psychoanalytic therapy. The techniques should *not* be applied because of some blind adherence to tradition and authority, to some personal or professional need of the therapist, or to some definitional boundaries. The means to the end should not be valued more than the end for which those means were implemented to serve.

What comes to my mind is the analogy, suggested by Kenneth Frank (1977), of technical guidelines in psychotherapy being like a road map. The road map provides some general guidelines for how to proceed, some general directions for how to reach one's destination and some estimate of the length of time the trip will take. The road map does not, and cannot, predict traffic or weather conditions, detours, accidents and numerous other exigencies idiosyncratic to one specific journey. So it is with psychoanalytic psychotherapy. If the means to the end, that is, the instruments or techniques, are overvalued (as so often is the case by the SD proponents), then other legitimate techniques applied to the same psychoanalytic goals often get contemptuously labeled as being non-psychoanalytic and arouse the suspicion that the therapist is poorly motivated, uninformed, inadequately trained or "acting out the counter-transference." It is a sad fact that many SD therapists, while proudly claiming to be followers of Freud, do not in fact follow his exhortations to remain empathically flexible and free from technical rigidity.

> The extraordinary diversity of the psychical constellations concerned, the plasticity of all mental processes, and the wealth of determining factors oppose any mechanization of the technique [of psychoanalysis]; and they bring it about that a course of action that is as a rule justified may at times prove ineffective, while one that is usually mistaken may once in a while lead to the desired end (Freud, 1913a, p. 123).

2.432 TRANSFERENCE

As mentioned above, SD proponents assert that only in psychoanalysis proper can a regressive transference neurosis occur to a significant degree so that a constructive therapeutic experience results.

In contrast to the SD view, I am defining and conceptualizing psychoanalytic psychotherapy as entailing a regressive, useful and complete transference neurosis that can be thoroughly investigated, undergo verbal mutative interpretations, and be worked through and resolved in the treatment setting in such a way that the consequences of the resolution entail major structural changes of the mind. The psychoanalytic therapist will, by definition, take over various roles of introjected and identified images, but will *not* assume that such transference phenomena are limited to classical analysis with its relatively fixed technical guidelines. If the relationship to the therapist lacks the transference neurosis and consists solely of a real relationship, a narcissistic alliance, or a therapeutic alliance (see Chapter 4), then that therapy, however helpful it may be, is not, by definition, psychoanalytic psychotherapy.

Working through of the transference neurosis usually requires interpretations from the psychoanalytic therapist and meaningful cognitive insight from the patient. As a general rule, the transference cannot be significantly effective without some verbal interpretations. Verbal interpretations are usually the most effective means to help the patient fully understand the causal relationships between the present and the childhood antecedents. In keeping with an avoidance of technical restraints, however, verbal interpretations of the transference will not be a definitional boundary of psychoanalytic psychotherapy as the term is being used here.

The reader will note, as he proceeds through this volume, that I oppose manipulation along the lines of the "corrective emotional experience" as recommended by Alexander and his followers (1944, 1953, 1954a, 1954b, also see Section 4.11). The psychoanalytic therapist cannot, and should not, facilitate the development of the transference by changing his own behavior. Only through a constant caring and uncovering of the unconscious and the resistance to the unconscious can the transference develop in a helpful and meaningful way. How can the therapist help the patient get in touch with his inner self and learn the truth about his psychic life if the therapist practices deception? How can a therapeutic alliance be established if the therapist practices deception? The only way for the patient to face the inner truth is for the therapist to be truthful in his own behavior. Such truthfulness demands that the therapist be himself and not play roles such as recommended by the proponents of the "corrective emotional experience." The relationship between patient and therapist (therapeutic relationship) is the most important curative factor. This relationship must, however, be based on total truth and must involve significant amounts of cognitive understanding and active utilization of the transference.

2.433 GOALS

Although the SD proponents consistently maintain that only classical psychoanalysis can engender a useful regressive transference neurosis and major intrapsychic changes, the SD theorists themselves still imply that even what *they* define as psychoanalytic psychotherapy has goals similar to those of classical psychoanalysis. For example, Gill, at one time a strong SD advocate, once wrote that psychoanalytically oriented psychotherapy involves ". . . the whole range of more ambitious goals up to analysis, the most ambitious of all" (Gill, 1951, p. 63). It is unclear from Gill's statement whether or not intrapsychic changes are involved in the "whole range."

Another example of SD obscurity is demonstrated by Stone who, although strongly committed to the SD perspective, points out that ". . . even brief psychotherapy properly conducted may exert an influence which could significantly permeate the character structure" (Stone, 1949, p. 61). In another presentation, Stone expresses the view that psychotherapy could be very useful if we could realize its ". . . enormous but uncontrollable potentialities" (Stone, 1949, p. 61). Still another example is that of the report of the American Psychoanalytic Association's Panel on Psychoanalysis and Psychotherapy which concluded that ". . . relatively brief [psychotherapeutic] contacts may lead to some fundamental changes in character structure" (Chassell, 1949, p. 64).

Gill tries to reach a middle of the road position by referring to those goals as "intermediate" that are between rapid symptom resolution and character change (Gill, 1954). He believes that these "intermediate" goals require "intermediate" techniques such as ". . . transference dealt with though not a regressive transference neurosis" (Gill, 1954, p. 789). In my opinion, labels of "intermediate" only further serve to confuse the issue and are of no more value than concepts such as "modified psychoanalysis" (see Section 2.42).

The goals of the BD psychotherapist vary from those of supportive treatment to that of the more investigative therapy. The primary goal of supportive psychoanalytic therapy is symptomatic relief. This goal is based on the underlying assumption that derivative intrapsychic conflicts and symptoms can be significantly reduced without resolution or even awareness of the primary and more basic intrapsychic conflicts. In essence then, the intermediate goal of supportive therapy is to create a therapeutic situation that promotes the synthetic capacity of the ego.

In contrast, the intermediate goal of psychoanalytic psychotherapy, as I am using the term in this book, is to uncover the deepest intrapsychic conflicts and mental elements as conceptualized from a Freudian model of the mind. Such a treatment modality includes a constant and progressive emotional uncovering of the unconscious and the resistance to the unconscious; also included is a breaking down of defense mechanisms in order to discover the psychogenesis of the symptoms and to reintegrate the ego. All of these procedures are directed towards the working through of profound and relatively permanent structural changes of the mind and the resolution of the transference neurosis. Although, of course, the ultimate goal of any psychotherapy is peace of mind and a decrease of the ego-alien symptoms, symptomatic relief and an immediate strengthening of the defense mechanisms are not the intermediate goals of psychoanalytic psychotherapy.

Since I am defining psychoanalytic psychotherapy as dealing with the unconscious, resistance to the unconscious, and transference neurosis, it must naturally mean that I am referring to the investigative type of psychoanalytic psychotherapy rather than the supportive type, and it is to be assumed that this is what I refer to henceforth when I use the term "psychoanalytic psychotherapy."

2.5 SUMMARY OF THE USE OF THE TERM PSYCHOANALYTIC PSYCHOTHERAPY

What I am calling psychoanalytic psychotherapy is very similar to what is described above in the Transference and Goals sections of the SD definition of psychoanalysis. In essence then, a treatment can be considered psychoanalytic psychotherapy if the therapist conceptualizes the psychic functioning and human behavior in Freudian terms and if the goal of the treatment is for the patient to: 1) be exposed to intrapsychic conflicts that could not be solved in the past and are causing symptoms in the present; 2) achieve an intense and regressive transference neurosis; 3) observe and resolve the transference neurosis through the therapeutic relationship so that the unsolved unconscious intrapsychic conflicts are resolved; and 4) undergo constructive alterations of the psychic structures as a result of the newly acquired emotional, physical and cognitive awareness of the unconscious.

The major difference between my definition of psychoanalytic psycho-therapy and that of most SD proponents is that my definition is not limited by the technical elements which are included in most SD pro-ponents' definition, if not explicitly, then at least implicitly, in informal discussions and explanations. Specifically, the reader will note, for ex-ample, that my definition of psychoanalytic psychotherapy is almost identical to Rangell's (see page 27) and Gill's (see page 27) definitions of psychoanalysis despite the fact that they would probably identify those specific definitions as representative of an SD view. Furthermore, my definition of psychoanalytic psychotherapy is almost identical to Stone's (see page 26) definition of modified psychoanalysis. The major difference between my definition of psychoanalytic psychotherapy, Rangell's and Gill's definition of psychoanalysis and Stone's definition of modified psy-choanalysis is that Rangell includes a "systematic interpretive attack" and Gill includes "interpretation alone" as essential to their definitions of psychoanalysis and Stone includes "favorable changes . . . as a result of interpretation" as essential to his definition of modified psychoanalysis. In contrast, I consider interpretation as well as other technical elements as nonessential definitional ingredients of psychoanalytic psychotherapy. My approach is not as divergent from the traditional analytic stance as some readers may think. For example, regarding the necessity of em-ploying primarily interpretation in classical psychoanalysis, the eminent analyst Joan Fleming writes:

> Is it possible that the structural changes we hope for from the psychoanalytic experience can be facilitated by responses from the analyst other than interpretation in the usual sense of the term? My experience in trying to understand the clinical phenomena that commonly appear in the course of psychoanalytic therapy have led me more and more insistently in this direction. The object need in many adults reproduces in many ways the functional relationship between mother and child—the diatrophic feeling, without which the analytic process meets with difficulty (Fleming, 1975, quoted by Erle & Goldberg, 1979, p. 65).

Brenner (1976) takes a similar approach when he defines psycho-analysis by describing the therapist's "analytic attitude" (p. 132) rather than techniques or components of the psychoanalytic process.

Since I assume no sharp difference between psychoanalysis and other forms of intensive investigative psychoanalytically oriented psychotherapy from this point on, most of what is discussed about psychoanalysis can equally be applied to psychoanalytic psychotherapy (psychoanalytic therapy). In fact, the classical psychoanalytic literature as well as the psychotherapy literature are about equally cited. Some authors (for example, Stone, 1954, p. 573) would no doubt suggest that we use the term "modified psychoanalysis" with the type of therapy that I am calling psychoanalytic psychotherapy. As noted above, however, the introduction of yet another term would only complicate an already obscure subject. What is needed is not a change of words. What is so desperately needed in the psychoanalytic literature and teaching is precise and agreed upon definitions of the words that we commonly use and a usage of those words that is consistent with those definitions. This process is the same one that a therapist explores with his patient—it is not the word the patient uses that is most important, it is the *meaning* that the word has for him. If therapists can do that for their patients, why not for themselves?*

2.6 SOME CONCLUDING COMMENTS

In many ways the degree to which a given therapist favors the SD or BD view depends on both the personality of the patient and the therapist, and the therapeutic context in which the patient is being treated. For example, a young psychiatrist beginning his first "control" case as part of his institute training to be a psychoanalyst is much more likely to lean in the direction of the SD perspective than would a psychoanalyst with 30 years of clinical experience practicing and teaching in a community where there are no psychoanalytic institutes and no psychoanalytic comraderie.

One of the major reasons I have chosen to adopt a BD perspective is because the BD approach challenges the tendency among *some* SD theorists to manifest, at times, blind adherence to technical doctrines to the degree that the means to the end are valued more than the therapeutic goal to which those means were originally implemented.** It should be emphasized, however, that psychoanalysis as described by the SD proponents, and psychoanalytic psychotherapy as I have described it here are in many ways identical. Both therapeutic modalities involve a

---

* I am grateful to my colleague Susan Zuckerman for reminding me of this similarity following her reading an early draft of the manuscript.
** A similar blind adherence is sometimes seen among people engaged in religious rituals who, in other areas of their lives, behave in ways that are quite the opposite to the essence of their religion.

relationship between patient and therapist in which: 1) both patient and therapist are devoted to discovering the psychic truth about the patient; 2) both patient and therapist engage in a professional relationship characterized by a combination of intimacy and social abstention unlike any other form of human relationship; 3) there is a constant attempt to uncover the deepest intrapsychic conflicts and mental elements as conceptualized from the Freudian principles of psychic functioning and human behavior; 4) the therapy involves uncovering the resistance to the unconscious and breaking down defense mechanisms so as to achieve an awareness of the unconscious, insight into which is expected to lead to constructive alteration of psychic functioning; 5) the therapist takes over various roles of introjected and identified images; and 6) the therapist has the intermediate goal of creating within the treatment setting the transformation of the current intrapsychic conflicts into the original childhood interpersonal experiences—these conflicts are then expected to be resolved through the therapeutic alliance.

CHAPTER 3

SOME ESSENTIAL
PRINCIPLES

The fundamental language of psychoanalytic psychotherapy is through use of the metaphor. The metaphorical model has as its foundation a series of basic principles. The purpose of this chapter is to present some of those principles.

Webster's Dictionary (1967) defines "principle" as "a comprehensive and fundamental law, doctrine or assumption" (p. 676). I will use a slightly modified version of Webster's definition and consider a principle to be a fundamental working hypothesis or operational assumption. This working definition avoids any insinuations that psychoanalytic principles are enshrined in doctrines, although, unfortunately, some therapists practice and teach as though they were. Thus, by defining the essential principles as working hypotheses, we promote the view that psychoanalytic techniques and theories, like all scientific disciplines, must always remain flexible and responsive to our empirical observations which will strengthen, verify, weaken or disprove our operating assumptions.

It is an unfortunate fact that many therapists do not have a clear idea of the essential principles upon which they base the psychotherapy they are delivering. It is not at all uncommon for a self-identified psychoanalytic therapist to actually be delivering a kind of therapy that is far different from what some other therapist might be calling psychoanalytic. Furthermore, it is not uncommon that therapists who label themselves "non-Freudian" are doing things quite similar to those who consider themselves "Freudian." In fact, some self-proclaimed non-Freudians are more psychoanalytic than some therapists who label themselves Freudians.

48

3.1 Psychic Determinism, Symptoms and the Pathogenic Role of Unconscious Intrapsychic Conflicts

3.11 Psychic Determinism

The principle of psychic determinism is a fundamental presupposition to the psychoanalytic theories of symptom formation. The principle of psychic determinism (or psychic causality) is that a mental event is never a random phenomenon. Nothing happens by chance and every psychic event is determined by a preceding chain of mental events. As with the physical world, the mental world is incapable of random causation and incapable of discontinuity. Therefore, chance is nonexistent and every psychic symptom, whatever its nature, is the consequence of other mental or physical problems, all operating within the totality of natural law.

The concept of psychic determinism is a synthesis and abstraction of a multitude of observations and can, of course, be applied to theories and treatment other than those with the psychoanalytic perspective. For example, psychic determinism is also fundamental to the sociological, behavioral, and systems theories of human behavior and treatment approaches as would logically be expected since ". . . scientific investigation would indeed be pointless if the order it strove to ascertain did not exist" (Jones, 1953, p. 365).

3.12 Symptoms

"Symptoms" have exceedingly complex and varied sources and manifestations, a comprehensive discussion of which is beyond the scope of this chapter. I will use the term "symptoms" for *both* those experiences of which the patient complains plus those "abnormalities" observed by the clinician but not areas of complaint by the patient. The latter phenomena, in nonpsychiatric medicine, are called "signs," but it is not necessary to make that distinction for the purpose of our discussion. Regardless of the source and form, all symptoms reduce the patient's self-image, peace of mind and capacity to cope.

An emotional or mental problem or diagnosis is the final common pathway that results from the collection of psychic symptoms. No matter how one conceptualizes psychic functioning and human behavior, a symptom is always a multidimensional phenomenon that possesses symbolic and communicative values. According to psychoanalytic theory, all psychic symptoms must be understood from five metapsychological perspectives: dynamic, economic, structural, genetic, and adaptive (Rapaport & Gill, 1959). All five perspectives of psychoanalytic metapsychology presuppose that psychic symptoms are the symbolic consequences of the mind's effort to adjust to unconscious intrapsychic conflicts and to the signal anxiety that is generated from such conflicts (Freud, 1926).

Symptoms are unpleasurable and/or detrimental to the patient. They do their greatest damage by requiring psychic energies to maintain them or oppose them, thus depleting the mind of energy for pleasurable or constructive tasks (Freud, 1916-1917g). A psychic symptom serves three mental functions: 1) it economizes the attempt of the psychic apparatus to resolve an intrapsychic conflict; 2) it reduces anxiety; and 3) it escapes the hazards signaled by the anxiety. The ineffectiveness and maladaptiveness of these three functions are what identify the thought, feeling or behavior as a symptom. Psychoanalytic psychotherapy is based on the presupposition that an alleviation of symptoms can result from a conscious recognition *and* emotional awareness of these mental processes.

Symptoms are the secondary adaptive phenomena that represent the reaction to the primary psychological cause of the psychic problem. A major component of many symptoms is the ego's response to the instinctual demands of the id and the moralistic prohibitions of the superego (Nunberg, 1933). A logical conclusion to this concept is that although symptoms engender emotional pain and suffering, they also serve a practical purpose in that they prevent the conscious awareness of thoughts and feelings that are consciously or unconsciously considered by the patient even more frightening and painful than the symptoms.

Thus, a mental illness is far more than a collection of symptoms, and the cure of the disease must entail more than a technical removal of symptoms. If only symptoms are eliminated and not the underlying intrapsychic conflicts causing those symptoms, then there remains the likelihood that new symptoms will form or the old symptom will reappear when the external factors responsible for removing the symptom are themselves removed. This concept of "symptom substitution" is fundamental to psychoanalytic psychotherapy and is in direct opposition to the essential principles of many forms of nonpsychoanalytically oriented psychotherapy such as behavior modification. In essence, then, a fundamental principle of psychoanalytic psychotherapy is that spontaneous cures to a psychological problem do not exist and no cures can be engendered solely by the manipulation of the external environment without accompanying intrapsychic structural change.

3.13 *The Pathogenic Role of the Unconscious*

An intrapsychic conflict is a phenomenon whereby different parts of the psychic apparatus of the same person oppose each other. A basic theme that starts with Freud and continues with all subsequent adherents is that the mind is simultaneously attracted towards and repelled by the same objects. It makes no difference whether Freud is discussing dreams (1900), the history of civilization (1913b), the neurological mind (1895), religion and mythology (1939), psychological theories of the mind (1900, 1923b), or the pathogenesis of neurosis (1916-1917g, 1920a); there is always the basic concept that there is some force drawing the mind away from some specific object while some other force is attracting the same mind to that object. The interaction of the opposing forces results in all intrapsychic conflicts containing, to various degrees, the elements of wish, anxiety, guilt and defense mechanisms (Brenner, 1976). In summary then, psychic symptoms are: 1) the result of multiply determined intrapsychic compromise formations; 2) the consequences of the mind's attempt at cure; and 3) the internal or external manifestations of any psychological disorder.

It is not uncommon for critics to complain that psychoanalytic therapists avoid or minimize current stress and the developmental intrapsychic tasks that occur at all stages of life. Although the developmental aspects of psychoanalytic theory focus on the psychosexual stages up to six years of age, it is grossly inaccurate to say that psychoanalytic therapists avoid the importance of current situations. The psychoanalytic therapist never denies the obvious fact that life continues after the age of six. Following the pioneer writings of Erikson (1950, 1978), Neugarten (1964), Gould (1972), Gutmann (1975), Vaillant (1977), Levinson (1978) and others, the psychoanalytic therapist is deeply committed to the principle that every human life cycle from birth to death creates new intrapsychic conflicts, new psychological tasks and new inner normative crises.

The various normal and abnormal solutions to each developmental crisis markedly influence the psychological resources available for subsequent developmental phases. During adolescence, the partial solutions achieved in latency are weakened by the stress of onset of sexual maturity leading to the many disorders of adolescence, although, of course, the reemergence of repressed conflicts also allows for more mature and permanent solutions. Early adulthood brings its own special tasks such as choosing a life partner and career. Parenthood often elicits repressed conflicts of dependency wishes, sharing and the burden of responsibility —issues often seen in their pathological form in postpartum depressions. Middle or late life requires the mastery of tasks such as menopause, failure to achieve one's goals, frequent sickness, retirement, loss of loved ones and imminent death—all intrapsychic conflicts that are so often observed as central to involutional melancholias or depressions among the aged that often are mistakenly diagnosed as "senile dementia" (Berezin & Cath, 1965; Zetzel, 1970).

Psychoanalytic therapy does more than just passively accept the significance of current situations and developmental psychic tasks; a fundamental presupposition is that the key to the understanding and treatment of unconscious pathogenic conflicts lies in the interaction between the various external and internal stressful experiences and the multitude of preexisting psychic processes. The psychic elements are not static. Symptoms gain new meaning as the mind interacts with various aspects of the current situation. In order to comprehend the genetic aspects of the specific clinical material under study, the therapist and patient must not only be aware of the developmental and intrapsychic variables, but must also understand the central problem with which the patient is currently dealing ("context," Langs, 1973). This equal importance attached to past and present can be contrasted with primal therapy's exclusive focus on past events and gestalt therapy's exclusive involvement in the present.

The psychoanalytic patient often resists an awareness of the context itself, in which case the primary therapeutic task is to discover the specific context which will lead to the underlying pathogenic psychic components. In the same way that the day residue is the nidus around which a dream is constructed, so is the current internal or external stress the day residue that serves as the organizer of specific defense mechanisms, symptoms and other manifestations of adaptive and maladaptive ego function (Langs, 1973).

3.2 THE TREATMENT GOAL OF MAKING THE UNCONSCIOUS CONSCIOUS

The goal of the psychoanalytic therapist is to focus on interactions with the patient that make the patient conscious of the unconscious pathogenic intrapsychic conflicts. The patient then assimilates this awareness so that there is a constructive mobilization of psychic drives, a decrease in tolerance of the superego and a more adaptive ego function. This results in a reduction of intrapsychic conflicts and the unpleasant affects that accompany such conflicts. If this goal is reached, there is a permanent end to the psychic struggles producing the symptoms. It is presupposed that resolution of intrapsychic conflicts maximizes the patient's capacity to cope with environmental factors by accepting limitations, altering that which is changeable and finding substitutive gratifications.

3.21 *Early Freudian Theory*

The fundamental theories of contemporary psychoanalytic therapy are in some ways very different from those of the early Freud and his contemporaries during the birth of the psychoanalytic movement. One of Freud's earliest therapeutic principles was that all that was necessary for cure was to make the unconscious conscious (for example, see the case histories discussed in *Studies on Hysteria* [Breuer & Freud, 1895]). By "the unconscious" Freud was referring not only to forgotten memories but also to current psychic processes within the patient of which the patient was unaware. The high priority assigned to making the unconscious conscious was the result of the belief that a major cause of psychopathology was the separation from conscious awareness of anxiety-arousing thoughts and feelings. According to this concept, the primary task of the therapist is to observe the various abnormal and normal preconscious and conscious derivatives of the unconscious, formulate the contents of the unconscious and its relationship to preconsciousness and consciousness, and then verbally communicate this knowledge to the patient. The therapist then expects a cure, provided the patient possesses the capacity to understand cognitively the therapist's communications.

3.22 *Later Freudian Theory*

It was not long before Freud learned that an automatic cure would not simply appear following the making of the unconscious conscious. Repeatedly, Freud listened closely to his patients and interpreted their unconscious motivation. Occasionally the patient agreed with the interpretation and would even change his cognitive outlook on the symptoms. The emotional nature of the condition, however, usually remained unchanged and sometimes deteriorated in response to the new awareness of the unconscious. Freud learned early in his psychoanalytic career what all competent contemporary psychoanalytic therapists now realize— namely that merely remembering a forgotten past experience or merely achieving intellectual insight does not change the forces responsible for intrapsychic conflict. The major difference from the earlier theories is the added presupposition that if there is to be any clinical change resulting from the psychoanalytic treatment, an emotional experience must be associated with the intellectual self-awareness. The patient must not only know the forgotten wish or idea but he must also bodily and psychologically experience the associated emotions, the wish's adaptive function and the realities which continue to enforce it (Langs, 1973). By keeping the feeling-idea complex from again becoming unconscious, the patient has the opportunity to learn how to readjust to the situation in a more adaptive way than he originally did.

Hendrick (1958) gives some excellent examples of the difference between the basic therapeutic principles of the earlier psychoanalysts and the more current theories: It is not the idea that the patient wants his mother and envies his father that so drastically influences behavior, but rather it is an idea-feeling conflict that he wants her for his own. It is not the thought that the patient's mother told him not to touch his penis in public; it is the thought that he *fears* severe punishment from his mother whom he loves. It is not the picture of an athlete that is a forceful event; it is the thought that the patient has of wanting to be strong and powerful like him.

In summary then, later Freudian theory asserts that the symptomatic relief results from more than just making the unconscious conscious. Contemporary psychoanalytic psychotherapists believe that, no matter how painful the insight, an increased awareness of the unconscious combined with the appropriate bodily and emotional experience can lead to a more peaceful, effective and mature resolution or adaptation of the intrapsychic problem.

3.3 The Therapeutic Effects of Thoughts and Feelings as Opposed to Action

Psychoanalytic psychotherapy is based on the fundamental principle that a combined verbal and emotional expression of thoughts and feelings is more clinically effective than the influence of overt behavior. This principle is in direct opposition to the various nonverbal therapists such as emotivists, psychodramatists, and body therapists. This principle is also, at first glance, in direct opposition to the behavior modification approach, although there certainly are areas of convergence between learning theory and psychoanalytic theory that have useful clinical applications (Ainslie, 1975; Ainslie & Schaefer, 1981; Feather & Rhoads, 1972; and Wachtel, 1976).

The psychoanalytic therapist wants the patient to verbalize and feel thoughts and feelings rather than act out those thoughts and feelings. An understanding of the means by which a patient resists a psychological rather than behavioral expression of his inner self will provide an understanding of the patient's usual forms of resistance.

The psychoanalytic therapist also proposes that it is often psychically and behaviorally dangerous for the patient to employ behavioral solutions to intrapsychic conflicts and anxiety. Emotional insight must come first, then behavioral changes are expected to follow. Of course, most psychoanalytic therapists acknowledge that there are specific cases where behavioral treatment may be indicated and may achieve immediate symptomatic relief. Psychoanalytic therapists doubt, however, whether any permanent solution is possible without some awareness and alteration of the unconscious pathogenic intrapsychic conflicts.

> We [psychoanalytic therapists] do not deal with the happenings in the external world as such, but with their repercussions in the mind (Freud, A., 1960, p. 54).

The psychoanalytic psychotherapist has learned from clinical experience that patients sometimes employ behavioral attempts at resolution as a way to avoid the psychic pain of dealing with the intrapsychic conflict. Such "acting out" (see Section 5.345) frequently is associated with destructive denial and maladaptive repression (Langs, 1973). If the acting out is discouraged, then the verbal and emotional expressions stimulate additional thoughts, feelings and insight that possess a curative force that is considered to be superior to direct action.

Another reason the psychoanalytic therapist prefers verbal expression over behavior is that he wants to create the psychoanalytic atmosphere in which the patient learns that there is nothing to fear from any thought or feeling no matter how irrational that thought or feeling may seem. Unlike behavior, thoughts and feelings have no limitations. If behavior is encouraged as a substitute for thoughts and feelings then the patient who lives in dread of his feelings and hidden thoughts will perceive the behavioral approach as confirming that fear. Such perceptions will in time reinforce suppression and repression.

3.4 THE SIGNIFICANCE OF FREE ASSOCIATIONS

He that has eyes to see and ears to hear can convince himself that no mortal can keep a secret (Freud, 1905a, p. 77).

Free association occurs when the patient reduces external, perceptual and cognitive functions, focuses on intrapsychic (mostly preconscious) stimuli, abandons the conscious processes of editing what he thinks and says, and learns to freely express feelings, thoughts, fantasies, attitudes and wishes with a minimum of the usual secondary process influence. Free association must operate in spite of what Freud called the four objections to such behavior: that they are 1) senseless, 2) irrelevant, 3) distressing, and 4) unimportant (Freud, 1916-1917d). In essence, then, free association is difficult to do since the person must perform in a manner that is the complete opposite of what has, since earliest childhood, been taught as proper behavior.

Free association refers not only to the patient's attitude, but also to the therapist's expectation that the patient will verbalize everything that comes to mind during the session. In fact, since it is rare for any patient to *completely* abandon censorship, it is safe to say that free association refers more to the therapist's expectation than the patient's actual verbalizations (Langs, 1973).

3.41 *Historical Perspective*

The meaningfulness of spontaneous mental associations certainly did not originate with Freud. As with many other of Freud's concepts, they were elaborations of ideas that were introduced by brilliant poets, novelists and philosophers who laid the cornerstones of contemporary psychology (Zilboorg, 1952). Aristotle, in his writings on logic, was the first to discuss the concepts of mental associations such as the triad of similarity, contiguity and contrast, often referred to as the primary law of association (Bellak, 1961; Ramzy, 1974). Hobbes, Locke, Mill, Browne and other English physicians and philosophers introduced the term "associations" when they pioneered the school of British Associationism and the secondary laws of association such as the duration of the original experience, frequency and connected affect (Bellak, 1961; Boring, 1950; Ramzy, 1974; Zilboorg, 1952).

Frances Galton experimented with the method of free association by practicing it on himself:

> ... ideas present themselves by association either with some object newly perceived by the senses or with previous ideas ... They [the associated ideas] gave me an interesting and unexpected view of the number of the operations of the mind, and of the obscure depths in which they took place, of which I had been little conscious before (Galton, 1879, quoted in Zilboorg, 1952, p. 493).

Even as a 14-year-old youth, Freud was influenced by the writer Ludwig Borne who recommended to prospective writers that they write down everything that came into their mind so that self-censorship would not interfere with creativity (Freud, 1920b; Jones, 1953). Later in his life, Freud noted that Schiller, the great poet he much admired, recommended in 1788 that any writer who wants to be creative and productive must use the method of free association (Freud, 1920b).*

The application of free association to psychoanalytic psychotherapy was first mentioned in the psychoanalytic literature in 1895 when Freud observed that there is a conscious or unconscious sense to everything the patient says or does (Breuer & Freud, 1895). In his earliest clinical years (1887-1896), still adhering to the traumatic event theory of hysteria, Freud employed free association merely as a method by which to uncover the specific traumatic event that caused the hysterical neurosis. Freud believed that, whether or not the patient was hypnotized, if she freely associated enough, she would eventually "remember" the pathogenic episode. Freud noticed that ideas and feelings were always occurring in the patient's mind. He observed that his insistence (suggestion) was not

---

* Another example of the artist's appreciation of free association is that of the novelist Virginia Woolf who wrote:

> I have just reread my year's [1918] diary and am struck by the rapid haphazard gallop at which it swings along, sometimes indeed jerking almost intolerably over the cobbles. Still if it were not written rather faster than the fastest typewriting, if I stopped and took thought, it would never be written at all; and the advantage of the method is that it sweeps up accidentally several matters which I should exclude if I hesitated, but which are the diamonds of the dustheap (Virginia Woolf, *A Writer's Diary*, Leonard Woolf, ed., 1953, p. 7).

necessary and could even inhibit free associations (Laplanche & Pontalis, 1973).

At the same time that he noted that it was unnecessary for him to suggest or hypnotize, Freud observed that something inside the patient unconsciously fought against free association. This Freud was eventually to call "resistance" (see Section 3.5). Free association, however, at this earliest stage of his clinical career was used only to achieve the technical goal of abreaction. It was assumed that if abreaction were achieved, then cure would result.

By 1896, Freud had rejected the traumatic event theory of neurosis, stopped asking patients to close their eyes, avoided touching them altogether, and abandoned hypnosis and classical catharsis in favor of clarification and interpretation as a way of overcoming those resistances that kept the patient from free association.

Freud's move from suggestion, catharsis and manipulation to clarification, free association and interpretation occurred simultaneously with his interest in the more profound matters of psychopathology. In other words, as his theories of neurosis involved deeper layers of the mind and more profound concepts, so also did his technique change to facilitate access to those areas of the mind. Likewise, as his techniques changed, he was able to collect more data, which in turn led to the development and refinement of his various theories.

An experience that was a major factor in this shift of technique from catharsis to free association was Freud's self-analysis, which was at its height during the years 1896-1900 (Laplanche & Pontalis, 1973). Freud especially used free association in his analysis of his own dreams. By using elements in his dreams as stimuli, Freud employed free associations that led him to the latent content of the dreams. This was to play a crucial role in the development of his theories of neurosis.*

In summary, instead of free association as a means to facilitate the therapeutic goal of abreaction, free association itself became the technical goal of interpretation and is now conceptualized as continually under attack by resistance (Loewenstein, 1963). In contemporary psychoanalytic psychotherapy, the prime targets of things to interpret are those phe-

---

* Another factor in the development of free association was the work of Jung and his associates in Zurich and its influence on Freud (Laplanche & Pontalis, 1973). Jung's experiments consisted of a study of the time it took to react to specific words. The subjects took more time to react to those word stimuli that elicited the most affect or the most troubled associations.

nomena that interfere with free association (for a comprehensive historical perspective on free association, the reader is referred to Zilboorg, 1952).

3.42 Further Comments on Free Association

Free association can now be considered as representative of the fundamental psychological and philosophical principles which underlie all of psychoanalytic psychotherapy. Freud clearly points out that it was only after he introduced the use of free association that he began to call his treatment the "psychoanalytic method" (Bergmann & Hartman, 1976; Zilboorg, 1952) and, in fact, free association is often called "the fundamental rule" of psychoanalytic psychotherapy. It is the fundamental rule for contemporary psychoanalytic psychotherapy for the same reasons as were believed by Freud (1925a). Spontaneous uncensored expressions reveal thoughts and feelings that more rational expressions conceal. Free association minimizes the risk of both patient and therapist overlooking significant material; minimizes the compulsive production of data; maximizes the patient's contact with the current therapeutic relationship; and maximizes the probability that the therapist will not influence the emergence or quality of data by suggestions, needs or expectations (Freud, 1925a). The more the patient adheres to the fundamental rule, the faster will be the rate of establishing the transference neurosis, a necessary component of therapy. The more quickly the patient free associates, the more quickly the patient will begin to express directly those mental elements and intrapsychic conflicts that possess the greatest intensity and are the most significant.

Another way of looking at free association is that it is the best method by which we can be sure that the data being produced come from the patient and not from anyone else, including the therapist. In this light, it is clear that free association is the complete opposite of suggestion.

Although the patient and therapist agree that it is up to the patient to choose *when* material is shared, there can be no exception to the *expectation* that *nothing* is to be considered irrelevant or censored and that the patient must consider that the therapist can be trusted with anything that comes to (the patient's) mind. (The patient must also feel that the therapist can be trusted with whatever free associations come to the therapist's own mind.) No exception can be made to the fundamental rule since the unconscious and the mind's resistance to the unconscious themselves make no exception. Finally, provided the resistance is interpreted, free association is always possible. As long as the therapist does not stipulate the nature of the free association, then the patient can follow the fundamental rule since it is a law of human behavior that in ordinary states of consciousness ideas never cease coming into the mind.

In essence, then, the psychoanalytic therapist presupposes that associations that follow one another within the clinical material have some conscious or unconscious connection to each other. In fact, it is assumed that *every* expression of the patient during the session has one or more unconscious meanings although, of course, the therapist does not expect to learn the full meaning of all the clinical material. A corollary of the basic concept of free association is that every one of the patient's uninhibited, uncensored and freely expressed communications could lead to underlying intrapsychic conflicts causing the symptoms for which the patient seeks treatment.

Mrs. O is a 25-year-old woman with a long history of fear of sex to the point that she experienced severe pain during all attempts at intercourse. In discussing one of her recent unsuccessful attempts, she associated to her husband inadvertently hurting her during intercourse; a childhood incident in which one of the other children hit her on the head with a hammer; another childhood incident when she was struck on the head with a stone; and then another childhood incident in which her father spanked her. All of these associations to sex have one thing in common —violence. Thus, she associates violence with sex, thereby giving some clue as to the reason for her fear of sex. The therapist had suspected that such was the case well over a year before this series of associations. However, it wasn't until the patient associated herself in this way that she became meaningfully, consciously aware of the relationship between sex and violence in her mind and she essentially made the interpretation herself.

The psychoanalytic therapist carries this basic concept of serial associations even further and assumes that each psychotherapy session may, and usually is, in some way related to a previous session or sessions. Of course, not all of the various associations, communications or meanings are of equal importance, and one of the primary tasks of the therapist is to assess from careful listening which material is of most clinical significance.

In many ways free association is never totally free. The concept of genuine free associations that reflect deeply unconscious disconnected ideas is a myth, a fallacy of the same magnitude as the concept of the uncontaminated transference discussed in Section 2.4311 (Gill, 1980). In accordance with the principle of psychic determinism (see Section 3.1), every thought or feeling is a departure from a previous unconscious or conscious psychic stimulus. If the therapist provides a stimulus word or idea such as, "What are your thoughts about that dream?", then such associations can be considered "controlled associations" (Bellak, 1961, p. 11). The degree of freedom attached to controlled associations is not as great as if no point of departure is designated by the therapist. Even if the therapist does not indicate a point of departure, there are innumerable, inadvertent stimuli arising out of a variety of factors (for example, office furnishings) that are idiosyncratic to that specific therapist-patient relationship. These inadvertent factors are to some degree uncontrollable and not only stimulate the production of free associations but influence the content itself. The associations, however, can still be considered free, as long as 1) the patient's self-perceptions to the stipulated word or idea are not overtly directed by the therapist or censored by the patient; 2) the therapist's inadvertent influences are kept at a minimum; and 3) the therapist is fully aware of the influence he has on his patient's "free" associations (Gill, 1980).

There are other ways in which free associations are never totally free. First, none of our thoughts or feelings is ever totally free of unconscious wishes, psychic conflict, repression and other defense mechanisms (Brenner, 1976; Freud, 1916-1917e). Furthermore, every thought or feeling that occurs to the patient in psychoanalytic psychotherapy is in some way relevant to the therapeutic situation (Freud, 1925a). The patient's past and present life history and symptoms often serve as conscious or preconscious factors in the organization of free association (Bellak, 1961; Zilboorg, 1952). The associations are considered free, however, as long as they arise from within the patient and are not imposed by external factors such as rules or suggestion (Zilboorg, 1952).

Even after the patient overcomes the conscious reluctance to free associate, he will still reveal a resistance to the fundamental rule. This second kind of resistance will manifest itself by distorting the repressed material so that the free association will only *approximate* its unconscious representative. In other words, free associations are actually verbal expressions of preconscious representations of unconscious psychic elements (Glover, 1928). The determinant order of the unconscious is no freer than the flow of conscious thought. By eliminating the censorship and selection, the patient is actually circumventing only the *conscious* censorship, or to put it in Freud's earliest topographical (see Section 3.61) terms, by free association, the patient attempts to avoid the censorship between the system *conscious* and the system *preconscious* but cannot by definition consciously evade the censorship between the system *preconscious* and the system *unconscious* (Laplanche & Pontalis, 1973).

It should be made clear that free associations do not represent instant and complete access to the unconscious. Neither does free association mean that the patient has completely transferred his mode of thinking to that of the primary process. What free association does do is promote the appearance of associations or absences of associations which, when perceived, make the unconscious determinants more accessible to clarifications and interpretations. Another way of saying this is that the technical goal of free association is to promote a kind of communication between the patient and therapist that overcomes the resistances that restrain unconscious thoughts and feelings (Laplanche & Pontalis, 1973) and facilitates clarification and interpretation.

The degree of distortion between the manifest free association and the unconscious element is directly proportional to the amount and force of the resistance as it is served by repression, censorship and the variety of other defense mechanisms. In this regard, Freud had a favorite analogy (1900). If a political writer has things to say or write, criticisms must be disguised to a degree determined by the degree of censorship imposed by the government and to the degree to which the writer wishes to protect his own well-being. If the political writer expresses criticisms in a verbal and undisguised form, certain governments may prevent his words from reaching the printed form. Also, the undisguised expression of content in the face of a harsh censorship may endanger the writer himself, just as production of clinical material could endanger the patient's ego.

The therapist is left with two ways to assess the free association. If the substitutive associations are only slight distortions of the unconscious, then the therapist may be able to employ clarification to reveal the unconscious idea. If, however, there are major distortions, that is, if there is strong resistance, then the therapist uses interpretation both to reveal the resistances and to infer the meaning of the association.

Perhaps the most important consequence of free association is that it forms the foundation on which the entire therapeutic relationship between patient and therapist develops. Free association is the fundamental principle by which the patient and therapist agree to a linguistic relationship (Laplanche & Pontalis, 1973). In this sense, then, the free association is more than a procedure that is allied with interpretation. Free association promotes a relationship in which the therapist requires that the patient try to express in words all aspects of the patient's mind. The greater the amount of free association, the more the patient becomes committed to verbal communications such that feelings, recollections and bodily sensations are all conveyed in expressed words which, in turn, allows the patient and therapist to trace the origin of these psychic elements.

The direct relationship between free association and interpretation is nicely described by Freud when he writes that the task of interpretation is:

. . . extracting the pure metal of the repressed thoughts from the ore of the unintentional ideas (Freud, 1904, p. 252).

We should bear in mind that the "unintentional ideas" of free association provide only one source of the data to be interpreted. Other clinical material that facilitates access to the repressed material comes from dreams, jokes, the transference, resistance, and of course, parapraxes.

Despite its value as a therapeutic tool, free association may occur as a way to avoid painful unconscious or conscious material more upsetting than the free associations (a concept pioneered by Ferenczi [1919] and Anna Freud [1936], the former attaching the label of "association resistance" to the phenomenon [Bergmann & Hartman, 1976]).

Greenson (1965) gives an excellent example of the use of free association to avoid the real relationship and therapeutic alliance. Greenson asked his analytic patient what his middle name was and the patient responded "Raskolnikov." Greenson was surprised at this response and questioned the patient about it. The patient said that when Greenson asked for his middle name, the first name that came to him was Raskolnikov. The patient went on to say that he thought he was supposed to free associate as much as he could in the analytic session and so he simply responded with the first name that came into his mind. Greenson analyzed this material more thoroughly and discovered that the patient was compliantly forcing himself in his attempt to free associate 100%

of the time during the analytic session. The patient was using free asso-ciate as a way to ". . . reduce the doctor's request to an absurdity" (Ferenczi 1919, quoted by Bergmann & Hartman, 1976, p. 90). This "spiteful obedience" (p. 164) became a means by which the patient avoided the real relationship and the therapeutic alliance, two experiences that frightened the patient even more than the irrational free associa-tions. Greenson notes that free associations in this patient facilitated a regressive transference but at the expense of the alliance and real rela-tionship with the analyst, thereby setting up a situation that was in fact a "caricature of psychoanalysis" (Greenson, 1965, p. 164).

3.5 THE ROLE OF RESISTANCE

The resistance accompanies the treatment step by step. Every single association, every act of the person under treatment must reckon with the resistance and represents a compromise between the forces that are striving towards recovery and the opposing ones which I have described (Freud, 1912, p. 103).

As thoughtfully discussed by Schafer (1973), the concept of resistance can, and does, have multiple definitions and meanings within the litera-ture as well as in clinical practice. For the purposes of this book, re-sistance can be defined as anything that the patient says or feels that interferes with gaining awareness of the unconscious psychic elements (Freud, 1900, 1915b). We can further categorize resistance into primary and secondary resistance. Primary resistance is aimed directly at the unconscious. Secondary resistance is directed at anything that attempts to uncover resistance (Eissler, 1953; Freud, 1920a, 1937).

The definition of resistance is sometimes misunderstood by the unini-tiated. When referring to the concept of resistance, the psychoanalytic therapist is referring to thoughts, feelings and behaviors over which the patient has conscious or unconscious control. Certainly, there are some external events over which the patient has *no* control, such as the death of a loved one, that significantly interfere with the treatment. These events cannot legitimately be called resistance although patients some-times *focus* and *capitalize* on external events in a way that serves the function of resistance.

Resistance is an overdetermined phenomenon and various manifesta-tions develop automatically from unconscious sources and independent of conscious volition. Forms of resistance often appear unexpectedly and then mysteriously vanish.

Freud (1923a, 1937) and his followers believe that resistance is a phenomenon that occurs naturally in all people in or out of therapy. Other theorists (e.g., Rogers, 1942) hypothesize that resistance is not an inevitable part of psychotherapy but is the consequence of the therapist's technical errors, such as introducing material into the session with which the patient is not ready to deal. The various theories of why resistance exists each reflect the theorists' concept of human behavior and psychic functioning; therefore they often disagree about what is being resisted and why. Most psychoanalytic therapists would agree that some commonly observed sources of resistance are: transference; fear of the therapist; fear of unconscious fantasies and the feelings of anxiety, guilt and anger associated with those fantasies; fear of getting symptomatically better in opposition to masochism and self destruction; fear based on the realities of the therapy (Langs, 1973) ; and an unconscious belief that there is no real alternative to the current psychological condition and all therapy will do is deprive the patient of his current psychological state which is, as problematic as it may be, his only means for psychological survival (Singer, 1970). All psychodynamic theorists agree that resistance in any form serves to avoid unconscious and unpleasant thoughts and/or feelings (Singer, 1970).*

The various manifestations of resistance are observable throughout all stages of psychoanalytic therapy and take many forms. It can be safely said that the silent, unobtrusive resistance is usually more difficult to overcome than the more obvious forms (Glover, 1928). Some ways that resistance reveals itself in therapy are: difficulty free associating characterized by silence or by complaining of having nothing to say; talking about the past to avoid the present or vice versa; slips of the tongue or ear; lateness; missed appointments or other forms of "acting out"; production of confusing thoughts or dreams; blaming others; questioning the value of therapy or the integrity of the therapist; creating a crisis situation outside of the therapy; shame; ruminating or overtalkativeness; avoiding specific subjects; or being remote or unclear (Hendrick, 1958; Langs, 1973). In fact, just about any thought, feeling or behavior can be utilized in the service of resistance.

---

* For a review of the psychoanalytic literature on resistance see Munroe (1955) and Singer (1970).

3.51 Freud's Models of Resistance and the Relationship
of Resistance to Repression

Very early in his psychoanalytic research, Freud recognized the hindrance of resistance to therapy. " (It is) resistance that finally brings work to a halt . . ." (Freud, 1897, p. 266). Freud, in 1895, is the first to mention resistance in the psychoanalytic literature (Strachey, 1955). At first, Freud attempted to overcome resistance by persuasion and insistence which are, of course, forms of suggestion. He then switched to other forms of suggestion such as pressing the patient's forehead with his fingers. Freud later tried catharsis but found these methods useless as a means to overcome resistance and he eventually switched to free association (Breuer & Freud, 1895; Freud, 1905b).

3.511 REPRESSIVE RESISTANCE

Repression can have two psychoanalytic meanings: 1) the strict definition, and 2) the generic usage. According to the strict definition, repression is an ego defense mechanism in which unacceptable ideas or feelings, especially those directly bound to an instinct, are unconsciously repelled from consciousness.*

> . . . the essence of repression lies simply in turning something away, and keeping it a distance from the conscious (Freud, 1915c, p. 147).

The confinement of what is repressed to the unconscious prevents an instinct from being satisfied. The ego puts repression into action because the satisfaction of that particular wish or instinct is considered potentially more painful than the deprivation of that satisfaction. This specific application of repression occurs in a variety of normal and abnormal behaviors, especially hysterical neurosis, and manifests itself in a variety of ways from apparently unexplainable naiveté and minute memory lapses to a severe pathological lack of perception of internal (intrapsychic) events. The "forgetting" aspect of repression is unusual in that clearly symbolic mental activity frequently accompanies the memory loss, thus indicating that the repressed elements are not totally forgotten.

As for the generic application, the term repression is essentially synonymous with "defense" and is the precondition for the pathogenesis of all

---

* "Suppression" is the name given to the phenomenon of a *conscious* attempt to repel a feeling or thought from consciousness.

symptoms (Freud, 1916-1917a). The generic usage implies that repression is an initial stage as well as the prototype for *all* defense mechanisms. Although defense mechanisms are not always employed in the service of resistance (Langs, 1973), they certainly are frequently used for that purpose.

During the period from 1911 to 1915, Freud described three distinguishable phases of repression (Freud, 1915a, Laplanche & Pontalis, 1973). These three phases are in essence the three ways that repressive resistance operates. Phase One is "primal repression" whereby the psychic *instinctual* representatives are kept from *ever* reaching consciousness. The unconscious material resulting from primal repression serves as an unconscious nucleus attracting other psychic elements destined to be repressed.

Phase Two is the "repression proper" and can be considered an "after pressure" in that the mind repels unwanted material that has managed to gain entrance to consciousness. Also, since the second phase operates by expelling material *from* consciousness, it can be said that, from a systemic perspective (see Section 3.61), this phase of repression (that is, repression proper) operates from the psychical locality that is topographically higher than that of primal repression.

Phase Three is the "return of the repressed" whereby the mind represses by disguising the unconscious material so that its assent to consciousness occurs in other forms, for example, dreams, symptoms or parapraxes.

A few words should be directed towards the psychic elements upon which repressive resistance acts. Freudian theory proposes that, strictly speaking, it is not instincts but rather their psychic representatives that occupy the unconscious. The psychic representatives that have undergone primal repression have done so because they either originated from the instinct that is the primary target of the repression or they have accidentally become associated with the targeted instinct.

Repression is distinguishable from denial, although the two mechanisms frequently occur together. Denial interferes with the perception and recognition of *external* events. In contrast, repression interferes with the perception and recognition of *internal* (intrapsychic) events, i.e., thoughts, feelings and instincts. For example, if a person were angry at someone for hitting him but he denied his anger or forgot the name of the person towards whom he felt angry, this would be repression. In contrast, if he denied the existence of his clenched fist or of the chair that he just broke in anger or if he denied the existence of the wound inflicted by the attacker, this would be denial.

3.512 TRANSFERENCE RESISTANCE

Transference resistance is similar to repressive resistance but is distinct in that it is specific to the analytic situation.

> . . . [Transference resistance] is of the same nature [as repressive resistance] but which has different and much clearer effects in analysis, since it succeeds in establishing a relation to the analytic situation or the analyst himself and thus reanimating a repression which should only have been recollected (Freud, 1962a, p. 160).

The transference itself, whether positive or negative, is a product of resistance since the transference is an acted out repetition of memories that the patient wishes not to consciously remember; in other words the patient relives rather than remembers (Freud, 1914a). The false connections between the past and present manifest themselves in the transference, obscure the true connections, and thus function to serve resistance. Furthermore, the patient is more interested in immediately satisfying his needs through the transference and has less interest in overcoming the resistances to remembering (Fenichel, 1945). In essence, then, transference is not only the vehicle of cure, but can be a hindrance to the adjustive changes that are the ultimate goal of the therapy.

3.513 SECONDARY GAIN RESISTANCE

Secondary gain resistance is also an ego resistance, but it is quite different from transference resistance and repressive resistance since secondary gain resistance arises out of a gain from illness and is a result of the ego's assimilation of the symptoms. These benefits of the illness give rise to a disinclination to give up the pleasurable aspects of the symptom. In other words, this is a kind of resistance that is trying to prevent glimpses into the unconscious so that the illness will not be alleviated, the symptoms remain and the secondary gain will therefore continue.

3.514 SUPEREGO RESISTANCE

Freud called the resistance emanating from the superego the "last to be discovered, as well as the most obscure, though not always the least powerful one" (1926a, p. 160). This form of resistance stems from a sense of guilt or self-punishment and expresses itself as a hindrance to any form of success including the success of the psychoanalytic therapy.

3.515 Id Resistance

The resistance coming from the id is what makes "working through" an indispensable part of a successful psychoanalytic psychotherapy. Freud observed that after the ego and superego resistances are completely dismantled, the material still remains unconscious. As a result of this observation, Freud postulated a resistance of the unconscious. The repressed material must be worked through in order to overcome this id resistance. The id resistance gives rise to a "compulsion to repeat" (Freud, 1926a, p. 159) which Freud says is a result of the unconscious's attraction for the repressed instinctual derivatives (see Section 3.66 for a definition and discussion of id, ego and superego).

3.52 *The Contribution of the Concept of Resistance to Models of the Mind*

Although this book is not primarily concerned with metapsychology, there are unavoidable overlaps between a discussion of the techniques of psychoanalytic psychotherapy and the functional anatomy of the psychic apparatus. The development of the concept of resistance is an excellent case in point.

Freud's first theory of the mind was the systemic (topographical) model and it was only in 1923 (Freud, 1923b) that he introduced the opposing structural theory.* After proposing the systemic functional anatomy of the mind, Freud observed that some resistive forces were inaccessible to consciousness and thus must be in the unconscious, not the preconscious, as the systemic theory claims. Freud came to this conclusion following repeated observations of patients in analysis during which time he focused not only on sexual instincts, but on the anti-instinctual forces of the psychic apparatus. The patients frequently manifested various ways of resisting an awareness of unconscious material, while showing no awareness of the resistive activity. Hard work by the therapist and patient

---

* See Arlow and Brenner (1964) for a comprehensive monograph on the differences and similarities between the systemic and structural models of the mind. A summary of Arlow and Brenner's superb monograph is incorporated in Section 3.6 as well as in the next few paragraphs.

may or may not make these repressive forces accessible to consciousness. The critical point to be made at this point in our discussion is as follows: according to the systemic (topographical) theory of the functional anatomy of the mind, psychic forces responsible for repression are *only* in the preconscious and thus accessible to consciousness. Anything that is inaccessible to consciousness is by definition a sexual wish (or a psychic representation of a sexual wish) in the unconscious. Freud's clinical observations proved that the functional anatomy of the mind cannot be delineated in accordance with whether or not the psychic component was accessible to consciousness. Clinical observations revealed that resistive forces are *also* inaccessible to consciousness and thus more than sexual instincts existed in the unconscious. Thus, Freud was faced with a contradiction between his systemic (topographical) model and his clinical observations. Freud had no choice other than postulating a different model of the mind, a model that was to be called the "structural" model (see Section 3.66).

3.53 *Further Comments on Resistance*

Freud discovered that the resistance itself could reveal the contents of the unconscious. Wilhelm Reich (1933) expands these ideas to the extreme by proposing that "character" consists of resistance *only,* and that psychoanalytic psychotherapy consists of nothing more than uncovering the various layers of resistance. Although most contemporary therapists do not go to the extremes proposed by Reich, it can be safely said that the success of the therapy parallels the success in overcoming resistance. We know from clinical experience that the manifestations of resistance frequently sustain the maladaptive defenses which we call "symptoms." For example, a patient who suffers from a phobic avoidance is more likely to resist through avoidance in therapy. In interpreting the resistances to therapy, the therapist is also exploring the deepest layers of psychic structures by which the patient has attempted to resolve the intrapsychic symptoms that led him to therapy in the first place. The unconscious issues related to the resistances are the same issues, defenses, complexes, traits and repressive forces that are behind the pathogenesis of the neurosis itself (Langs, 1973).

> . . . they [the symptoms] represent not only the repression, but also the repressing force [and thus the resistance] which had a share in their origin (Freud, 1916-1917a, p. 301).

In essence then, by aggressively analyzing resistance the therapist achieves two goals: 1) removing obstacles to the progress of therapy, and 2) gaining insight into the unconscious intrapsychic processes that have given rise to the illness itself.

Paradoxically, the very technique of minimizing resistance is not just responsible for the superiority of psychoanalytic psychotherapy; rather, because the process consumes so much time, the attempt to reduce resistance is also responsible for the length of psychoanalytic treatment and one of the major reasons for the preference for other forms of therapy. If a psychotherapist has many patients and little time, he cannot afford the time that it takes to overcome resistance. In these brief therapies, the therapist gains the patient's confidence and cooperation mostly through the techniques of suggestion, abreaction, manipulation, clarification and confrontation. These techniques may yield symptomatic relief, but they should not be confused with the process of reducing resistance in an attempt to make the unconscious conscious. The psychoanalytic therapist believes that teaching (suggesting) or manipulating a patient does not effectively elicit permanent psychic change. The psychoanalytic therapist believes that only through meaningful insight into the unconscious can permanent curative changes be achieved. Thus, the reduction of resistance (often through interpretation) is necessary for a successful psychoanalytic therapy.

3.6 The Concept of Regression and the Psychoanalytic Models of the Mind

The concept of regression presupposes that the mind is constantly maturing both genetically and functionally, and that the developmental path of the individual remains within the mind.

The concept of regression was introduced into psychoanalytic literature by Freud (1900) as one of the ways to explain dream phenomena. Later on, Freud elaborated and revised his concept of regression and applied it to the concepts of pathogenesis and the disruption of normal development. Accordingly, Freud's concept of regression often implies something unhealthy or foreboding. In recent years, beginning with Kris (1952), regression has also been shown to have an adaptive as well as an ominous meaning. These healthy (adaptive) forms of regression are inextricably combined with normal psychic growth, insight and learning.

Freud presents six conceptualizations of regression: 1) topographical regression, 2) genetic-systemic regression,* 3) instinctual regression, 4) phylogenetic regression, 5) biogenetic regression, and 6) genetic-structural regression. Although the six categories will be presented in this section separately, the reader must remember that many of the concepts overlap, and in fact it is often difficult to distinguish whether an author is discussing—or when a patient is experiencing—one type or another.

3.61 *Topographical Regression*

According to the concept of topographical regression, the mind must first be conceptualized as having abstract, spatial and functional relationships to each other. The psychic layers ("agencies") are labeled the "systems" of perception (*Pcpt*), memory (*Mnem*), unconsciousness (*Ucs*), preconsciousness (*Pcs*), and consciousness (*Cs*) (see Figure 3.1). The emphasis on the five systems accounts for this model to be labeled the "systemic" perspective or "systemic" model of the mind (also synonymously called the "topographical" model of the mind).

According to the topographical model, psychic excitations travel from the sensory system *Pcpt* through the systems *Mnem, Ucs, Pcs* and *Cs*. The *Cs* is the part of the mind that provides us with conscious awareness of both the internal and external world and is also the source of stimulation of the conscious motor activity. Thus, psychic movements function in a reflex arc, beginning with internal or external perceptual stimuli of the mind and terminating in a discharge of motor activity. "Topographical regression" is the term given to the reverse of this flow of energy. Dreams and hallucinations are examples of topographical regression whereby psychic excitations travel *from* the *Mnem* to the *Pcpt* instead of to the *Cs*. Freud used the concept of topographical regression to explain the process whereby unconscious wishes express themselves as hallucinatory experiences in sleeping (dreams) and waking (psychotic) life. One of the major deficiencies of the concept of topographical regression is that it offers little understanding of the development of the mind of the infant into the mind of the adult.

---

* Arlow and Brenner (1964) originated the idea of distinguishing genetic-systemic regression, a concept that arises from Freud's systemic model of the mind, from the genetic-structural regression, a concept that results from Freud's structural psychic model which has, of course, replaced the systemic model.

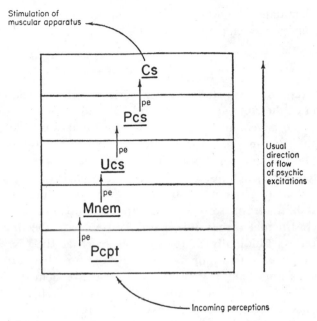

FIGURE 3.1. Schematic drawing of Freud's topographical perspective of the mind. The usual direction is the "progressive" direction as opposed to its opposite, "regressive" direction. The abbreviation "pe" stands for "psychic excitations." [Modified after Freud (1900). *The Interpretation of Dreams.* London: Hogarth Press, 1953, Chapter VII.]

3.62 Genetic-Systemic Regression

"Genetic-systemic" regression is the name for the concept that presupposes that the psychical systems or agencies of the mind are related to a series of causally related temporally successive events. In genetic-systemic regression, the person returns partially or symbolically in thought, feeling or behavior to one of the previous developmental phases. The concept of genetic-systemic regression attempts to offer some developmental understanding that is lacking in the concept of topographical regression. Freud informs us in his autobiographical study (1925a) that as far back as in his early reports on hysteria, he realized that all neuroses manifest to some degree some mental phenomena that were more frequent at an early time in the patient's life. The mind characteristically reacts to stress by attempting to reexperience past pleasurable experiences. This primordial tendency dominates the waking life of an infant, the waking life of hallucinating psychotics, and the sleeping life of normal adults.

3.63 *Instinctual Regression*

The concept of instinctual regression is actually a refinement and elaboration of the concepts of topographical and genetic-systemic regression. With the advent of his libido theory, Freud was able to expand the topographical and genetic-systemic meaning of regression to include more specific functions of the mind and the relationship of those functions to neurotic symptoms. Instinctual regression is the name given to the redirection (regression) of libidinal cathexis to instinctual wishes already established and stored within the unconscious. The regression to earlier instinctual wishes may manifest itself by cathecting an object that was once a libidinally charged object (such as the case in Freud's earlier concept of hysteria), or by returning to an earlier form of sexual organization as a whole (e.g., obsessive-compulsive neurosis is a return to anal-sadistic organization [Freud, 1916-1917b]). When these unconscious wishes receive additional psychic energy from the redirected libidinal cathexis, the previously repressed infantile wishes gain the energy to overcome the anti-instinctual forces of repression and neurotic symptoms result. Thus, neurotic symptoms are the consequences of primal repression, fixation and instinctual regression (see Section 3.511 for a definition of primal repression). The primal repression and fixation set the stage for the instinctual regression to take place, usually in response to stressful situations in later life. Another way of looking at this is that if it were not for primal repression and fixation, the misdirected libidinal cathexis would not find any repressed instinctual wishes that could be recharged.

Freud postulated that the original cathexis, attached to a specific point of fixation, determines the relationship between regression and fixation. During the long period of infancy, childhood and adolescence, the instinctual energy passes through critical periods of psychosexual development usually called oral (0-1 year), anal (2-3 years), phallic (Oedipal) (4-5 years), latency (6-12 years) and genital (over 12 years) psychosexual stages. In order for normal psychosexual development to occur, intrapsychic conflicts must be resolved during the course of interactions between the instincts, other intrapsychic processes and external environmental events. If these intrapsychic conflicts are resolved and an optimal amount of gratification is achieved at each stage, then there is a normal flow of cathexis from object to object or from one means of gratification to another. If the intrapsychic conflicts are not resolved, a "fixation" (psychological bondage) may occur at a specific stage or mode of development.

The concept of fixation is explained by Freud through the use of analogies. Freud compared the similarities of fixation to a migrant horde of people who, having left their domicile to find a new home, inevitably left certain members by the wayside during their difficult journey (Freud, 1916-1917b). Another analogy offered by Freud is, interestingly enough, the embryonic migration of sex glands from their origin in the abdominal wall through the inguinal canal to a position immediately beneath the skin of the pelvic cavity (Freud, 1916-1917b). If we consider the migration of the people or the migration of the sexual gland to be analogous to the development of an instinct or a part of the psychic apparatus, then fixation is the word designated by Freud to represent the phenomenon whereby there is a lagging behind of some part of the developing process. People left behind, or an undescended testicle, are thus analogous to the fixation of the developing instinct. It is at this conceptual point that fixation and instinctual regression are so closely related. The greater the amount of fixation experienced by an instinct during its development, the more likely it is the instinct will regress to the fixation point when the organism encounters internal or external stress.* Thus, fixation and regression go hand in hand.

It is plausible to suppose that fixation and regression are not independent of each other. The stronger the fixation on its path of development the more readily will the function evade external difficulties by regression to the fixations—the more incapable, therefore, does the developed function turn out to be of resisting external obstacles in its course. Consider that if a people which is in movement has left strong detachments behind on the stopping places on its migrations, it is likely that the more advanced parties will be inclined to retreat to the stopping places if they have been defeated or have come up against a superior enemy. But they will also be

---

* Arlow and Brenner (1964) point out that Lewin (1950) has reminded us that Freud and many of his followers such as Abraham were serious students of embryology and were no doubt influenced by the concept of progressive development from antecedent germinal layers (analogous to psychic development) as well as the biological concept of atavism and functional disinvolution (analogous to instinctual regression).

in the greater danger of being defeated the more of their number they have left behind on their migration (Freud, 1916-1917b, p. 341).

The concept of instinctual regression is not only an expansion of the concept of topographical and genetic-systemic regression, but for a period during Freud's writings, the concept of instinctual regression largely overshadowed the other types of regression. According to the concept of instinctual regression, normal psychosexual development involves nongenital sexual activity that is the sole sexual activity *before* the phallic psychosexual stage. When adult genitality is achieved, the pre-phallic sexual activity diminishes, although it frequently serves as fore-play. If, however, instinctual regression occurs, for example, in response to the threat of castration anxiety, the prephallic sexual activity may become the primary sexual focus or the activity the person seeks for orgasm. This then is called "perversion" and is actually an instinctual regression (provided, of course, that the genital stage was reached at one point in the developmental history).

According to the theory, instinctual regression plays an important role in determining the specific types of mental symptoms that may arise. For example, a precondition and major contributory cause of obsessional neurosis is an instinctual regression to the anal-sadistic psychosexual stage. Another example is Freud's (1911) idea that psychotic symptoms are the result of instinctual regression to the narcissistic phase of psycho-sexual development.

There are many mental phenomena and symptoms that Freud initially explained in instinctual-regression terms, of which he changed his explanation when he switched to the structural theory of the mind. For example, the phenomena of conversion, isolation, undoing, reaction formation, ambivalence, magical thinking and schizophrenia were first attributed to instinctual regression when Freud was operating from the topographical perspective of the mind and then switched to a structural explanation involving ego mechanisms of defense after he proposed his structural theory of the mind.

According to the instinctual-regression concept the union between libidinal phases and modes of psychic functioning results in regression being an all or none process involving the total personality rather than only certain parts of the psychic structure. (This concept is a major way in which the instinctual regression concept differs from the genetic-struc-tural theory). For example, sadomasochistic patients are significantly involved with no sexual interest other than sadomasochistic ones. Or, the obsessive-compulsive patients unconsciously associate feces to *all* people and things.

Another example of the close connection between instinctual regression and modes of psychic functioning can be seen in the depressed patient. *According to the instinctual regression concept,* depression is the result of regression of cathexis to a point of oral instinctual fixation within the *Ucs.* The oral instinctual fixation is of the whole mind, not just part of it. The depressed person is expected to assume the position of orality as if he were once again an infant, always behaving in a passive dependent manner and encountering all people and things as if they were mother and breast objects.

3.64 *Phylogenetic Regression*

Phylogenetic regression is a concept that has only historical significance, although it is occasionally mentioned in the current literature. The concept of phylogenetic regression operates on the presupposition that within each person's mind, in addition to memories of his infancy and childhood, are memories of the development of the human race (Freud, 1900, 1916-1917f). In other words, each human mind contains representatives of the human race's archaic heritage. Thus, a person can regress not only to childhood memories but also to forms of mental life that represent earlier evolutionary developmental stages of the human race. A corollary to this notion is that phylogenetic regression is a mental phenomenon by which we can learn more about the evolution of our race. The most meaningful way by which we get to view phylogenetic regression is through normal dreams and mental illness.

Freud (1921) tried to explain the dominance of the hypnotist over the subject as the manifestation of the subject's phylogenetic regression to the evolutionary period in which the father of the primal horde ruled absolutely over subordinate family members. Freud also used the concept of phylogenetic regression in trying to explain castration anxiety in people who never encounter, as far as psychoanalysis could determine, any actual castration threats.

Phylogenetic regression is no longer considered scientifically acceptable. There are better ways to explain mental phenomena that were previously attributed to phylogenetic regression. For example, the experiences of the phallic period offer a more plausible explanation of castration anxiety. Also, and this is the most severe criticism, the concept of phylogenetic regression can be neither validated nor invalidated by clinical observations. Thus, the concept has no useful clinical application.

3.65 Biogenetic Regression

The concept of biogenetic regression is as scientifically unacceptable and as clinically useless as that of phylogenetic regression, and for the same reasons. Nevertheless, for the sake of completeness, as well as to help the reader understand something about the way Freud and some of his followers thought during that time, it will be briefly discussed.

Biogenetic regression assumes that specific human psychic elements evolve from the evolutionary circumstances of subhuman organisms. Regression to these parts of the mind extend far beyond ontogenesis and even phylogenesis. Examples of an ego mode of functioning that are explained by biogenetic regression are the following: Organ alienation and self-castration have been associated to the anatomy of salamanders (Fenichel, 1945; Rado, 1939). Trances and stupors have been associated to unconditioned reflexes in nonhuman animals (Bonaparte, 1952), and the masochistic nature observed in female sexual activity has been associated to the "painful" penetration of a cell (Bonaparte, 1952).

3.66 Genetic-Structural Regression

After proposing the topographical (systemic) model of the mind, Freud (1900) observed that the conceptual model did not fit his clinical observations of mental conflict. Freud (1923b) proposed the structural theory which was more consistent with his clinical observations. The reasons for the abandonment of the topographical model have been discussed briefly in Section 3.52. What is relevant to our present discussion is how the structural model results in a new concept of regression, a concept that can be labeled "genetic-structural regression."

According to the structural model, the mind consists of three major structures ("macrostructures") : the id, ego and superego (see Figure 3.2). The *id* is the reservoir of all unconscious instinctual needs. These needs relentlessly strive for direct and indirect, open and disguised gratification. The *ego* both gratifies and governs the instincts, perceives and interacts with the external and internal environment, and in general, protects the total self. The *superego* is the name given to that part of the ego that deals with morality, conscience, guilt, self-evaluation, self-criticism and

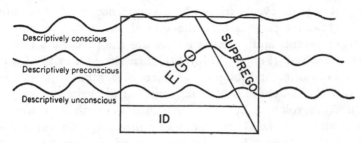

FIGURE 3.2. Freud's structural model of the mind. Straight lines indicate the boundaries of the psychic macrostructures. Wavy lines indicate a descriptive sense that attributes the specific quality of conscious, preconscious, or unconscious to the macrostructures.

self-punishment. This tripartite perspective of the human mind is in accordance with what Freud considered to be the two categories of intra-psychic conflicts: 1) the conflicts between the instincts and their related thoughts and feelings on the one hand and the defensive ego and moral superego on the other hand; 2) the conflicts between the defensive ego and the moral superego.

This conceptual focus on psychic structures is the major way in which the genetic-structural regression differs from genetic-systemic regression. The concept of genetic-structural regression is centered around the concept of evolving mental structures. This approach presupposes that the psychic structures are constantly maturing and evolving. Genetic-structural regression is the name given to those psychic phenomena that represent a shifting of some part of the psychic structures to a less mature mode of functioning. This concept applies to the operation of every part of the psychic structures, that is, to all components of the id, ego and superego, with the focus on developmental aspects. In accordance with this logic, genetic-structural regression consists of one or a combination of three subtypes of regression: 1) ego regression, 2) id regression and 3) superego regression.

Perhaps the example presented by Arlow and Brenner (1964) will help the reader distinguish genetic-structural regression from the three (topographical, genetic-systemic, instinctual) systemic perspectives of regression. This example is, in fact, one of the clinical observations that first led Freud to switch from a systemic to a structural model of the mind. I am referring to the delusion of being observed. Freud explained the delusion of being observed as the result of a genetic regression of conscience back to the past psychic events from which conscience (and thus superego) evolved. Freud's theory is that the ethical demands and moral prohibitions of parents and parental figures are the precursors from which conscience evolved (Freud, 1914b; 1917). In the memories of all of us are critical censoring and judgmental voices of significant people. Freud's theory is that the delusions of being watched are genetic regressions to those parental voices such that the memories of those voices are recathected and reactivated to perceptions that are then experienced as auditory hallucinations. Thus, the adult conscience, normally perceived as an intrapsychic phenomenon, undergoes regression and is perceived as an interpersonal relationship (between the person and the voices).

What is so new about the above example and how can we relate it to our current discussion? The answer lies in a comparison to the concepts of instinctual regression. At the height of his systemic perspective period of writing, Freud (1911) explained psychotic symptoms as the result of instinctual regression to the narcissistic phase of libidinal development. The new theory (Freud, 1914b; 1917) proposed that regression of libido is not enough to explain the delusions of being observed. In other words, genetic-structural regression is a concept that loosens up the previously tight conceptual connection between instinctual regression and psychic modes of activity. For example, conversion is no longer considered an instinctual regression but rather a defense mechanism that is the result of the conflict engendered by an oedipal wish in the phallic psychosexual stage.

In summary, then, the conceptual switch from the concept of a systemic regression to a genetic-structural regression represents a change in the conceptualization of the very essence of pathogenesis. No longer are development and regression exclusively a matter of instinctual development and instinctual regression. Psychosis is no longer viewed as the manifestation of a specific kind of regression of libido back to the stage of libidinal development called the narcissistic phase. Neuroses, too, are no longer viewed as manifestations of a global regression of the total personality. The genetic-structural concept of regression, in accordance with the structural perspective of the mind, allows for greater specificity and flexibility that is in accordance with clinical observations.

3.661 FOUR FUNDAMENTAL CHARACTERISTICS OF GENETIC-STRUCTURAL REGRESSION

It is helpful to follow the suggestions of Arlow and Brenner (1964) and conceptualize genetic-structural regression as comprised of four fundamental characteristics: 1) ubiquity; 2) the existence of primitive modes alongside mature ones; 3) the reversible and short-lived characteristics; and 4) the specific rather than global nature.

3.6611 *The Ubiquity of Genetic-Structural Regression*

Genetic-structural regression is one of the most characteristic attributes and universal features of all psychic operations. This concept was also well described by Piaget (1937) and by Anna Freud (1951, 1963) who proposed that every step towards a more mature level of psychic functioning is accompanied by some associated regressions.

3.6612 *Primitive Modes Existing Alongside Mature Modes*

The less mature modes of psychic functioning permanently exist alongside more mature forms of psychic activity. A corollary to this concept is that a new level of functioning reached by the mind will not always be maintained. In fact, normal regression is quite common, and there are numerous examples, with sleep-dreams and daydreams perhaps being the most traditional examples. Thus, when the mind evolves into a more mature mode of operation, the earlier mode does not disappear, but rather succumbs to the dominance of the newer form, always ready and able to reemerge in the appropriate situation.

3.6613 *Short-Lived and Reversible*

Genetic-structural regression is usually short-lived and almost always reversible. This characteristic of regression has profound practical implications. Clinicians are usually faced with the less transient types of genetic-structural regression. We sometimes tend to forget that most regressions, both normal and pathological, are temporary and easily reversible, such as is manifested in short-lived disturbances of orientation, transient depersonalization and derealization, déjà vu and its variants, and the variety of regressions observed during psychoanalytic therapy. *The severity or prognostic value of a specific form of regression is not its depth but rather its degree of reversibility, persistence and adaptability or maladaptability.*

3.6614 *Specific Rather Than Global*

This characteristic applies to all three psychic structures: id, ego, and superego. Distinct rather than global regression is logically consistent with the structural perspective that the id, ego and superego are not whole entities but rather are collections of specific functions responding to specific principles, demands, etc. This idea can perhaps be better understood if we take a closer look at each major psychic process.

Id Regression. According to the libido theory, an uncomfortable fantasy directly associated with a childhood instinctual wish is central to every neurotic symptom. The neurotic symptom is a manifestation of the cathexis of an oral, anal or phallic stage instinctual wish. Also, the fantasy behind the symptom is a wish for some *specific distinct* instinctual satisfaction. This concept has been illustrated by Arlow and Brenner (1964, p. 75).

The patient is an accountant whose work habits reveal a reaction formation and sublimation against anal instinctual wishes. A neurosis develops and is characterized by obsessive-compulsive symptoms which psychoanalysis shows to be a defense against a wish to kill or impregnate by using anal gas.

The relevance of this example is that even though the symptoms exist, that is, the anal regression has occurred, the character traits manifested in the professional success and normal sexuality persist without being impaired by the regression to the anal psychosexual stage. In other words, the *entire* organization of drives within the patient has not regressed, but rather only a *discrete* component has regressed such that the primitive anal instinct now exists side by side with reaction formations and sublimation which still maintain their autonomy and influence. Of course, in other illnesses such as severe schizophrenia, there is more regression of the total drive organization. But even in schizophrenia, certain instinctual drives persist in their most mature and adaptive forms. This concept has enormous practical clinical application to the concepts of treatability discussed in Chapter 5.

Ego Regression. Thoughts, feelings and behavior can sometimes be hierarchically categorized according to form, function and differentiation. Ego regression can be conceptualized as a retreat along this hierarchy to lower levels of expression.

Freud wrote relatively little about ego regression compared to his discussions about instinctual regression. This is probably because the concept of ego regression had to await Freud's development of the structural perspective of the mind which was not fully explained until

1923. Anna Freud, Hartmann and their followers have contributed more to the concept of ego regression than Freud himself.

Hartmann's Ego Autonomy and Differentiation Between Primary and Secondary Autonomy. In order to understand ego regression, the reader should have some understanding of the basic concepts of ego growth since ego regression is in many ways the reverse of ego development (I am referring now to the genetic-structural concept of regression). Thus, Hartmann's (1939, 1950, 1956, 1958) theories of ego autonomy are relevant at this point. In order to appreciate Hartmann's theories of ego evolution, we should perhaps briefly review part of the systemic perspective of the mind.

According to the systemic model of the mind, the psychic apparatus is fundamentally the instrument for the discharge of instinctual excitations. The external environment frustrates the drive reduction purpose of the mental apparatus. The psychic functions that we now call "ego" are a result of this environmental restraint on the satisfaction of instinctual drives.

According to Hartmann, simple observation shows us that certain ego functions are *not* necessarily the result of some instinctual circumstances. *Hartmann proposes that some ego activities are autonomous and independent of the instincts from the beginning of life. The primary autonomous ego functions are not consequences of frustrated instinctual drives, but rather are part of the genetic constitution that is a part of maturation in all human beings regardless of instinctual vicissitudes.*

The concept of primary autonomous ego functions certainly does not preclude the existence of *secondary* autonomous ego functions. In fact, Hartmann clearly states that there *are* secondary ego functions that achieve autonomy but are derived from, and are the result of, the frustration of instinctual drives. These ego functions may resolve intrapsychic conflicts and thereby be adopted as reliable and durable psychic structures that are governed by the ego and that show no resemblance to the unrestrained and illogical nature of the original instinct from which they derived. Some examples of secondarily autonomous ego operations are sublimations, intellectualizations, and a variety of characterological traits.

The normal ego tends to undergo a regression of its secondarily autonomous activities during intrapsychic conflict or external stress. Of course, in all psychopathological conditions there is a certain amount of regression of secondarily autonomous ego activities. In psychoses, ego functions that at one time enjoyed a significant amount of secondary autonomy regress to the point of being reinstinctualized. However, even in these cases, the regression is distinct and not generalized as would be proposed by the systemic perspective of topographical, genetic and instinctual regression. In other words, even in psychoses, most ego activity does not regress. This is a concept that has enormous practical clinical value since the therapist must use that healthy part of the ego in order to form the therapeutic cooperation necessary for just about any kind of psychological treatment.

In summary, then, the structural perspective clearly presupposes a direction of ego maturation in which the ego progressively achieves more secondary autonomy (primary autonomous ego functions exist at birth), gains more dominance over the derivatives of instinctual drives, and more successfully converts the impulsive drive energy into more adaptive secondary process modes of thinking.

Thus, it is clear what to expect if the ego regresses, that is, if the direction of ego growth is reversed. One can expect less secondary autonomy, less control over the id, and less successful adaptiveness of instinctual drives. Some examples of ego regression are the inability to differentiate daydreams from external perceptions or the conversion of sublimation into its instinctual precursors.

Defense Mechanisms. The concept of ego regression from one defense mechanism to a more primitive defense mechanism is an excellent illustration of genetic-structural regression. Defense mechanism is the name given to the mental process by which the ego wards off anxiety and other psychic dangers and attempts to resolve unconsciously the intrapsychic conflicts that result from mutually incompatible instinctual drives, external realities, and internal demands and prohibitions (Sjoback, 1973; Vaillant, 1971). Defense mechanisms are components of ego functioning and thus can be categorized along a hierarchical structure (Vaillant, 1971).* Such a categorization presupposes that mature defense

---

* Vaillant (1971) defines 18 defense mechanisms so that each defense mechanism is, by definition, mutually exclusive (15 of the 18 were defense mechanisms described by Anna Freud [1936]). Vaillant categorizes these 18 defense mechanisms into four groups along a hierarchical organization that theoretically correlates highly with degrees of mental illness. The most primitive group of defense mechanisms are associated with the most severe and most primitive illnesses. Group One is called the "Narcissistic Defense"; Group Two is called the "Immature Defenses"; Group Three, the "Neurotic Defenses"; and Group Four the "Mature Defenses." The four categories of defense mechanisms roughly correspond to the four classifications of abnormal behavior—psychosis, character disorder, neurosis, and normal coping reactions to normal stress situations.

mechanisms correlate positively with successful environmental adjustment. The conceptualization of defense mechanisms also presupposes that regression involves the falling back to less mature defense mechanisms. This type of regression usually involves those specific ego functions associated with intrapsychic conflicts, but the regression also influences the quality of many other ideas and feelings that are only loosely related to the intrapsychic conflicts (Moore & Fine, 1968).

A predominance of primitive defense mechanisms occurring in an adult is the result of either a developmental arrest *or* a regression of the ego as viewed from a genetic-structural perspective. Many Freudians conceptualize different stages of severe mental illness as corresponding to the patient's use of different groups of defense mechanisms (Engel, 1962; Menninger, 1963; Vaillant, 1971). For example, Semrad (Mann & Semrad, 1959; Semrad, 1967) conceptualizes the recovery of schizophrenia in this way. Semrad views schizophrenics as abnormally sensitive to loss. The illness is precipitated by a loss and the most regressed and decompensated stage of schizophrenia is when the person uses the defense mechanisms of denial, projection and distortion. As the patient begins to recover and compensate, he employs less primitive (more adaptive) defense mechanisms, such as conversion, hypochondriasis, incorporation and obsessive-compulsive behavior.

In essence, then, Semrad's and others' approach to schizophrenia and other diagnostic categories can be expanded and refined so that the defense mechanisms employed by anyone are correlated with the level of ego maturity at that point in time (Vaillant, 1971). In periods of stress, the ego may regress to defense mechanisms that are less mature, less adaptive, less sophisticated and more primitive. For example, a normal person may respond to an overwhelming personal loss by regressing to the point of *denying* that loss. This phenomenon is what we are calling genetic-structural regression. The ego regression to denial is more pathological and less adaptive than, for example, the ego's use of intellectualization.

The concept of regression of ego defenses presupposes not only that the mature defense mechanisms can regress to less mature ones, but also that the immature defense mechanisms that were once adaptive will not necessarily be abandoned but can, and will, evolve into the more mature defense mechanisms as the organism develops. Such an evolutionary process can be highly specific such that a given defense mechanism may evolve into some specific defense mechanisms and not into others. For example, the *denial* of infancy and childhood may evolve into *repression* in later childhood and then be replaced in adulthood by *suppression* (Vaillant, 1971). If this evolution does not take place, the specific defense mechanism will become maladaptive. For example, excessive denial, which is adaptive to the infant, is rarely adaptive and usually maladaptive in adult life. The evolution of defense mechanisms is the result not only of psychosocial maturation, but of biological maturation as well (Vaillant, 1971).

Superego Regression. We have already touched upon the subject of genetic-structural regression of the superego when we discussed the delusion of being observed in our discussion of the distinction between a systemic versus a genetic-structural perspective of regression (see Section 3.66).

As with the concept of ego regression, we must be familiar with some concepts of superego *development* before we can fully understand the meaning of superego genetic-structural regression, since this concept of regression is, for the most part, temporal. Since the superego develops out of the ego, our previous discussion about the directions of ego development is applicable to our explanations of the direction of superego development with, of course, important refinements. *Whereas the direction of ego development is towards more secondary autonomy, control over instincts, and more realistic conversion of instinctual energy, the direction of superego maturation entails substitution of judgment for guilt and the substitution of moral prohibitions and demands for purely affective activities.* When referring to the ego maturation there is a familiar dictum: "Where id was, there shall ego be." Regarding the superego, this maxim can be changed to "where superego was, there shall ego be."

Just as with the regression of id and ego, regression of superego is also distinct rather than global. As with id and ego regression, the distinctness of superego regression can be clinically observed. For example, one manifestation of superego regression may be a shift in values or sudden lapse of ethics. The specific nature of the regression may be manifested by distinct delusions, hallucinations or dreams that correspond to various stages of superego regression. Also, people can be observed to have strong feelings of guilt and needs to be punished associated with certain objects or situations and not associated with others.

3.7 THE THEORY OF CURE

The theory of cure is a very complicated subject beyond the scope of this chapter and has been a source of much controversy and writing (for comprehensive discussions on this subject, see Glover, 1937; Knight, 1941-42; Loewald, 1960; Pfeffer, 1963; Strachey, 1934). We can summarize, however, by saying that there has been, among theorists and clinicians, a gradual and continuous shift from emphasis on catharsis and the therapist's role as a reflecting mirror (Breuer & Freud, 1893) to the therapist and patient reciprocally interacting in an active and evolving psychoanalytic process (Dewald, 1976).

According to psychoanalytic theory, cure is achieved in psychoanalytic psychotherapy through a complicated process during which the patient freely expresses verbal and nonverbal communication. The therapist verbally and nonverbally examines the unconscious so that the patient becomes aware of the previously unconscious intrapsychic forces and conflicts. The patient then assimilates this awareness so that there is a constructive mobilization of psychic drives, a decrease in tolerance of the superego and a more adaptive ego function resulting in a reduction of intrapsychic conflicts and the unpleasant affects that accompany such conflicts so that there is a permanent end to the psychic struggles producing the symptoms.

The previous paragraph describes a process by which cure is achieved but does not tell us why cure results. The fact is that no one really knows why the patients get better from psychoanalytic psychotherapy. The following is a comment that I think is one of the more intelligent and honest on the subject of goals and theory of cure.

> One of the as yet unsolved problems of psychoanalysis [psychoanalytic psychotherapy] is concerned with the essential nature of psychoanalytic cure. It is not insight; it is not the recall of infantile memories; it is not catharsis or abreaction; it is not the relationship to the analyst [therapist]. Still, it is all of these in some synthesis which it has not yet been possible to formulate explicitly. Somehow, in a successful analysis [psychoanalytic psychotherapy] the patient matures as a total personality. Somehow, a developmental process which has been halted or side-tracked, resumes its course. It is as though the person, re-experiencing his past and the transference, finds in the new conditions a second chance and "redevelops" while he is "reliving" (Gitelson, 1951, p. 285).

CHAPTER 4

THE COMPONENTS OF
THE THERAPEUTIC
RELATIONSHIP

> You can go on analyzing forever and get nowhere. It is the personal
> relation that is therapeutic. Science has no values except scientific
> values, the schizoid values of the investigator who stands outside of
> life and watches. It is purely instrumental, useful for a time but then
> you have to get back to living (Fairbairn, quoted by Guntrip, 1975,
> p. 145).

The therapeutic relationship is as complicated and complex as any
other kind of human relationship. The therapeutic relationship is of
greatest importance in psychoanalytic psychotherapy since it is not only
the means by which the patient's intrapsychic conflicts are explored
and resolved, but also the means by which are created the major obstacles
to treatment. Although there is universal agreement among psychoanalytic therapists on the critical importance of the therapeutic relationship, there are enormous divergences of opinion on almost every
theoretical and technical aspect. This chapter provides this writer's
perspectives on some of the basic concepts as they relate to our previous
discussion and to the discussion of treatability in Chapter 5.

In psychoanalytic psychotherapy, the therapeutic relationship operates
in four dimensions: 1) transference, 2) therapeutic alliance, 3) narcissistic alliance, and 4) real relationship. This chapter consists of four
sections, each section devoted to a definition and discussion of one of
the four dimensions of the therapeutic relationship. We will discuss the
four components again in Chapter 5 but only as they relate to the issue
of treatability.

In order for psychoanalytic psychotherapy to be clinically successful, all four dimensions of the patient/therapist relationship must be fully recognized and equally, actively utilized by therapist and patient as media for intrapsychic change. Furthermore, these relationships can and should be used as part of the basis of our nosology (Kohut, 1971; Modell, 1975). Most elements of these four components exist to some degree in most personal as well as professional relationships (for example, teacher/student or lawyer/client); what makes psychoanalytic psychotherapy so unusual is that in no other professional dyadic relationship are the two people determined to make the relationship a major object of intense scrutiny.

The phenomena of transference, therapeutic alliance, narcissistic alliance and real relationship are separated only for expository purposes. Although a relatively distinct separation is always considered the idealized goal of psychoanalytic therapy, all patient/therapist relationships consist of overlapping mixtures of the four aspects of the therapeutic relationship. For example, most, if not all transferences are adaptive or maladaptive responses to some current stimulus within the real relationship (Langs, 1974). The real aspects of transferences and all real relationships are influenced by past experiences with significant others. The experience of a regressive transference certainly creates very real experiences for the patient, some aspects of which may be experienced for the very first time. Furthermore, the very fact that the patients present themselves for psychotherapy is proof of some degree of therapeutic alliance in every patient being seen, although it may not be enough to sustain a course of psychoanalytic psychotherapy. Needless to say, there is a certain amount of narcissism in all interpersonal relationships. Thus, when we speak of the transference, the therapeutic alliance, the narcissistic alliance, or the real relationship, we are speaking relatively and identifying the relationship by separable elements that predominate based on the definitions presented below that identify those elements. At any point in time, one or the other of the four types of relationships may predominate but the core of the other three relationships will still exist. In order to identify the predominant component of the therapeutic relationship, it is often necessary to gather large amounts of information, not only about the patient but about the therapist and the external environment.

Before proceeding with the discussion of the four components of the therapeutic relationship, there is another introductory concept of critical importance, namely, that in the dyadic therapeutic relationship there are *two* people involved. Accordingly, there are two people independently making evaluative judgments about whether or not a specific behavior fits any definition of transference, therapeutic alliance, narcissistic alliance, or real relationship. Hopefully, the two people will agree most of the time whether they, for example, conceptualize a specific behavior as a part of the transference rather than the real relationship. Nevertheless, there may be times when one person considers the patient's behavior as a manifestation of one of the four components of the therapeutic relationship whereas the other person is dealing with that behavior as a manifestation of one of the other components. It cannot be overemphasized that there are multiple combinations of these potential discrepancies. For example, most therapists are familiar with the numerous literature and clinical examples that deal with the problems of helping a patient perceive that what the patient sees as real relationship is actually transference. Few papers or clinical discussions, however, deal with the possibility (and frequent actuality) that the patient views his behavior as transference but the therapist is perceiving and acting as if the behavior is a manifestation of the real relationship (see Szasz, 1963, for an eloquent discussion of this important concept).

4.1 THE CONCEPT AND THERAPEUTIC RATIONALE OF TRANSFERENCE AND TRANSFERENCE NEUROSIS

I now come to the description of a factor which adds an essential feature to my picture of analysis [psychoanalytic psychotherapy] and which can claim, alike technically and theoretically, to be regarded as of the first importance. In every analytic treatment there arises, without the physician's [therapist's] agency, an intense emotional relationship between the patient and the analyst [therapist] which is not to be accounted for by the actual situation. It can be of a positive or of a negative character and can vary between the extremes of a passionate, completely sensual love and the unbridled expression of an embittered defiance and hatred. This *transference*—to give it its short name—soon replaces in the patient's mind the desire to be cured, and, so long as it is affectionate and moderate, becomes the agent of the physician's influence and neither more nor less than the mainspring of the joint work of analysis. Later on, when it has become passionate or has been converted into hostility, it becomes the principal tool of the resistance. It may then happen that it will paralyze the patient's powers of associating and endanger the success of the treatment. Yet it would be senseless to try to evade it; for an analysis without transference is an impossibility. It must not be supposed, however, that transference is created by analysis and does not occur apart from it. Transference is merely uncovered and isolated by analysis. It is a universal phenomenon of the human mind, it decides the success of all medical influence, and in fact dominates the whole of each person's relations to his human environment. We can easily recognize it as the same dynamic factor which the hypnotists have named "suggestibility," which is the agent of hypnotic *rapport* and whose incalculable behaviour led to the difficulties with the cathartic method as well. When there is no inclination to a transference of emotion such as this, or when it has become entirely negative, as happens in dementia praecox or paranoia, then there is also no possibility of influencing the patient by psychological means (Freud, 1925a, p. 42, italics in the original).

Of all of the countless phenomena intrinsic to psychoanalytic psychotherapy, the unavoidable reality of transference is one of the most awesome experiences, is the most theoretically and technically burdensome, and has required repeated clarification and reclarification throughout the psychoanalytic literature (e.g., Bird, 1972; Brenner, 1976; Breuer & Freud, 1895; Freud, 1905a, 1910, 1912, 1914a, 1915b, 1916-1917j, 1920a, 1925a, 1937; Greenacre, 1954; Jackel, 1966; Kepecs, 1966; Lagache, 1953; Loewald, 1971; Macalpine, 1950; Nunberg, 1951; Orr, 1954; panel discussion, 1956; Sandler et al., 1969; Silverberg, 1948; Szasz, 1963; Weinshel, 1971; Wolstein, 1954, 1960; Zetzel, 1956).

The first use of the term transference in the psychoanalytic literature was by Breuer and Freud (1895). Their use of the term to denote the "false connection" (p. 302) to the person of the therapist was much narrower than Freud's later concept of transference which began with the publication of the Dora case (Freud, 1905a; Strachey, 1953).

Until his treatment of Dora, an 18-year-old woman whom Freud treated in 1900, Freud and others considered transference as something that got in the way of the therapeutic alliance and had to be recognized so that it could be eliminated in order for the therapy to continue successfully. Even with Dora, Freud did not recognize the importance of the transference and countertransference while actually treating her (Lewin, 1973-74; Marcus, 1976; Muslin & Gill, 1978; Rogow, 1978). In fact, Freud speculated when writing her case history that had he recognized and interpreted the transference and transference neurosis, the abrupt and premature termination after only three months of therapy might have been prevented.

There is in the psychoanalytic literature no unified conceptualization of transference and transference neurosis and, as noted in the excellent reviews by Macalpine (1950), Orr (1954) and Kepecs (1966), there is wide divergence among clinicians. In essence, the difference between transference and transference neurosis is a quantitative one. The problem with making this distinction on a quantitative basis is that there is no agreement among theorists and clinicians as to what are the measuring parameters. Furthermore, psychoanalytic researchers and therapists lack the luxury of measuring instruments and standards of measurement. Thus, as so often happens with psychoanalytic concepts, we have concepts that are distinguished quantitatively but we lack means to quantitate. Such a situation leaves the distinction between transference and transference neurosis to arbitrary impressions (Szasz, 1963). I have tried to minimize this pitfall by defining in the next few paragraphs what I mean by transference and transference neurosis and then by using those terms in this book in accordance with those definitions.*

The term transference can be defined as referring to any phenomenon, no matter how sporadic or transient, that fits all of the following five criteria: that it 1) is an interpersonal relationship; 2) is largely determined by previous relationships with significant people, especially significant infantile and childhood relationships; 3) is an unconscious and/or preconscious repetition of past intrapsychic conflicts and *early* pathogenic relationships—transference is a reexperiencing without memory, and when reexperienced in the therapeutic setting, occurs in a psychic rather than a motor sphere; 4) is relatively anachronistic and inappropriately relevant to the current situation in which it occurs; and 5) involves the psychic mechanism of displacement (Greenson, 1967; Langs, 1974).

There is limited understanding as to why transference occurs. Freud (1905a, 1914a) emphasized that psychoanalytic therapy does not *create* transference since transference occurs with all people at all times and is, in fact, an unavoidable part of all human relationships.

A capacity for direct libidinal object-cathexes onto people must of course be attributed to every normal person. Dependency to trans-

---

*See Alexander and French (1946) for an opposing view that proposes that we discard the term transference neurosis and consider all these phenomena as those of transference.

ference of the neurotics I have spoken of is only an extraordinary increase of this universal characteristic (Freud, 1916-1917j, p. 446).

The various psychoanalytic theories about transference entail a spectrum of opinion that extends from the extreme that considers transference as a phenomenon that occurs only in psychoanalytic psychotherapy, to the extreme that proposes that the transference is a ubiquitous human phenomenon occurring to some degree with all interpersonal relationships (Kepecs, 1966). According to this latter view, transference is so ubiquitous that it can be conceptualized as a "primitive social instinct" (Greenacre, 1954, p. 672).*

Most theorists and clinicians agree that, at least within the psychoanalytic situation, transference is relatively spontaneous and is founded on two basic inherent human tendencies: 1) the tendency to regress and 2) the tendency to manifest a repetition compulsion (Singer, 1970). The transference serves to fulfill repressed frustrated needs while simultaneously serving the resistance, since remembering and working through are compulsively and repetitively replaced by the thoughts, feelings and behavior of the transference.

Many patients in psychoanalytic psychotherapy develop intense transference to their therapist but never develop a transference neurosis. The difference between transference and transference neurosis is that the latter describes a relatively intense, permanent, and stable neurotic condition that arises out of the ungratified instinctual demands of the psychoanalytic situation (Blum, 1971). The transference neurosis is characterized by the therapist's becoming one of the most important people, if not the most important person, in the patient's life. In the transference neurosis, the therapist is the person with whom the patient reexperiences the intrapsychic conflicts that cause the symptoms for which the patient sought treatment (Freud, 1914a, 1916-1917j; Greenson, 1965). The transference neurosis, then, can be conceptualized as a specific clinical entity limited to the psychoanalytic therapeutic relationship, whereas transfer-

---

* For divergent psychoanalytic views, see Macalpine (1950), Waelder (1956), Gill and Brenman (1961) and Marmor (1962), who assert that transference is not a spontaneous phenomenon but rather is an artificially evoked form of regression imperceptibly induced by the readiness of the therapist and the rigid infantile setting imposed by the therapist in a manner comparable to the hypnotist's induction of hypnosis. Szasz (1963) responds to Macalpine, Waelder and others by arguing that to say transference is limited to psychoanalytic psychotherapy because that is where it is most closely scrutinized is as illogical as saying bacteria only exist under a microscope.

ence in the more general sense can be viewed as a phenomenon occurring to some degree in all relationships. The transference neurosis is more pervasive and organized than the isolated transference phenomena. It is characterized by tenacity, capriciousness and intensity (Greenson, 1965), and is the prototype by which the neurosis is expressed within the therapy.

> [In the transference neurosis] all the patient's transference symptoms have abandoned their original meaning and have taken on a new sense which lies in a relation to the transference [transference neurosis]; or only such symptoms have persisted as are capable of undergoing such a transformation. But the mastering of this new, artificial neurosis coincides with getting rid of the illness which was originally brought to the treatment—with the accomplishment of our therapeutic task (Freud, 1916-1917j, p. 444).

The reexperienced intrapsychic conflicts represent unconscious, infantile and childhood unsatisfied libidinal needs and conflicts. These previously unconscious object libidinal urges, with their preconscious strivings and accompanying intrapsychic conflicts, are directed towards the object of the therapist, remembered, reexperienced, worked through and resolved in the current treatment setting (Freud, 1912, 1914a) . The transference neurosis is always ambivalent (positive and negative) towards the therapist since the displaced thoughts and feelings have an infantile origin and all infantile object relationships are ambivalent (Freud, 1912; Greenson, 1967).

Starting with his discussion of Dora, Freud gradually realized that a transference neurosis must occur and be resolved in every successful psychoanalytic psychotherapy. At first Freud limited consideration of the transference neurosis as responding to the Pleasure Principle in search of libidinal satisfaction (1914a, 1915b). Later on, however, Freud expanded his ideas so that the transference neurosis was also seen as a compulsion-to-repeat response to the urges of the aggressive instinct (Freud, 1920a; Greenson, 1967) .

Many Freudians consider the exploration of transference neurosis to be Freud's major contribution. First, the transference neurosis is the indispensable driving force behind the curative elements of the psychoanalytic process. Second, if it were not for the concept of transference, the therapist would probably be drastically less able, if not unable, to remain scientifically detached and observant within a format which he so actively experiences as a person (Szasz, 1963). Third, clinicians have found transference neurosis to be the most effective procedure by which the patient surmounts the resistance to the repressed and painful unconscious.

Transference is a rejuvenation of intrapsychic conflicts that manifest themselves in the patient-therapist interpersonal relationship. Thus, a cognitive and emotional reality is achieved for the patient. Of course, transference neurosis is an artificially generated interpersonal phenomenon. Furthermore, the totality of one's life can never be totally resurrected in the transference neurosis. Clinical experience has shown, however, that if the therapist has the knowledge and technical skill, the most significant pathogenic intrapsychic conflicts that were once reflected in a child-significant other relationship will invariably be reflected in the relationship between the adult patient and therapist (Alexander, 1954a).

If we assume that transference is a universal interpersonal phenomenon, we can then say that psychoanalytic psychotherapy differs from all other therapies (or for that matter, from all other interpersonal relationships) in that psychoanalytic psychotherapy: 1) contains a recognition of and attempt to overcome the initial preformed transference resistance; 2) technically facilitates the intensification of keenly sensitive transferences so that the transference neurosis develops; and 3) contains an expectation that the patients will learn from the transference phenomena without acting them out.

An intermediate goal of psychoanalytic therapy is for the patient to resolve various components of the transference neurosis in response, at least in part, to interpretations or to the equivalent of interpretations. As already mentioned, the patient in psychoanalytic therapy experiences the intrapsychic conflicts within the current transference neurosis as if the conflicts were the original pathogenic problems. A concept that cannot be overemphasized, however, is that the transference neurosis is more than a replication of old conflicts and relationships in a new setting (Blum, 1971; Weinshel, 1971). The transference neurosis is also a *transformation*, that is, the transference neurosis has some qualities of its own that are quite distinct from the *original* neurosis, or as Freud stated, ". . . new editions of the old disorder" (Freud, 1916-1917j, p. 444).

The resurrected primary conflicts are less intense than their original (usually childhood) situations. In response to the therapist's empathic and interpretive interventions, the patient develops a therapeutic alliance and a real relationship and is able to apply more mature secondary process modes of thinking and reality testing to the original problems. The patient is less helpless and less impotent to find resolutions to the conflicts that he experienced as a child, since he is now an adult who has undergone ego development and maturation. Furthermore, since the transference neurosis is a less forceful duplication of the original intrapsychic conflict, the patient not only has a stronger ego with which to work, but also is confronted with a weaker conflict.

Another favorable component within the treatment setting is the therapist's reaction to the patient's transference. The therapist usually is less intimidating and less punitive than the parents of childhood, and so once again the transference neurosis situation facilitates resolution of the earlier intrapsychic conflicts. A resolution of the conflicts this second time around may not only alleviate symptoms but may free the patient from previous maturational retardation (fixation) that may be a consequence of the original conflict so that the patient progresses ontogenetically.

Mrs. B is a 28-year-old housewife in thrice-weekly psychoanalytic psychotherapy for excessive anxiety and a phobic avoidance of sexual intercourse. Although Mrs. B's mother and father never divorced and always lived together, one of the major traumatic events of Mrs. B's childhood was her mother's periodic escapades with other men, which on three occasions resulted in mother unexpectedly running away with another man, staying away for a few months and then, just as unexpectedly, returning. These three "abandonments" all occurred between the ages of five and 11, leaving Mrs. B very ambivalent about allowing herself to be close to anyone for fear that they would also abandon her.

After two years of the psychotherapy, Mrs. B's therapist, Mrs. X, a very skilled 35-year-old psychiatric social worker, had to move to a city hundreds of miles away because Mrs. X's husband received a very significant promotion and job transfer. Mrs. X was able to announce the move six months in advance. Needless to say, Mrs. B was very upset by the imminent move and, as a result of the transference, fully expected Mrs. X to behave in the same way as her mother. During the course of the last six months of therapy, Mrs. B was able to deal with the issues of "abandonment" with someone who was not acting impulsively and selfishly as Mrs. B's mother had done.

The issues of separation from the therapist were dealt with through the context of the transference but this time the maternal object (the therapist) was able to respond in a caring and sensitive manner, thereby allowing Mrs. B to express the full range of emotions towards the maternal object in an appropriate and therapeutic fashion. This was in great contrast to Mrs. B's childhood where the maternal object left unexpectedly, was not present so that the child could give vent to the feelings in a direct fashion, and then when she returned was not emotionally available to allow the child to express the feelings. As in the case of Ms. A, which follows, we see an example of the transference being ". . . new editions of the old disorder" (Freud, 1916-1917j, p. 444).

Ms. A was a 26-year-old novelist in twice-weekly psychoanalytic psychotherapy because of depression of neurotic proportions precipitated by memories that emerged while writing a fictional novel with autobiographical elements. The specific memories that precipitated the depression involved the death of her mother, a cancerous death after two years of terminal illness that occurred when the patient was 13 years old. During her mother's illness and after her death, her father was so overcome with grief that he was unable to be supportive and help Ms. A with her grief. For example, Ms. A was so overwhelmed by the death that she could not bring herself to attend the funeral services, and father was so overwhelmed that he could not take the advice of friends and relatives and insist that Ms. A go through the burial ceremonies as a way to help her mourn the loss of mother. Furthermore, Ms. A ran away from home a few weeks after the death and again, father's own grief and depression interfered with his handling the situation in a helpful manner.

During the psychotherapy, Ms. A developed a very intensive transference neurosis involving full-blown oedipal issues. She cognitively and emotionally reexperienced the death of mother and fully expected the therapist to respond in the same way that her father had responded. This time, however, she experienced "new editions of the old disorder." The "father" this time, being reexperienced through the therapist in the transference, was not emotionally unavailable, but rather, was able to sit with the patient so that she could deal with the issues that she repressed at the age of 13. Then father did not go after her when she ran away, but rather let her come back on her own, a passive response that the patient always perceived as a lack of concern. It became quite clear during the course of the therapy that one reason Ms. A ran away from *home was that she was afraid to be alone with her father since she not only feared his grief, but she feared his love for her and fantasized that he would expect her to somehow replace mother. In the psychotherapy, when Ms. A "quit" therapy, the therapist called the patient at home on three separate occasions and finally the patient agreed to come back into treatment.*

One of the ways of looking at this case is that the therapist was able to respond to Ms. A through the paternal transference in a healthier way than the original paternal object responded. This allowed the patient to work through some of the issues about mother's loss and some of the anger and love that she felt towards her father. The transference experience was certainly not an exact replication of the original parental experience. In the transference situation, the patient did not have to deal with the oedipal issues and the ambivalence towards father in the same real sense that they existed during the original experience. This gave her the distance that she needed to work on the issues and to resolve them intrapsychically.

4.11 *Corrective Emotional Experience*

The concept of "corrective emotional experience" promotes role playing on the part of the therapist. Corrective emotional experience is in opposition to the value placed on verbal interpretations and conscious understanding of the transference neurosis.

Ferenczi and Rank (1925) deserve credit for introducing this concept to the psychoanalytic literature. It was Alexander and his followers (Alexander, 1944, 1953, 1954a, 1954b; Alexander & French, 1946), however, who vigorously promoted the idea that certain *behavior* by the therapist has a greater curative influence and greater impact in making the unconscious conscious than do verbal interpretations, abreaction, insight and working through the insight. For example, if the patient as a child was intimidated by a tyrannical father, the therapist may choose to be outspokenly permissive; or, if the parent of childhood was over-indulgent to the point of evoking guilt in the patient, the therapist may choose to be more detached. In other words, Alexander and his followers recommend that the therapist facilitate the formation of the transference in a desired direction by manipulating the external environment through use of specific attitudes, feelings, role playing, and other behavior shown by the therapist towards the patient (Orr, 1954).

The concept of corrective emotional experience has had a profound impact on the psychoanalytic literature and has been the subject of numerous papers, panel discussions and debates. Lipton (1977) has even submitted the interesting possibility that the modern psychoanalyst's techniques have arisen, in part, as reactions against Alexander's promotion of corrective emotional experience. Lipton suggests that the classical analyst's (see Section 2.42) attempt to erradicate all personal influence that the therapist has on the patient, in itself, exerts a profound impact.

A thorough discussion of Alexander's provocative ideas is beyond the scope of this chapter. For a thorough and harsh critique of Alexander's perspectives, the reader is referred to Eissler (1950) who disdainfully refers to corrective emotional experience as "magic psychotherapy" as opposed to the "rational therapy" of *verbal* interpretations of the transference.

Although it is important for us to understand the concept of corrective emotional experience, I would like to emphasize that I do not support role playing on the part of the therapist. This book supports the value of cognitive understanding, as well as emotional and bodily experience of the treatment, as necessary for psychoanalytic psychotherapy to be clinically successful. The concept of corrective emotional experience, in my view, incorrectly assumes that the interpersonal relationship with the therapist can be a substitute for the emergence of the unconscious transference elements. It is incorrect in its assumption that a current relationship can by its very existence undo the effects of past relationships. The current relationship with the therapist and the past relationships differ in time, place, situation and attitude, and thus it is wrong to assume that one relationship can be exchanged for another (Stone, 1961). The transference must be expressed and experienced, but the patient must gain conscious affective insight into the past relationships so that the previously unconscious conflicts can be resolved.

Despite my disagreement with Alexander's concepts of corrective emotional experience, clinicians should not "throw out the baby with the bath water" with regard to Alexander's ideas on these matters. The proponents of corrective emotional experience have an important lesson to teach in emphasizing the enormous corrective value of the therapeutic relationship. This value will be discussed in more detail in this chapter and will also be explicitly and implicitly emphasized throughout this volume.

4.2 THERAPEUTIC ALLIANCE

The concept of therapeutic alliance originated with the pioneering work of Sterba (1934) and Bibring (1937) who described the ego split that must occur for the relatively mature part of the patient's ego to identify with the real aspects of the therapist as both people share common goals of treatment (Modell, 1975).

There have been numerous terms for the concept of therapeutic alliance. For example, Greenson prefers the term "working alliance" (Greenson, 1965, 1967) because it focuses on *work* that the patient must do, sometimes despite the neurosis and transference. Other terms used are "rational transference" (Fenichel, 1941); "mature transference" (Stone, 1961); "therapeutic dissociation" (Sterba, 1934); "the analytic pact" (Freud, according to Pfeiffer, 1972); "allying rationally" (Schafer, according to Gutheil & Havens, 1979) ; "prosthetic alliance" (Kernberg, 1968). These authors define therapeutic alliance in accordance with their own clinical and conceptual perspectives and often in accordance with the specific clinical and conceptual dilemmas which have led them to formulate the terms and definitions and to share their ideas with the psychoanalytic readership. All of these terms encompass the same fundamental concepts and for the purposes of uniformity this book will consistently use the term "therapeutic alliance," which was introduced by Zetzel in 1956 (Zetzel, 1956).

As has been eloquently discussed by Friedman (1969) and Gutheil and Havens (1979), therapeutic alliance is a complicated subject upon which there is much disagreement and many paradoxes among Freudians. For example, Freud (1937) conceptualized the therapeutic alliance as the result of the patient's libidinal attachment to the therapist. According to Freud, the therapeutic alliance is the primary motivating force behind the treatment and is indistinguishable from the nonsexual positive transference (see Freud quote on first page of Section 4.1) although, of course, Freud observed that all transferences are a mixture of positive and negative transference phenomena (1912, 1916-1917j).

Sterba (1934, 1940) considered the therapeutic alliance as more of a *consequence* of the treatment than a motivating force. Sterba conceptualized the phenomenon as one that results from the therapist and patient sharing the same goals and expectation of the treatment. Sterba's concept places great emphasis on the patient's *identification* with the therapist so that the patient's perceptions of himself are relatively uninfluenced by transference and neurosis. One part of the patient's ego is allied with the therapist as both people team up against the instinctual and defensive energies. This concept of therapeutic alliance utilizes martial metaphors, as if there is a war occurring between the instinctual forces and the defensive forces, both forces interfering with the psychoanalytic process (Gutheil & Havens, 1979). The alliance, according to Sterba, is as if there is an ally within the enemy camp, the ally being a team composed of the therapist and that part of the patient's ego that is realistic and seeks psychic health and growth. Thus, Sterba's concept of therapeutic alliance involves intrapsychic structure (ego split), object relations and psychoanalytic process (identification with the therapist).

Another way of describing Sterba's concept of therapeutic alliance is to say that the patient consists of two people, one driven by instinctual and repressive (defensive) forces that can only interfere with psychoanalytic psychotherapy. The other person within the patient is realistic, rational, and seeks self-understanding, psychic change and psychic growth. The therapist forms a partnership with the latter person of the patient and even makes interventions in order to allow the emergence of the "rational" person within the patient (Gutheil & Havens, 1979).

In contrast to Sterba, Nunberg (1926, 1928, 1955) conceptualized the goals of the patient in treatment as much different from those of the therapist. Nunberg proposed that the patient's alliance with the therapist is based on the patient's *distortions* of the realistic aspects of the therapeutic relationship. The distortions themselves are the consequences of the very neurosis which the therapeutic alliance will eventually help to remove. Such distortions engender the patient's unobtainable wishes, such as the wish for complete symbiosis with the therapist. Nunberg proposes that, despite the fact that the therapist is not allied with the patient in the way that the patient thinks, the *illusory* alliance still promotes the patient's cooperation in doing the work of psychoanalytic psychotherapy by decreasing anxiety and creating an atmosphere of safety necessary to probe the deepest parts of the mind.

The threat of the therapist losing interest in the patient is also, according to Nunberg, a large part of the motivating force behind the therapeutic alliance. Despite the fact that neurotic wishes are the foundation of Nunberg's therapeutic alliance, the threat of loss of the therapist forces the patient to constructively participate in the treatment. In other words, in disagreement with Sterba (1934), Nunberg proposes that the patient can be directed to do the right work toward achieving mental health even if the patient is doing the work for the wrong (pathological) reasons and goals.

A helpful way to conceptualize these ideas is to follow Gutheil and Havens' proposal (1979) that the opposing concepts of therapeutic alliance, represented by Sterba and Nunberg, be conceptualized as the categories of "rational therapeutic alliance" and "irrational therapeutic alliance." This can be summarized as follows:

Rational therapeutic alliance is the bond between therapist and patient that is based on the patient's reason, reality orientation, intellectual capacities and needs for psychic health, all of which are relatively uninfluenced by the irrationality and unreasonableness of the neurosis and transference neurosis. In contrast, the irrational therapeutic alliance is founded on neurotic wishes in which the patient sees himself as helpless and overestimates the power of the therapist to unilaterally, magically cure the illness. *Both the rational and irrational therapeutic alliance entail ego splits plus an object relationship with the therapist that are integral to the psychoanalytic process.* The difference is that in rational alliance the patient allies the healthy side of his ego with the therapist, whereas in irrational alliance it is the unhealthy side that forms the alliance. Both forms of alliance are therapeutic, however, since both can, within the therapeutic relationship, be utilized towards symptomatic relief, and both constructively contribute to the therapeutic relationship, although they differ in the process by which they contribute to the therapeutic relationship. For example, in the rational alliance, the patient collaborates with a friend (the therapist), whereas in the irrational alliance the patient surrenders to a loved and frightening adversary.

4.21 *Definition of Therapeutic Alliance*

As stated above, psychoanalytic technique and theory are encumbered by inconsistent and imprecise definitions and conceptualizations of identical terms. For our purposes therapeutic alliance will be defined in terms that would fit Sterba's concepts (1934, 1940) and Gutheil and Havens' (1979) criteria of a rational therapeutic alliance. In accordance with these authors, therapeutic alliance entails a relationship between the rational and reality-oriented components of the patient as these components relate to the treatment setting.*

For the remainder of this book, unless otherwise noted, the term

---

* The "real relationship" (see Section 4.4) is more involved with the real aspects of the relationship that are not exclusive to the treatment.

therapeutic alliance will be used in accordance with the following rationally oriented and reality-oriented definition:

A therapeutic alliance is a relationship between patient and therapist that is characterized by the following conditions:

1) The patient has made an identification with the real person of the therapist so that the patient views himself in the same way that the therapist observes the patient and deals with the patient's resistances.
2) The therapist and patient agree to observe the patient's psychic functioning and behavior in an attempt to achieve a deterministic understanding of such behavior.
3) The therapist and patient agree that the format for such treatment is a verbal and not behavioral interaction during the treatment sessions.
4) There is a real congruence between the patient's and therapist's concepts of mental health and psychic growth.
5) Unlike the transference neurosis, there is a contemporary relationship characterized by a non-neurotic, rational rapport that is desexualized and deaggressivized and functions despite occasional impulses from the transference, real relationship, narcissistic alliance and the symptoms themselves.
6) Although the patient and therapist accept the patient as he currently is, the patient and therapist do not settle for the patient being the way he is.
7) Both patient and therapist share confidence and hopefulness in the treatment, are enthusiastic about their work together, and highly value the fundamental role of free association, the profound role of the unconscious and the goal of maximal awareness of bodily feelings.
8) The patient is capable of transferring to the therapist total responsibility for the patient's coping and defensive adaptive psychic devices; that is, the patient is capable of "secondary trust" (see Section 4.225 for a definition and discussion of secondary trust).

Of course, the therapeutic alliance is rarely attained in its ideal entirety. Nevertheless, the elements of this definition must be present to a significant degree in order for the full course of psychoanalytic psychotherapy to be clinically successful.

4.22 Trust

In order for the patient to be capable of a therapeutic alliance, the patient must possess the capacity to trust, a phenomenon more profound than rapport and distinctly separate from transference.

Trust, as it is used in general vocabulary, refers to ". . . an unquestionable reliance on the integrity, character, ability, strength or truth of someone or something" (Webster's, 1967, p. 952). The problem with understanding trust as it relates to the therapeutic alliance is that, like so many concepts in psychoanalytic therapy, it has multiple definitions and meanings. Zetzel (1965, 1970) and many others (e.g., Corwin, 1974) have proposed that the capacity for a therapeutic alliance is essentially equivalent to the capacity for basic trust. I propose that we go one conceptual step further and follow Mehlman's (1976, 1977) suggestion to distinguish between "basic trust" and "secondary trust," each type of trust possessing a separate, though related, ontogeny and *both* types being required for there to be a therapeutic alliance.

4.221 THE DEFINITION OF BASIC TRUST

Basic trust entails the capacity to tolerate painful anxiety, depression and frustration while maintaining reality testing and confidence in a therapy and therapist that most likely are unproven to the patient. Through basic trust the patient establishes a barrier to destructive regression and at the same time allows himself to observe the various primitive fantasies, memories and feelings that are engendered by the transference neurosis. As will be discussed later in this chapter and in Section 5.36, basic trust is necessary for there to be a transference neurosis instead of a transference psychosis. Even if basic trust is present, however, without secondary trust the transference neurosis would be unworkable within the psychoanalytic process.

4.222 THE ONTOGENY OF BASIC TRUST

Erikson (1950) and Zetzel (1965, 1970) have pioneered the developmental concepts of basic trust and their ideas can be briefly summarized as follows: The degree of development of basic trust and the capacity to maintain basic trust in the absence of immediate gratfiication are determined by the quality and stability of preoedipal maternal relationships. Up to the age of two the life of an infant is almost totally involved in the one-to-one relationship with the mother, a relationship that is characterized by a symbiosis in which the infant's ego boundaries are unclear. Archaic fantasies of omnipotence predominate, and primary identification with the mother prevails.* It is after the preoedipal stage (age two), but before the achievement of stable reality testing and the oedipal period (ages four to five), that basic trust develops. Thus, the child is developing basic trust at a time when his life is still mostly involved in the mother-child, one-to-one relationship. At this time (between the ages of two and four) the child is learning to tolerate separation and delay, and to control feelings such as rage, anxiety and frustration at unmet needs. Also, the child is beginning to rely on his own ability to control destructive urges so that he will not harm objects that are frustrating. The child is simultaneously gaining awareness of the distinction between self and others and between the internal and external phenomena, so that mother becomes "an inner certainty as well as an outer predictability" (Erikson, 1950, p. 219). This capacity engenders the ability eventually to distinguish introjection and projection. The child is acquiring independent skills and is developing the process of secondary identification. During this time, the child is also learning to accept limitations without feeling devalued or rejected, learning to find substitutive gratifications, developing the capacity to renounce the omnipotent self-image, and developing the capacity to simultaneously tolerate love and hate toward the same object.

4.223 Object Constancy

For basic trust to exist, there must be "object constancy." This term was first used in the psychoanalytic literature by Heinz Hartmann (1952) and is closely associated with Piaget's (1937) "object concept." that is, the concept of an object external and autonomous from the self and the person's perception of it (Fraiberg, 1969).

Object constancy arises from early infant-mother relationships and is determined by the degree of enduring infantile fixation and the degree to which genital primacy is achieved. According to psychoanalytic theory, if psychosexual development has been significantly impaired, then object constancy (self-object discrimination) has not been achieved and a constructive therapeutic relationship is difficult if not impossible to obtain (Aarons, 1962).

---

* Throughout this book, whenever the terms "mother," "maternal," etc. are used, it is assumed that there could be, and indeed often are, mother substitutes providing the same roles. For example, the "preoedipal" mother could be a single parent father, a grandmother, etc.

4.224 Evocative Memory Capacity

In addition to object constancy, another component necessary for basic trust is "evocative memory." Evocative memory can be defined as the evoking of a cathected mental representation of the object irrespective of the object's external presence or absence (Adler, 1979; Fraiberg, 1969; Freud, 1925b; Piaget, 1937). The evocative memory capacity is not the same as the capacity for "recognition memory." Recognition memory merely requires that the object perceived has characteristics that stimulate memory traces laid down from past experiences. Recognition memory does not involve the evocation of *cathected* mental representations.

Normal childhood development involves a progressive capacity to maintain a cathected mental representation (memory) of a person even if that person is absent (Fraiberg, 1969; Piaget, 1937). The capacity to remember an object and also to maintain cathexis of that object even if it is not externally present is not normally fully developed before 18 months of age (Schlessinger & Robbins, 1974). If "good mothering" cannot be internalized, then the capacity for object constancy never develops, and the person usually has an unstable evocative memory capacity (Adler, 1979).

4.225 Definition of Secondary Trust*

Secondary trust is a separate but equally essential component of the therapeutic alliance. It can be defined as the mental state of willingness and maintenance of a condition of openness whereby a person can allow himself to fluctuate from total acceptance of coping responsibility to transferring that responsibility and control over one's thoughts, feelings or behavior to another person, depending on the exigencies of the current reality. The absence of secondary trust reflects a closed system of previously internalized, archaic parental psychic images. If the person possesses only the primitive parental objects, then the ceding over

---

* Rather than reference each idea discussed on the subjects of secondary trust and narcissistic alliance, I would like to state at the outset that, unless otherwise noted in the context, all such discussions in this book condense, paraphrase and elaborate the contributions of Robert Mehlman (1976, 1977). The 1976 paper was awarded the Boston Psychoanalytic Society and Institute Helene and Felix Deutsch Essay Prize. It was presented at the scientific meetings of the Boston Psychoanalytic Institute, February 1976. Also, as a supervisee of Dr. Mehlman, I had the privilege of discussing these ideas with him on numerous occasions as these concepts related to the clinical case being supervised.

of adaptive and defensive ego functions to parental objects will not occur, and a meaningful therapeutic alliance will never develop. Another way of saying the same thing is that secondary trust must be present for the child to allow the parent to parent.

Furthermore, the person who has prematurely closed and solidified the parental images will be unable to make the structural modifications (for example, superego) necessary for the transference neurosis to be resolved. Although the transference neurosis does not evolve from secondary trust, without secondary trust the transference neurosis cannot be resolved within the therapeutic relationship. In other words, whereas basic trust is a necessary precursor to the transference neurosis (as opposed to the undesirable transference psychosis), secondary trust is a necessary precursor to the therapeutic alliance.

4.226 THE ONTOGENY OF SECONDARY TRUST

A deficiency in secondary trust, often seen in the obsessive-compulsive neurotic, is *not* the result of inadequate mothering, but rather, is the result of a developmentally *premature* closure of parenting. The premature closure of parenting is the child's way of coping with situations such as trauma, intrapsychic factors, parental demands, or parental failure to set limits or meet needs. *The premature closure occurs at a developmental stage much later than the preoedipal stage when primitive parental images are introjected and when the basic trust develops.*

The closure of the parental system in a *normal* child occurs in early adolescence (around age 15) and is part of the normal adolescent process (Zetzel, 1965). In the obsessive-compulsive prototype, the child develops basic trust, but then prematurely closes down the earlier open trusting relationships with the parent. The child becomes for the most part his own parent, preconsciously or consciously abandoning the universally desired ideal parent and viewing the parents as they realistically exist, with all their realistic limitations and weaknesses. Such children often impressively achieve during the latency period, although through a process of manipulation or intimidation of others. These "little adults" go through most of their latency with the underlying feeling that they are parentless and, even in dangerous situations, can themselves handle things better than their parents. The lack of secondary trust is a defense against affects while maintaining object relationships and a relatively secure sense of self. Such people may appear to possess secondary trust but a closer inspection reveals a pseudo-trust characterized by an unwillingness to allow themselves to be taken care of by someone else.

Mehlman (1976) offers the following example to clarify these ideas: A normal latency child will follow his parent down the most dangerous ski slope or across the busiest of streets without thinking of the danger or, in the case of the street, not even looking for cars. This willingness to be led represents the basic readiness to keep an open, trusting relationship in the bodily presence of a parent, even in the face of danger and even when the child knows that he has the potential capacity to take the adaptive responsibility himself. The same normal child, however, if not with his parents, would, out of a sense of self-preservation, not attempt the ski slope, look carefully both ways before crossing the street and, in general, avoid situations beyond his coping abilities except under special conditions such as the influence of group supported carelessness. The prototypical obsessive-compulsive latency child, in contrast, does not follow the parents and does not use the parents to overcome mild realistic fears, but rather, tyranically retains control of the situation, forcing the parents to conform to the child's fears. In this way, the child gains control over the parent-child relationship.

Mrs. J was a 33-year-old housewife in twice-weekly psychoanalytic psychotherapy because of dissatisfaction with her eight-year-old marriage combined with fears of being on her own and lack of confidence that she could manage her life without the husband with whom she was so unhappy. Throughout the course of the therapy it became clear to Mrs. J and to her therapist that her marriage was based on strong neurotic needs and weaknesses. As the weaknesses became less intense, she gradually became confident enough to end the marriage. She did, however, have a great problem in sharing her decision with her therapist as this decision was being made. The separation from her husband involved a series of steps, for example, the decision to sleep in another room, the decision to tell her parents and her children, the physical separation itself and the various legal and financial arrangements. In each and every incident where a decision had to be made, the patient would struggle with the decision within herself, reach a decision and then share in retrospect that decision with her therapist. This process was very subtle and at first the therapist was not aware of it. It became very clear after a few months, however, that the patient was keeping the therapist out of the experience of sharing the decision before it was made. She needed the therapist for support once the decision was made but she was afraid of sharing the uncertainty with the therapist during those times before she had made up her mind. She later reflected on these periods and became aware that making the decision first and then sharing it with the therapist was a way of keeping the therapist at a distance as well as a way of keeping a certain amount of control over the therapeutic relationship.

Mr. W was a 20-year-old college sophomore in once-weekly psycho-analytic therapy that began a month after he dropped out of college because of progressive dissatisfaction with school work and with himself and a fear that he would not be able to compete with the other students. The therapy went well during the one year that he was out of school. He focused on his competitiveness, strong performance orientation to the point of not being able to tolerate anything less than all A's, conflicts with his father, and some other issues often seen in adolescence. The sessions were always quite intellectual and he had a great deal of trouble experiencing the therapist within the relationship. After the year's interruption of his schooling, he went back to school. Mr. W made the decision to return to school within himself and then informed the therapist. Furthermore, during the crucial few weeks in which he returned to school, Mr. W cancelled his therapy sessions, the first sessions that he had missed in the year's psychotherapy. He said he could not make the sessions because of school work, class schedule, etc. But both therapist and patient realized that there was more going on since the therapist was very flexible with regard to time, and the therapist's office was less than a mile away from the school on public transportation. After missing three or four weeks of sessions (the first three or four weeks of returning to school), Mr. W returned to therapy. He told the therapist about how difficult it was returning to school and the many fears and doubts that he had in the classroom as well as in the dormitory. He also informed the therapist that things were much better after three or four weeks, the crucial three or four weeks during which time he was not in therapy. It became very clear to both therapist and patient that he felt very uncomfortable being with the therapist at a time when his life was so uncertain and he could only return to therapy once he had things back under control.

In the cases of both Mrs. J and Mr. W, we see evidence of a lack of secondary trust. The patients needed the therapy and made good use of it. Although it was not mentioned in the clinical example, both people had made effective use of the real relationships and developed intensive transference neuroses which were utilized effectively. Both cases, however, did not make *full* use of the therapy because of a defect in the therapeutic alliance in the area of secondary trust. Both Mrs. J and Mr. W were afraid to share the uncertainties of their life prospectively with the therapist. To use the metaphor described above, they were afraid to cross the street holding the parent's hand without looking both ways. To continue with this metaphor, they had to look both ways alone, cross the street alone, wait for the therapist to cross the street and then discuss the experience.

4.3 NARCISSISTIC ALLIANCE

The concept of a narcissistic alliance can be traced back to Aichhorn (1935), who described his therapeutic relationship with a 17-year-old delinquent boy who developed an attachment to Aichhorn. Aichhorn notes that it was the attachment alone, without insight, that allowed the boy to increase his adaptive activities, abandon his symptoms and eventually no longer need Aichhorn's presence. Although Anna Freud (1946) also alludes to the concept of narcissistic alliance, the first published use of the term occurred in Corwin (1972), although, as noted by Corwin (1974), Mehlman (1976) originated the term in his work with colleagues and students at the Boston Psychoanalytic Institute. The most comprehensive discussion of narcissistic alliance occurs in Mehlman's (1976) as yet unpublished manuscript, which has been briefly summarized by Mehlman (1977).

The narcissistic alliance can be defined as that aspect of the relationship between patient and therapist whereby the bodily presence of the therapist serves as a substitute for some of the patient's previously used major coping and defensive psychic devices.* The narcissistic alliance can be distinguished from the transference since (as discussed in Section 4.1) the transference is determined by previous relationships, is a repetition

---

* Narcissism is an extraordinarily complicated subject with multiple definitions. For the purposes of this book, narcissism will be used in a way that refers to the psychology of the self as opposed to an interpersonal psychology or psychology that involves the interaction between the self and the environment. Any attempt to further define "self" would take us beyond the scope of this book and into the realm of philosophy, religion and the very essence of human existence. (The author is grateful to John Mack, M.D. for his helpful comments on this issue).

of past relationships, is anachronistic, and requires displacement from significant others onto the therapist. In contrast, the narcissistic alliance requires no more than the presence of the therapist with little emphasis on the past or present interpersonal factors since the narcissistic alliance is comprised of an unidentifiable incorporation of the therapist into the patient's mental structure. In order for the narcissistic alliance to develop, the therapist has to do no more than what Freud recommended for "proper rapport" to develop with the patient:

> . . . Nothing needs to be done but to give him time. If one exhibits a serious interest in him, carefully clears away the resistances that crop up at the beginning . . . he will form . . . an attachment . . . (Freud, 1913a, p. 139).

The narcissistic alliance, by definition, entails both the primitive aspects of narcissism along with a systematic adaptive timely function. Although all narcissism is, in a developmental sense, "primitive," we must remind ourselves that the pejorative sense of the term narcissism derives from its association to psychotic and severe character disorders. Narcissism is, however, also quite active in healthy individuals, and in fact may be impressively adaptive, facilitate normal sexual pleasure and indeed may even insure biological and mental survival (Corwin, 1974; Rochlin, 1973).

In order to be able to distinguish between the irrational therapeutic alliance and narcissistic alliance, it is crucial to bear in mind that the therapeutic alliance, whether rational or irrational, involves an object relationship and an ego split (Gutheil & Havens, 1979). (See Section 4.2 for a discussion of irrational and rational therapeutic alliances.) To be sure, the irrational therapeutic alliance may be quite unreasonable and magical, but there still exists the patient's ego split, with a component of the ego forming an object relationship with the therapist. In contrast, the narcissistic alliance, albeit irrational, involves the incorporation of the bodily presence of the therapist so that the object of the therapist becomes a component of the patient's adaptive-defensive psychic mechanisms. This process is founded on preoedipal capacities that predate the development of true object relationships (see discussion of the ontogeny of basic trust, Section 4.222). As will be discussed in this Section, a premature push for a therapeutic alliance could frighten away the patient and destroy all chances of an eventual therapeutic alliance.

In essence, as noted by Gutheil and Havens (1979), the difference between irrational or rational therapeutic alliance on the one hand, and narcissistic alliance on the other hand, is that in the latter, the therapist ". . . becomes temporarily a part of an extension of the patient's self" (p. 473). In other words, the irrational and rational alliances are object relationships whereas the narcissistic alliance is a relatively subjective experience. Along these lines, Gutheil and Havens (1979) point out that Kohut's (1971) concept of "narcissistic transference" and Mehlman's (1976, 1977) concept of narcissistic alliance can only be distinguished in terms of their functions within the psychoanalytic process. The therapist's empathy reawakens archaic structures from which are formed the "amplifying mirrors" of the narcissistic transference in which the patient views the therapist as an extension of himself (patient). In contrast, the narcissistic alliance does not involve the patient viewing the therapist as an extension of himself, but rather, involves an incorporation of the therapist into the patient's psychic structure.

Along with the formation of the narcissistic transference, the narcissistic alliance develops and serves to stabilize the therapeutic relationship. The narcissistic transference provides the therapist with the opportunity for mutative interpretations but the whole process is held together by the narcissistic alliance. Gutheil and Havens point out that within the therapeutic situation eventually both narcissistic transference and narcissistic alliance evolve into the object relationships of the (rational) therapeutic alliance.

The narcissistic alliance is certainly not exclusive to psychoanalytic psychotherapy. In fact, it is a large part of all parent-child interactions around developmental tasks whereby parental empathy facilitates the child's development. Narcissistic alliance phenomena also often occur when a person enters into a newly formed relationship, either professionally or socially, and as a result of that relationship shows constructive behavioral changes and alleviation of psychic pain.

By including the narcissistic alliance as an integral part of the therapeutic relationship, we are assuming that the person of the therapist is incorporated into the patient's psychic apparatus. This model is in direct opposition to those therapists (for example, Rangell, 1954a, b) who propose that the psychoanalytic situation is, or should be, one in which the psychoanalytic therapist observes the patient from the periphery of the patient's mind and does not function within the realm of the patient's psychic apparatus.

Freud never explicitly wrote about the concept of a narcissistic alliance as that term is defined above. He did, however, report his observations that

> Often enough the transference is able to remove the symptoms of the disease itself, but only for awhile—only for as long as it itself lasts. In this case, the treatment is a treatment by suggestion . . . (1913a, p. 143).

In this quote, Freud is attributing the sudden symptomatic changes to transference. There have been numerous other authors who all have described the "transference cure" or "transference improvement" in ways that differ from each other but still emphasize the *transference* in the service of resistances as the vehicle for the cure or improvement (Alexander & French, 1946; Fenichel, 1945, 1954; Kolb & Montgomery, 1958; Oberndorf, 1946; Oremland, 1972; Singer, 1965). Mehlman (1976, 1977) points out that it is often the narcissistic alliance and not the transference that is responsible for this sudden loss of symptoms. The phenomenon of the narcissistic alliance is often called "transference cure," an erroneous label since the phenomenon has occurred *before* the transference and resistance have actually developed to a degree intense enough to elicit such changes.

It is the narcissistic alliance that, early in therapy before the development of the transference neurosis, provides the therapist with great influence over the patient's thoughts, feelings and behavior. This concept of narcissistic alliance presupposes that in any form of psychotherapy, even in the healthiest neurotics, it is not the therapeutic alliance that holds the patient in therapy during the initial stages of therapy, but rather it is the preformed transference and the narcissistic alliance which is the first cohesive force that captures the patient in the relationship (Corwin, 1974; Mehlman, 1976).

From a practical perspective, one of the most important lessons for the therapist to learn from the above discussions is that the predominant existence of a narcissistic alliance with a new patient should not lead the therapist to label the patient untreatable. Instead, the existence of the narcissistic alliance should be expected and allowed to flourish until a significant therapeutic alliance develops (Corwin, 1974). Of course, the longer it takes for a therapeutic alliance and transference neurosis to evolve out of the narcissistic alliance, the greater the probability of an unworkable therapeutic relationship (Greenson, 1967; Mehlman, 1976, 1977; Zetzel, 1965).

The narcissistic alliance is the precursor to the therapeutic alliance and transference neurosis. The degree of willingness and patience to wait out the development of the therapeutic alliance varies with each patient-therapist combination. What may take one week with one patient-therapist combination may take two years with another. Whether the patient is psychotic or neurotic, young or old, in crisis or not, the same process takes place in a successful psychoanalytic psychotherapy. The only difference is the timing. *If the therapist does not accept the narcissistic alliance, but rather forces the patient to resort to a rational understanding of why he wants treatment, then the patient may very likely be driven away before therapy has ever begun.*

Of course, the interventions employed to facilitate the narcissistic alliance must be determined by the current situation. For example, an interpretation may be necessary in one case or be avoided in another. The guidelines should be, however, that, for *all* patients, including the so-called healthy neurotic, the therapist must realize the value of the narcissistic alliance, allow his charisma and the patient's neediness to emerge, avoid adding to the patient's presenting fears, and in fact, diminish those fears by allowing the patient to irrationally incorporate the therapist as a part of the previously existing adaptive defensive devices.

Before proceeding any further in our discussion of the narcissistic alliance, a clinical example may help the reader to bring together some of the relevant concepts.

Mr. B was a 24-year-old, never married, only child in thrice-weekly psychoanalytic psychotherapy, which began in his first year of law school. Mr. B began therapy with the chief complaint of "an excessive self-criticism that interferes with my functioning at full capacity," "periodic depression," "an inability to gain psychological freedom from my parents," "a loneliness marked by no past or present romances despite numerous opportunities," and "a continuous obsessing about school work to the point of never allowing myself any fun." The patient had always been an outstanding, hard-working student although he reported that no matter how well he did, he was never satisfied with himself nor were his parents satisfied, all three people always expecting more.

Most of Mr. B's childhood memories were associated with observing almost daily arguments between his parents, both successful attorneys now living about 100 miles away from Mr. B. The parents would often

*use the child as a mediator around such issues as money, father's unavail-
ability, and mother's frequent extramarital affairs. The patient recalled
how often each parent would take him aside complaining about the
other parent and saying that if it were not for concern about the patient's
welfare they would seek a divorce. These arguments persisted to the time
of the patient beginning psychotherapy, and in fact, a large bulk of the
clinical material of the first year of therapy was talking about the parents
continuing to call the patient at all hours of the day and night, criticizing
the other parent and asking the patient his advice as to whether or not
they should divorce. When the patient refused to get involved, he was
often reminded about "all we have done for you," a pattern of instilled
guilt that was an integral component of the patient's neurosis.*

*When the psychotherapy began, Mr. B was traveling to his parents' home
every available weekend in order to serve as a mediator to their endless
marital problems, to do chores around their house, and to care for an
ailing grandparent whom the patient did not even like. Also, in the first
few months of therapy, Mr. B literally spent hours at a time unneces-
sarily worrying and planning what electives he should take, what his
professors thought about him, and whether or not he was adequately
prepared for an exam or for moot court presentations despite hours of
preparation. He also worried—I should say obsessed—about what law
speciality he should eventually choose, despite the fact that he had 18
months before such a decision had to be made. Another dominant symptom was that he would dutifully report things to his parents that he
knew they would criticize.*

*During the first year of therapy, all of the symptoms mentioned in
the previous paragraphs markedly decreased. Mr. B became more constructively assertive with his parents; took more time off for enjoyment;
increased his social life; chose not to decide about a speciality until
after several electives; went home far less often despite strong weekly
pleas from his parents; stopped trying to impress his professors as much;
completely stopped telling parents things that he knew beforehand they
would criticize; and in general became less guilty and less self-critical.*

*Since pre-law school days, the parents had been pressuring the patient
to commit himself to returning to his hometown after training in order
to take over the parents' law practice. The patient had never seriously
considered this move, but neither had he ever explicitly told the parents
his intentions, thus always leaving the parents with hope. By not being
explicit, and by being somewhat passive, Mr. B had been feeding the*

endless struggles, phone conversations and bitter arguments with his parents who were always hoping to convince him in their direction. After a weekend visit home after six months of therapy, the patient reported the following:

"This weekend I finally told my parents that I will not be returning home but will be looking for law firms in another city. I feel much better after this weekend. I feel like at least my parents, especially my father, know where I stand. Before I began psychotherapy I was never sure if they ever really heard me because I never really told them. I would be very passive and, although I would imply that I was not returning, I did not say it explicitly and they brushed it aside. Now they know that I am not going to return to their city. I'm not going to take any more of their abuse on this subject. I also feel better because I am not planning out everything anymore. It's good to feel that somehow the decisions will be made and that in time I will make the correct decisions. I never felt this way before psychotherapy."

Mr. B repeatedly told the therapist that he knew that it was "the therapy" that was responsible for his changed behavior, but he had no idea why, especially since he did not have any significant gain in psychological insight and he rarely thought about the therapy. Nor did he think about the issues discussed in therapy or about the therapist outside of the sessions. During his first year of therapy, there was very little feeling on the patient's part of any object relationship with the therapist.

It is accurate to attribute the symptomatic changes during the first year of therapy to the narcissistic alliance. During this period of therapy, there had been no interpretations on the patient's or the therapist's part, no significant revelations of the unconscious, and no psychic structural changes. The patient showed immediate constructive behavioral change and symptomatic relief, a phenomenon that cannot be accurately called "transference cure," since during the first year of therapy when these behavioral changes were taking place there was no clinical evidence within or outside of the sessions that indicated a significant transference. Furthermore, any evidence indicating a significant influence from the real relationship of the therapy was also absent. During this first year of treatment, it was not the therapeutic alliance that kept Mr. B in treatment, but rather, the narcissistic alliance captured him into the therapeutic relationship. His strong motivation which had driven him to be a reliable and hard-working patient had not been characterized so much by conscious control and logic, but was mostly determined by external necessities, regression, preformed wishes and expectations, nonrational motivations and therapist's charisma. It was the narcissistic alliance that allowed the patient to abandon the structured attachment to his parents and to abandon his excessive self-criticism and self-doubt. Of course, if the narcissistic defenses were not eventually subjected to mutative interpretation of the transference neurosis, then all the therapy would have accomplished would be to replace one form of narcissistic unreality with another. Complete and permanent reduction of the harsh superego, autonomy from parents accompanied by a loss of depression and isolation would never occur until the patient fully experienced the guilt and the anger and finally the infantile neurosis with its many layers of need and deprivations within the transference neurosis.

In agreement with Mehlman (1976, 1977) I support the following five assumptions (see Figure 4.1) which I will first list and then discuss:

1) Basic trust is not equivalent to therapeutic alliance;
2) Basic trust is necessary for the development of the narcissistic alliance;
3) Secondary trust gives rise to and is necessary for the development of the therapeutic alliance;
4) The transference neurosis evolves out of the narcissistic alliance;
5) The narcissistic alliance facilitates the development of the therapeutic alliance by contributing to the patient's secondary trust of the therapist.

4.31 Basic Trust Is Not Equivalent to Therapeutic Alliance

This proposition is in opposition to Zetzel, who originated the term therapeutic alliance (1956) and was a pioneer in developing the concepts of basic trust and its relationship to treatability. The definition of basic trust and its relationship to therapeutic alliance have been discussed in Section 4.21 and 4.22 and so will not be repeated here except to repeat the critical concept that it is basic trust that is responsible for the transference to be a workable neurotic condition (transference neurosis) rather than an unworkable psychotic experience (transference psychosis).

4.32 Basic Trust Is Necessary for the Development of the Narcissistic Alliance

Without basic trust, the patient will not make or maintain the initial therapeutic relationship. If the patient has not developed the capacities subsumed under the concept of basic trust, then the patient will be unable to establish reality testing within the one-to-one relationship. In

FIGURE 4.1 — The Functional Relationships Among Basic Trust (BT), Secondary Trust (ST), Narcissistic Alliance (NA), Therapeutic Alliance (TA), and Transference Neurosis (TN).

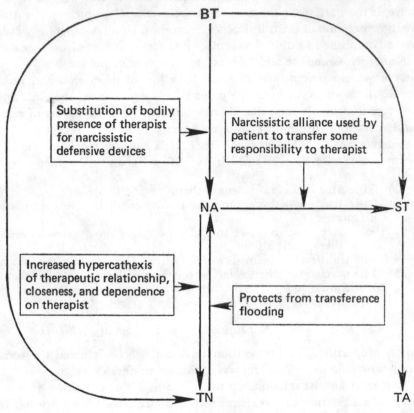

such patients, a psychotic transference may be formed, but either way, these patients will not allow the narcissistic alliance to emerge (Corwin, 1974; Mehlman, 1976, 1977).

4.33 *Secondary Trust Gives Rise to and Is Necessary for the Development of Therapeutic Alliance*

These concepts are defined and discussed in Sections 4.21 and 4.22.

4.34 *The Transference Neurosis Evolves Out of the Narcissistic Alliance*

The existence of the narcissistic alliance means, by definition, that the patient has relaxed his narcissistic defenses. The reduction of the narcissistic defenses allows an increase in dependence, closeness and hypercathexis towards the therapist. In essence then, the narcissistic alliance is a situation in which the narcissistic devices are replaced by the bodily presence of the therapist. The narcissistic alliance is a necessary precursor to the transference neurosis and is the situation from which the transference neurosis evolves.

If the transference neurosis does not develop out of the narcissistic alliance, then one of two conditions exists: 1) the therapist has interfered with its development through misapplied technical interventions; or 2) the patient's defensive structure is too rigid to allow abrogation of narcissistic devices and subsequent narcissistic alliance. Such people are labeled by Freud as having "narcissistic neuroses" and today comprise, for the most part, the psychotics and what many people call "borderline" or "severe character disorders."

If the transference neurosis with its closeness, dependency and hypercathexis develops out of the narcissistic alliance, then it must logically follow that the previous narcissistic adaptive-defensive devices become bound to the transference neurosis. If these therapeutically earlier developmental narcissistic defenses are not subjected to mutative interpretations of the transference neurosis, then all the therapy has accomplished is to replace one form of narcissistic unreality with another. In this regard, Mehlman (1976) quotes Myerson (1973), who describes this situation as ". . . better has become the enemy of best and a modus vivendi has become established" (p. 136). It is this very element of the psychoanalytic process that, perhaps more than anything else, distinguishes psychoanalytic therapy from the other forms of psychotherapy. The nonpsychoanalytic forms of psychotherapy, largely through manipulation and suggestion, result in various manifestations of relearning new adaptive-defensive styles, including the substitutions that result from the narcissistic alliance.

In summary, then, psychoanalytic therapy engenders: 1) a regressive opening of a previously closed psychic system; 2) a narcissistic alliance that gives way to the infantile trends expressed via the transference neurosis; 3) a therapeutic alliance which allows for a resolution of the transference neurosis, which in turn 4) engenders a reclosing of the psychic system leaving the therapist as an incorporated and introjected image unidentifiably integrated into the changed psychic structure (Mehlman, 1976, 1977; Zetzel, 1965).

4.35 The Narcissistic Alliance Facilitates the Development of the Therapeutic Alliance by Contributing to the Patient's Secondary Trust of the Therapist

As already mentioned, the transference neurosis evolves from the narcissistic alliance. With the development of the transference neurosis, there occurs increased anxiety that was originally associated with the intrapsychic conflicts which are now reexperienced in the transference neurosis. This phenomenon can lead to transference crisis or flooding, which in turn engenders a mobilization of narcissistic defensive, or narcissistic resistant psychic devices. The patient often uses the bodily presence of the therapist as a substitute for these narcissistic defenses.

The narcissistic alliance, then, serves to protect the patient from transference flooding (thus explaining the dual direction of the arrow between NA and TN in Figure 4.1). The patient utilizes the narcissistic alliance to allow an openness through which responsibility is ceded over to the parent substitute (therapist) (thus explaining the arrow from NA to ST in Figure 4.1). Through this process the therapist protects the patient and facilitates the approximation of narcissistic and therapeutic need. In some ways, the establishment of secondary trust is a result of a regressive mechanism (from transference neurosis to narcissistic alliance) that serves to resist the transference neurosis. Indeed, we often see in patients, especially "hysterics," a phenomenon of "overtrust" in the service of resistance.

The hysteric's overtrust is in some ways the converse of the "pseudotrust" described above in the prototypical obsessive. The hysteric's willingness to overtrust can be as much an obstruction to the therapeutic relationship as the obsessive's lack of secondary trust, and must be handled in the treatment in similar ways. In fact, the hysterical "immaturely patent" (Mehlman, 1976, p. 23) trust could represent a more primitive use of parents than the obsessive's lack of secondary trust. Thus, the developmental aspects of overtrust differ from those of pseudotrust.

The important point to be made is that, whether we are dealing with pseudotrust or overtrust, the process discussed in this Section and represented in Figure 4.1 is the same regarding the contribution of the narcissistic alliance to the therapeutic alliance, since both kinds of trust serve to expand the therapeutic alliance. The narcissistic alliance can serve to enhance the patient's secondary trust towards the therapist and, in this way, the narcissistic alliance serves as an intermediary between transference neurosis and therapeutic alliance.

4.4 THE REAL RELATIONSHIP

Now that we have defined transference, therapeutic alliance, and narcissistic alliance, there remains the difficult task of defining what is meant by the real relationship. The term "real" is here being used to connote an observation or experience that is actual, in accordance with observable phenomena and not illusory nor apparent. The term real refers to an observation or experience that is relatively uninfluenced by psychological distortions and psychic symptoms. As noted by Dewald (1976), this use of the term real is synonymous with the more ponderous concept of "actuality of perception and experience" (p. 216).

All psychoanalytic psychotherapy involves significant components of real relationships. Certain experiences and observations occur to both patient and therapist, as separate people, which contribute to the real relationship. A few examples are office furnishings, gait, posture, dress, style of speech, family illnesses and financial matters. Furthermore, the therapeutic relationship itself involves an experience for most patients which is unusual in a very real sense, perhaps experienced for the first time, and functions as a new way to relate to another person, which in turn may serve as a learning model for strengthening future interpersonal relationships (Dewald, 1976).

The real relationship can be distinguished from the transference neurosis by the fact that the former is relatively non-neurotic, appropriate and relevant to the current situation, less rigid and not characterized by an indiscriminate duplication of the past and distortion of reality so characteristic of the transference. Furthermore, environmental or intrapsychic realities have more influence on the real relationship than on the transference (Greenson, 1971). Whereas interpretations are the interventions employed to change the transference, noninterpretive interventions are used to modify the real relationship, although the noninterpretive interventions are still psychoanalytic techniques (Greenson & Wexler, 1969). Also, the real relationship and the therapeutic alliance are not as useful in the service of resistance and are not as idealized, eroticized and aggressivized as in the transference neurosis. (I should emphasize, however, that not only transference, but all aspects of the real relationship or therapeutic alliance, can be and often are used as a source of strong resistance.)

In both the therapist and patient, the real relationship is both genuine (that is, it is a psychic reality in that it reflects what the inner experience is) and realistic (that is, it is an external reality, not imaginary, really existing outside of the mind and the treatment situation). In contrast, in both therapist and patient, the transference neurosis phenomenon is genuine in that it is really felt, but is nonrealistic in that it does not exist outside of the mind. The therapeutic alliance is genuine but is an artifact of the treatment and does not exist outside of the patient-therapist relationship (Greenson, 1967).

A clinical fact that we sometimes overlook is that some patients can rather easily develop a transference neurosis but show enormous resistance to dealing with the real aspects of the relationship with the therapist. Both therapist and patient can, and often do, use the transference neurosis to disguise their difficulty in experiencing the real involvement of the interpersonal relationship that inevitably exists between patient and therapist (Greenson, 1972; Greenson & Wexler, 1969; Szasz, 1963). Both patient and therapist must possess the capacity to naturally and spontaneously move in and out of the real relationship so that they can utilize the real affects without interfering with the full force of the transference or alliance (Couch, 1979).

If the therapist focuses on transference to the exclusion of the real relationship, then there will undoubtedly occur times in the treatment when the therapist ignores crucial patient thoughts and feelings. Furthermore, an overfocusing on the transference and ignoring of reality tends to further reduce self-esteem, reinforce the patient's feelings that he is abnormal, impede the capacity to distinguish between the reality and fantasy, and indirectly suggest that all of the happenings of the world can be explained through the transference and other psychoanalytic theories (Greenson, 1971). If the real relationship is not actively recognized and utilized in the therapy sessions, then the patient is exposed to a relationship with the therapist that is interpersonally sterile and lacking the opportunity for the patient to develop a meaningful and therapeutic object relationship. By exposing the patient to a relationship that lacks the human component, the patient is in a situation that fosters a withdrawal of cathexis and maybe even results in "iatrogenic narcissistic disorders" (Lipton, 1977, p. 272).

Some psychoanalytic therapists consider dealing with the real relationship as "anti-analytic." If we define anti-analytic as those "procedures . . . which block or lessen the patient's capacity for insight and understanding" (Greenson & Wexler, 1969, p. 29), then what is anti-analytic is the *ignoring* of thoughts and feelings that are highly charged, and it should make no difference to the therapist whether the material arises out of the real relationship, the transference, the therapeutic alliance or the narcissistic alliance.

Mr. D was a 26-year-old architect in twice-weekly psychoanalytic psychotherapy because of excessive anxiety, moderate depression and a problem of never allowing himself a normal amount of physical or emotional intimacy with other people. Although Therapist X did not dress or act in any overt seductive way, she was one of those individuals who come across to most people as a very warm and gentle person, as well as being very sexually attractive. At one point in her life Therapist X was a gifted dancer as well as a fashion model. A great deal of the therapy focused on Mr. D's relationship with his mother, a woman who all of her life remained cold, aloof and sexually unattractive to others. Furthermore, it became quite clear that Mr. D's mother was especially distant to him in comparison to his three female siblings. In fact, Mr. D did not have one memory of his mother touching him at any point in his life.

Mr. D worked very hard in psychotherapy and things went very well. He achieved significant emotional insight, lost many of his symptoms, and made very significant changes in his job and interpersonal relationships. All of these changes appeared to result directly from the work in psychotherapy, and Mr. D and Therapist X were quite pleased with the way that therapy was able to help him.

During the first few months of the psychotherapy, Mr. D focused more on the real relationship of the therapy. He joked with Therapist X, felt relatively comfortable with her, occasionally commented about her attractiveness, his feelings for her and his wish to meet a woman as physically attractive as his therapist. He experienced sexual feelings for Therapist X which, as mentioned above, were not unusual for anyone who met Therapist X.

As the therapy progressed into the second year, however, an intense transference neurosis developed. Mr. D progressively treated Therapist

X more in a way that he treated his mother or, more accurately, he treated Therapist X in ways that his mother had treated him. He became distant, cold, aloof and ceased the sexual fantasies and feelings that he once had for Therapist X. He spent many, many months struggling with the transference issues, complaining about the lack of feelings that he had towards Therapist X, and yet it became clear to Therapist X that in many ways he was more comfortable within the transference because of his lack of feelings than he was within the real relationship which possessed more intense feelings.

Therapist X persistently and repeatedly interpreted the patient's resistance of the feelings he had in the real relationship and pointed out to him that his adherence to the transference neurosis, that is, that his treating the therapist as his mother, was serving to protect him from the sexual feelings that he had towards Therapist X before the transference neurosis developed. In addition to making these interpretations, Therapist X made every attempt not to seem distant and aloof and occasionally would even make some comments about herself in her own life in an attempt to help Mr. D no longer hide behind the transference. The interpretations as well as the openness were remarkably successful. Mr. D, although resisting at first, finally used the therapy as a way of dealing with those feelings he had avoided—regardless of whether or not those feelings happened to arise out of the real relationship or the transference.

The case of Therapist X and Mr. D is an excellent example of how transference neurosis can be used as a resistance to the real relationship. If Therapist X had allowed Mr. D to experience her only in the transference neurosis, Mr. D never would have had the intensive emotional and bodily experience within the therapeutic context. Therapist X was able to allow the real relationship to be experienced. Therapist X felt comfortable enough with her own sexuality to allow Mr. D to experience her within the therapeutic context as a real person, an experience that was most therapeutic.

Ms. A was a 23-year-old, very gifted artist who had been in thrice-weekly psychoanalytic psychotherapy with Dr. X for two years because of episodic neurotic depression, excessive anxiety, fears of dying and an unresolved grief reaction to father's tragic death when patient was 20 years old. These symptoms had caused an almost total cessation of her ability to continue her work, despite her enormous proven creative abilities. A very strong transference neurosis developed during the first year and persisted throughout the second year of therapy. Both the patient and Dr. X recognized the transference neurosis as a useful vehicle of treatment.

Towards the end of the second year of therapy, the patient had achieved several meaningful insights, experienced some symptom reduction and, in general, was progressing quite well. Although the patient had dealt with virtually all other aspects of her past and present life, she had never talked very much about the experience of having a sister born when the patient was one year of age and another sister born when the patient was four years of age. Towards the end of the second year of psychotherapy, a baby girl was born to Dr. X and his wife. The patient knew of the pregnancy but had not said much about it beyond the comment that she was jealous of the wife because she had many fantasies of marrying the therapist.

Following the birth, Dr. X took a week off from work and then returned to seeing his patients. Dr. X had noticed within himself that during the first few weeks back to work he was not as totally involved with his work as he had been before the birth. He was excited about the baby, was tired from 2 a.m. and 5 a.m. feedings, and was also concerned about some minor postpartum complications. Dr. X was convinced that his slight preoccupations and fatigue were not interfering with his therapeutic work and in fact, in restrospect, did not interfere with his therapeutic work except for the case of Ms. A. Ms. A was an extraordinarily perceptive person and could sense that Dr. X was not "connected" to her as he had been before the delivery. She became extremely depressed, expressed agonizing sadness mixed with rage towards Dr. X and accused him of "abandoning me," "not caring about me as much as before," and "not being the right therapist for me." This sadness and rage lasted several sessions.

Dr. X considered two alternatives: 1) He could point out to the patient that her reaction to the birth of his daughter was a reliving (transference neurosis phenomenon) of the abandonment that the patient felt when her siblings were born. 2) He could acknowledge to the patient that, indeed, he was somewhat preoccupied and not as in touch with her as before the birth of his daughter, but that this was because his mind, on occasion, was wandering to the problems and issues at home and that the patient's unusual capacity to be tuned into Dr. X was resulting in her being aware of this situation. Dr. X chose the first alternative, namely to make the transference neurosis interpretation. After he made the interpretation, the patient got even more enraged, more depressed and felt even more abandoned.

A few sessions later, Dr. X decided to finally acknowledge the real relationship aspects of the therapeutic relationship. He told the patient about the postpartum complications, and he explained to the patient that the baby was waking up two to three times a night and that he was sharing the feeding times equally with his wife. He also explained that because he and his wife had no family in the area, and because they lived a considerable distance from town where all their friends lived, they did not have the help that they needed at that time. Dr. X went on to say that although he was sure that this was a situation that would be resolved within a few weeks, at the present time he was not only mentally preoccupied but physically tired in the early morning when the sessions with Ms. A were held. Dr. X made it very clear, however, that despite these problems he still felt that he could be a useful therapist to the patient.

Ms. A showed an immediate response to Dr. X's acknowledgment of the real relationship aspects of the lack of connectedness. She displayed sudden relief, and expressed the warmth and understanding that had been so characteristic of her relationship with Dr. X before the birth of the baby. Within minutes of Dr. X's explanation of the real relationship, Ms. A free associated to her childhood and her feelings of abandonment when her siblings were born. She reexperienced the agony of being displaced with the birth of her siblings and felt free to associate to the intense envy and murderous rage at her siblings that she remembered feeling as early as four years of age. The sibling rivalry had never been discussed or felt at any point during the psychotherapy until this moment. The withholding of the acknowledgment of the real relationship was viewed by the patient as deceptive and was an obstacle to the process of treatment. It was very clear to Dr. X that his acknowledgment of the real relationship was the intervention that allowed the patient to continue insight and growth through the psychotherapeutic process.

CHAPTER 5

TREATABILITY AND ONGOING CLINICAL ASSESSMENT

5.1 INTRODUCTION

> The need for a better organized and more precise approach to the assessment of analyzability [treatability] became apparent from the reading of scant and scattered literature on this topic . . . (Waldhorn, 1967, p. 30).

So far in this book we have, in Chapter 1, discussed the capacities needed to be a psychoanalytic therapist and also discussed the need for a more consistent use of definitions and theory; in Chapter 2, we clarified the use of the term "psychoanalytic psychotherapy" as that term is used in this book and discussed the relationship of this usage to "psychoanalysis"; in Chapter 3, we discussed some essential principles, and in Chapter 4, we discussed some of the issues surrounding the therapeutic relationship. Now it is time to ask the all important question, "Who is treatable by (suitable for) psychoanalytic psychotherapy and why?" It is important to remember that, as noted in Chapter 2, I am defining psychoanalytic psychotherapy in a way that has many similarities to the traditional definitions of psychoanalysis, since this justifies my many citations of analyzability literature when discussing treatability for psychotherapy.

For purposes of space and conciseness, unless otherwise stated in the context, henceforth the word "treatable" will mean "treatable by psychoanalytic psychotherapy" as I have defined that therapy in Chapter 2. The reader must be very careful not to commit the all too frequent error of confusing "untreatable by psychoanalytic psychotherapy" with

127

"untreatable by any means." This is an erroneous conclusion that has stigmatized many patients in the past. To give just one example, alcoholics have been repeatedly described as poorly motivated or refractory to treatment or untreatable because of the conclusion by many psychoanalytically oriented psychotherapists (e.g., Blum, 1966) that alcoholics are not good candidates for psychoanalytic psychotherapy. These labels have been applied to the specific lack of motivation that for complex reasons alcoholics *as a group* have consistently shown towards psychoanalytic therapy. However, this certainly should not imply that alcoholics are not treatable by more environmentally oriented approaches. In fact, research literature has shown again and again that alcoholics have a very good prognosis when treated with other modalities such as behavior modification (Hunt & Azrin, 1973; Paolino & McCrady, 1977; Sobell & Sobell, 1973).

5.11 *Freud in Perspective*

Although Freud often referred to the issue of treatability, especially in his papers written between 1904 and 1924, many of his comments are brief clinical pieces of advice without much discussion of underlying theory. Most of Freud's clinical and theoretical papers can be applied to the various issues of treatability, especially if we include discussions of the psychoanalytic process and metapsychology. When discussing treatability proper, however, Freud focused his comments on practical and logical concepts of behavior and personality, emphasizing the motivation to relieve psychic suffering and the capacity to: avoid ego disintegration; form the transference neurosis, the ultimate curative factor; be introspective, able to articulate and of sound ethical character; be capable of withstanding the stresses of the treatment and not demanding immediate removal of symptoms (Waldhorn, 1960).

In his major theoretical paper on treatability, Freud (1937) used economic and dynamic concepts to propose that treatability can only be assessed if we examine the specific patient's relative freedom from severe infantile training, degree of libidinal adhesiveness, capacity for libidinal mobility, and relationship between his instincts and defense mechanisms. At any point in time the strength of these various forces vary and treatability varies accordingly. If during pathogenesis, cathexis becomes excessively fixed, the mind is incapable of undergoing shifts of psychic energy necessary for resolution of symptoms. At predictable times in life (for example, adolescence and mid-life) the instincts and intrapsychic conflicts are reinforced, and thus the symptoms are less treatable.

Freud urged the psychoanalytic therapist to question the treatability of all prospective patients who will not immediately begin treatment regardless of the reason. According to Freud, patients who delay beginning treatment tend to fail to appear when the time comes to begin or tend to drop out soon after treatment begins (Freud, 1913a; Stekel, 1940).

Regarding fee, Freud (1913a) believed that hours should be leased, that is, the patient should be expected to accept an arrangement whereby the patient paid whether or not he (patient) came to that specific session. Freud proposed that if the patient does not accept this arrangement then he is not suitable for psychoanalytic psychotherapy. Freud also believed that (as a rule) gratuitous psychoanalytic psychotherapy is not productive because of the feeling of mistrust, resentment, reluctance to discuss the negative transference, excessive dependence on the therapist, and increased resistance that free service tends to elicit in patients (Freud, 1913a). (See Section 5.222 for further discussion of and an opposing opinion about gratuitous therapy.)

Freud proposed that the ideal age for psychoanalytic psychotherapy is the mid-twenties to thirties. The more over 40, the more likely the volume of psychic material will be prohibitive, the time required for cure becomes too long, and the patient's educable capacity and elasticity for psychical reconstruction is diminished (Freud, 1898, 1904). At the age of 49, Freud wrote that people over 50 are "no longer educable" (1905b, p. 264). It is of some interest to note that despite Freud's pessimism about the minds of people over 50, he himself continued to study, learn about himself and others, and write creative and original material, including brilliant papers, in his octogenarian years.

Freud believed that sexual satisfaction is necessary for a maximally happy adjustment to life situations and that sexual life drastically decreases after middle age, as it did for Freud himself (Roazen, 1971). Freud thus concluded that middle-aged patients are less treatable.

Freud wrote that the best way to assess treatability is not to do a question-answer type of interview, but rather to suspend judgment of treatability for most patients until after the patient is seen in provisional therapy five or six times a week for two consecutive weeks. Freud preferred the gradual development of transference, and reasoned that the avoidance of the question-answer anamnesis minimizes the risk of a pretreatment transference developing during the history taking sessions

(Freud, 1905b). Another advantage of the trial period is that it gives the assessor ample opportunity to observe the patient functioning in the treatment setting (Freud, 1913a). During the trial weeks, Freud would say very little to the patient, essentially letting the patient do all the talking.

Another reason Freud employed the trial period is that sometimes a patient has a much more serious illness than is indicated by the initial few interviews, but which reveals itself in the two weeks of intensive therapy. Freud was referring specifically to the patient who presents with the early signs of "schizophrenia" but, because of no previous history, cannot be diagnosed in an initial few interviews (Freud, 1913a). It is interesting to note that, although Freud believed that only those patients with "transference neuroses" are treatable, many of his own analytic patients would be labeled by contemporary psychiatrists as "psychotic" or "borderline" and "untreatable." (See Section 5.222 for further discussion of a trial period.)

Freud did not worry very much about the danger of treatment itself, writing that in proper hands the risks are minimal (Freud, 1926b). Furthermore, Freud did not concern himself with the possibility that the patient was suitable for psychoanalytic treatment but would respond even more to some other therapy, since Freud was convinced that there were no other effective therapeutic modalities for the neuroses (Freud, 1905b).

A solid understanding of Freud demands a grasp of his ideas with a proper historical perspective. Freud's prejudice against other modalities, for example, existed before the development of any effective means of treating psychic and behavioral disorders (Wallerstein, 1969). When Freud first began his practice in the field of neurology and psychiatry, the disease known as "hysteria" was commonly attributed to various religious, moral or magical causes such as demons, witchcraft, the Hippocratic theory of a wandering uterus and malingering (Bromberg, 1975). In response to these theories, some physicians attempted to treat the "hysteric" by application of a mélange of anachronistic and nonsensical treatments such as: warm liquids passed by a funnel into the vagina (Bromberg, 1975); a bandage wrapped tightly around the abdomen (Bromberg, 1975); medicinal herbs which were supposed to produce an odor that drove back the wandering uterus; walking barefoot on wet grass (Strachey, 1962); threats of physical punishment (Breuer & Freud, 1895); various forms of hydrotherapy such as cold water poured on top of the head (Breuer & Freud, 1895); plaster applied to the navel (Bromberg, 1975); bloodletting (Bromberg, 1975); elaborate apparatuses such as one that spun the patient in a circle (Breuer & Freud, 1895); and even extirpation of the clitoris (Jones, 1953).

Freud did not participate in any of the nonsensical treatment modalities mentioned in the previous paragraph, but he did subscribe to: body massage; nutritious diet; some forms of hydrotherapy such as hot or cold baths (Breuer & Freud, 1895); long periods in sanitoria; the Weir-Mitchell "Rest Cure"; physical exercise; electrotherapy to stimulate the nerves and improve blood circulation (Bromberg, 1975); hypnosis and other forms of suggestion; and medications such as bromides, narcotics, mineral water and placebo (Andersson, 1962; Breuer & Freud, 1895; Jones, 1953).

If Freud were alive today, his commitment to observing the empirical evidence would lead him to seriously consider certain "nonpsychoanalytic" treatments for some disorders before he would recommend the longer and more expensive classical psychoanalytic psychotherapy of his day. Thus, Freud might accept the idea of lithium for mania; behavior treatment for many addictive disorders, circumscribed phobias and sexual perversions; "short-term" therapy; couples, family or group therapy for specific cases; and, of course, other forms of psychoanalytically oriented treatment.

5.12 *Purpose of Chapter*

My goal here will be to clarify and consolidate some of the major concepts used in assessing clinical appropriateness for psychoanalytic psychotherapy. This chapter is not so much a description of how to assess treatability as it is a description of the psychological and environmental concepts and processes that interact in order for a patient to be treatable or untreatable. To use an analogy, this chapter is more of a discussion of the anatomy and physiology of treatability than it is an exposition on the diagnosis of untreatability, although there are some recommendations as to how to diagnose with respect to the specific concept discussed.

If the reader has a thorough understanding of the various psychic and environmental factors that interact in order to make a patient treatable or untreatable, the degree of treatability at times may become readily apparent in the initial assessment sessions, whereas at other times it can never be properly assessed until the patient has been in treatment for a significant amount of time. Either way, a grasp of treatability concepts will give the assessor-therapist a better idea of the issues he will have to deal with once the treatment begins.

A note of caution and clarification is in order: There are innumerable unavoidable hazards and complexities in presenting a discussion on treatability. Every aspect of treatability must be considered absolutely specific for each patient and each situation and few, if any, generalizations can be legitimately made. Despite these uncertainties, a clinician should have as clear a grasp as possible of those factors determining treatability since such knowledge not only helps the assessor decide whether or not to ask a patient to undergo or to continue the burdensome expense of such an experience, but also may reveal that the psychoanalytic psychotherapy is contraindicated and even potentially dangerous to the patient's mental and physical well-being. "Above all, do no harm," the first command of medical ethics, applies to psychoanalytic therapy as well as to somatic medicine.

Even though the assessor can never be sure of treatability, another reason for maximizing the assessment skills is that the busy therapist who has more potential patients than time may be better able to serve his patient population as a whole by selecting, or having selected for him, for psychoanalytic therapy those patients who are most likely to benefit.

Before 1960, there were no quantitative methodologically controlled research studies on treatability. Since then there have been eight, but none of these studies present an organized categorization of the relevant parameters, and none have clearly delineated the relationships between the research findings and their criteria for treatability (Bachrach & Leaff, 1978). In essence then, psychoanalytic literature still has not provided the ". . . better organized and more precise approach" recommended by Waldhorn 14 years ago (1967, p. 30).

Bachrach and Leaff (1978) systematically reviewed the American psychoanalytic literature since 1954 on qualities of the patient as they relate to treatability and observed that there are 390 separate, although overlapping, parameters that various clinicians and researchers have thought important to evaluate in assessing treatability. In general, Bachrach and Leaff note that, when assessing treatability, most clinicians focus on "ego strength" and "object relations."

I will expand on the efforts of Waldhorn (1967), Bachrach and Leaff (1978), Erle and Goldberg (1979) and others by providing a context in which this complex subject can be approached. Hopefully my attempt to group or classify the concepts related to treatability will be of value as a working outline for clinicians and future researchers in the area of correlation, integration, systematization and empirical verification.

The psychoanalytic literature on treatability consists of writings that either do not define what is meant by treatability or define it in divergent, fragmentary or inconsistent ways (Erle & Goldberg, 1979). For example, the literature tends to reserve the term "indications" or "suitability" for psychoanalytic psychotherapy when referring to symptoms or diagnosis, whereas the term "treatability" seems to be favored when referring to the patient's capacity to do the work of psychoanalytic psychotherapy (Tyson & Sandler, 1971). To define how I will be using the term "treatability," I will borrow Limentani's (1972) definition which does not distinguish between "suitability," "indications" and "treatability." Treatability is a certain state of readiness that involves the capacity to understand psychodynamics plus the capacity for change as a result of the understanding.

> . . . "analyzable" [treatable] is taken to refer to the possibility that in the course of analysis [psychoanalytic psychotherapy], a given condition, life situation, symptom, etc. is capable of being understood by the analyst [psychoanalytic therapist] and patient alike. Furthermore, it is taken for granted that such understanding as may have been achieved will lead to increased insight on the part of the analyst [psychoanalytic therapist] with regard to the patient's personality and character accompanied by psychodynamic changes in the latter (p. 355).

Those therapists with the courage to be honest with themselves will acknowledge that the judgment of treatability is mostly made subjectively (Diatkine, 1968; Feldman, 1968; Kantrowitz et al., 1975; Knapp et al., 1960; Levin, 1960, 1962; Lower et al., 1972; Waldhorn, 1967). Freud's (1913a) well-known analogy of psychotherapy to chess is also applicable to treatability. We know only some of the opening and closing moves; we apply the rest of our techniques mostly as the result of intuitively applied guidelines. Many of the *intuitively* made judgments on treatability are most satisfying and have confirmed the wisdom of empathic intuition. Although I remain respectful of empathic intuition, my conviction is that the assessment of treatability is far too important a decision in the life of the patient to be made by such unreliable forces. It should, instead, be made with a cognitive and rational understanding of the relevant concepts.

I will use the term "assessor" for the person assessing treatability and "therapist" for the person who administers the psychoanalytic therapy once the patient is found to be treatable and is referred. The assessor-therapist dichotomy is, of course, somewhat artificial, but is, nevertheless, useful for purposes of presentation. Whether or not the preanalytic assessor becomes the therapist for a specific patient, the assessment session still should be considered the beginning of the treatment itself (Pollock, 1960).

We must logically assume that the assessment of treatability does not stop after the patient is found suitable by the assessor. The assessment must continue throughout the course of psychoanalytic psychotherapy since treatability may vary throughout. At any point, the previously treatable patient may become less treatable or more treatable. Whenever I use terms such as "refer the patient to psychoanalytic psychotherapy" or "find the patient treatable," I am assuming that the reader will know that this also applies to the referral that the therapist implicitly makes to himself each time he agrees to continue administering psychoanalytic psychotherapy to a particular patient.

Certain situations and capacities are more important than others at various phases of the psychoanalytic process. Furthermore, the judgment of treatability of any given patient varies with each assessor. In essence then, this chapter not only deals with the issues of treatability, but also involves concepts relevant to the ongoing psychoanalytic process. *In this sense, then, we touch in many places upon issues of psychoanalytic technique as well as the main topic of treatability.* For example, I wish to say more than that a patient must be able to free associate in order to make use of psychoanalytic therapy. I also want the reader to understand (from the discussions in Chapter 3 as well as Chapter 5) something about the concept of free association, what it is and why it is an essential element for successful psychoanalytic psychotherapy. I wish to do more than inform the reader that the patient must be able to regress constructively in order to make use of this therapy. The reader will not be able to recognize such a capacity without a solid idea about how regression plays a role in the psychoanalytic psychotherapeutic process.

My expansion into the theoretical side of treatability is the result of my firm conviction that the assessor of treatability has to have a solid knowledge of the theory and process of psychoanalytic psychotherapy in order to be able to recognize the presence or absence of the potential in a prospective patient to participate in such a psychotherapeutic process. The assessment of treatability by a clinician who does not understand the psychotherapeutic process makes as much sense as the evaluation of a patient for a surgery by an evaluator who does not understand surgical procedures.

5.13 *What is a Treatment Failure?*

A major function of the assessor is to refer to psychoanalytic psychotherapy only patients who have a good chance not to fail. The assessor cannot fulfill this function without an operational definition of "treatment failure." I suggest that we follow Waldhorn (1960) and describe a treatment failure as a situation in which a patient does one or more of the following: 1) permanently and prematurely quits in the middle of therapy; 2) gets significantly more symptomatic during the course of therapy; 3) chronically and progressively acts dangerously to self or others during the course of therapy; and 4) does not progress in therapy but is satisfied with remaining in treatment.

The reasons for all psychoanalytic psychotherapy failures fall into one or both of two major overlapping classifications: 1) The patient was not suitable; that is, the interaction of intrapsychic and environmental factors resulted in the patient being either not disturbed enough to need this expensive and time consuming treatment, or not capable of becoming an ally in the treatment in order to benefit from it. 2) The basic therapeutic techniques were incorrectly employed by the therapist. Although this chapter will focus on the first category, many of the concepts of treatability may be useful in clarifying the ongoing psychoanalytic process and technical concepts.

5.14 *The Categorization Model and Its Shortcomings*

Although the ultimate standard by which we assess treatability is the outcome of the treatment itself, the relevant concepts can be roughly categorized into two main classifications. Group One, labeled "Preanalytic Assessment" (see Section 5.2), consists of situations or capacities that can be judged within the initial assessment sessions. As noted in Bachrach and Leaff's (1978) review article, much of the psychoanalytic literature on treatability is presented in metapsychological terms (for a typical example, see Greenspan & Cullander, 1973) rather than as clinical observations of relatively unambiguous parameters. I have tried to avoid this tendency by presenting categories and subcategories that focus on the patient's interpersonal and external strengths and on his external environment, past history, current appearance, behavior and verbalizations.

Group Two, labeled "Postanalytic Assessment" (see Section 5.3), consists of capacities and situations that cannot, with any degree of certainty, be assessed until the patient has been in psychoanalytic psychotherapy for a considerable length of time. Group Two items are equally important as Group One for treatability, and although the final judgment cannot be made initially, the assessor must still begin evaluating these items in the initial sessions. Because of the absence of empirical research, I have had to be somewhat arbitrary in these groupings so that, for any given patient, categories in Group One may be more appropriately included in Group Two or vice versa. Perhaps this chapter will be of some use to empirical researchers who can test out the validity of whether or not a specific category should be in a preanalytic or postanalytic group.

This chapter is an attempt at presenting an organized *categorization* by which we can approach the subject of treatability, and does not, to any significant degree, attempt to dynamically integrate or synthesize the various categories. The system of categorization presented is a static model, although the discussion *within* each category is dynamically oriented. This approach certainly does not mean that the categories are *not* mutually dependent. To give just one example, the subjects of fee and psychic pain are discussed separately; and yet, the fee may be an insurmountable obstacle to the slight sufferer but no more than an inconvenience to someone experiencing large amounts of psychic discomfort.

There is another way in which the categorization of this chapter is artificially static: psychoanalytic psychotherapy is discussed as if it were a static treatment model not capable of multiple variations in response to therapist differences and individual patient needs. I chose to keep these complicated matters out of this chapter for the sake of clarity, hoping that there has not been any significant sacrifice of a truthful representation of the phenomena involved.

Also, the very essence of psychoanalytic psychotherapy is based on the assumption (discussed in Chapter 3) that unconscious intrapsychic conflicts directly cause psychic symptoms. Thus, it is impossible to accurately predict the outcome of psychoanalytic psychotherapy without knowing how a person will react to the experience of significant awareness and working through of unconscious psychic elements, an experience that usually requires psychoanalytic psychotherapy itself.

Why, then, have I written this chapter at all? There is, to my knowledge, no attempt in the literature to organize an approach to treatability by the method of categorization presented in this chapter. No matter how crude and inexact this approach may be, a relatively consistent categorization is, in my opinion, better than no organized approach at all.

Of course, no discussion of treatability can be considered definitive or comprehensive without a close inspection of the various influences that the categories have on each other, nor without taking into consideration the enormously complicated psychoanalytic process, the varieties of psychoanalytic psychotherapy and the different patient needs. *The problem, however, is that the relevant concepts of treatability are as comprehensive as human functioning itself and defy any comprehensive and systematic discussion without first establishing an organized categorization.*

> The true beginning of scientific activity consists . . . in describing phenomena and then in proceeding to group, classify and correlate them (Freud, 1915a, p. 117).

The categorization model has the potential to help clinicians in their daily work by: 1) directing attention to the relevant data; 2) facilitating the perception of the relevant data in a way that distinguishes untreatable from treatable; 3) clarifying assessor-patient and therapist-patient interaction in a way that promotes constructive assessor and therapist intervention; and 4) facilitating development of new perspectives on treatability.

5.2 Group One Categories—Preanalytic Assessment

5.21 *Patient Strengths*

The treatable patient must possess many strengths. For example, the patient must be able to regress yet undergo growth; abandon control yet maintain control; renounce yet maintain reality testing; articulate with order and logic yet free associate and regress to primary process thinking; communicate intimately with profound thoughts and feelings yet restrain from action; fantasize yet scrutinize; experiment yet observe; be passive yet active; involved yet detached (Greenson, 1967).*

By training medical clinicians are oriented towards disease and, accordingly, usually find it easier to identify defects and predict conflicts or psychological abnormalities than to identify psychological strengths and predict conflict-free functioning and the use of normal coping. This same tendency among clinicians perhaps explains why subjective impressions as well as empirical research (Lower et al., 1972) reveal that these practitioners tend to agree more on a patient's defects than strengths as they relate to treatability. In this Section and in Section 5.34, I have tried to avoid the tendency to focus on abnormalities and have tried instead to discuss strengths, although, of course, some strengths are more relevant than others and some mention of weaknesses is unavoidable.

5.211 Intelligence

There is little said in the literature regarding intelligence required for any forms of investigative psychodynamic therapy. Nevertheless, from Freud (1904) onward (e.g., Knight, 1949; Rogers, 1940; Wallerstein et al., 1956), it is assumed that at least normal, and perhaps even superior, intelligence is preferred if not required. The research literature strongly supports the hypothesis that education and verbal intelligence are highly correlated with psychological mindedness (Frank, 1974; Redlich et al., 1953). The American Psychoanalytic Association's report of 3,019 patients in psychoanalytic psychotherapy reveals that 88% had attended college and half of those had also attended graduate school (Hamburg et al., 1967). Furthermore, there is positive correlation between educational level and likelihood to complete the treatment (Hamburg et al., 1967). A review (Luborsky et al., 1971) of empirical research on the relationship between psychotherapy of any kind and intelligence as measured by the usual tests reveals that intelligence is highly correlated with good clinical outcome. Psychoanalytic psychotherapy is no exception to this generalization, especially since it requires a significant amount of abstraction and learning.

The assessor must bear in mind, however, that intellectual capacity does not remain static from crib to grave. Psychic problems may interfere

---

* The same strengths and capacities, or course, must be possessed by the therapist (see Section 1.5). See Greenson (1966) and Singer (1970) for insightful discussion of capacities and strengths that the therapist must have and/or develop.

with the intellectual abilities during the taking of IQ tests, schoolwork performance, or interpersonal encounters so that the patient, in fact, may be more intelligent than he seems at first. Some patients may even present with "pseudo-debility" (Fenichel, 1945, p. 180) that will yield to a condition of normal or above average intelligence as a successful psychoanalytic psychotherapy proceeds (Hellman, 1954; Klein, 1931; Mahler-Schoenberger, 1942; Schmideberg, 1938; Tyson & Sandler, 1971).

Related to the subject of intelligence is the complex issue surrounding the degree to which social class values tend to influence the assessor's judgment of treatability. Most psychoanalytic clinicians live their private lives in middle or upper social economic classes. Furthermore, most psychoanalytic clinicians were raised and/or currently live in social and professional environments in which intelligence is highly valued. We know that, in general, when compared to the higher socioeconomic groups, patients from the lower social economic classes tend to be less intelligent if we use the traditional measurements of intelligence. We also know that, in general, the patient from the lower social economic class is less likely to be referred to psychotherapy than equally disturbed patients from higher social economic classes (Blais & Georges, 1969; Brown & Kosterlitz, 1964; Gerson & Bassuk, 1980; Hollingshead & Redlich, 1958; Rowden et al., 1979; Shader et al., 1969; Yamamoto & Goin, 1966).

Also, there have been some impressive reports showing that the social class difference between the assessor and the patient is inversely related to the degree of self-exploration that the patient experiences during the assessment (Carkhuff & Pierce, 1967; Gerson & Bassuk, 1980). The social class difference between the preanalytic assessor and patient is also inversely related to the probability that the patient will be referred for psychotherapy (Kandel, 1966).

Of course, intelligence is not the only variable that accounts for these trends with regard to referral to psychotherapy and socioeconomic class. Nevertheless, it is unfortunate, but true, that psychoanalytic clinicians find patients with above average intelligence the most enjoyable with whom to work. Most people working in free or low-cost clinics that see patients from all socioeconomic classes would, I think, agree with my own subjective impression that the patient with above average intelligence who has no job and no income is more likely to be referred for psychoanalytic therapy than the patient with average or below average intelligence who may be classified in a higher socioeconomic group. There has never been well-controlled research on these issues so, at this level of our knowledge, they can only be subjects of speculation.

5.212 CAPACITY TO VERBALIZE

Words are used in secondary process thinking as: 1) a means to satisfy the basic human need to symbolize and communicate; 2) substitutes for action; 3) possessors of cathexis derived from instinctual origins (Rycroft, 1958); 4) the means by which a person forms the connection between psychic elements in the ego and the memory traces from the visual and auditory perceptions (Freud, 1940; Loewenstein, 1956); 5) a means by which ideas can be integrated and the mind can gain some conscious control over the frightening elements of the mind (Kanzer, 1961); and 6) a means of motor and emotional discharge, or abreaction (Hartmann, 1964). It is this six-part function of words that makes psychoanalytic treatment possible, although, of course, psychoanalytic psychotherapy is a peculiar dialogue unlike any other.

The term "verbalization" was originally coined in 1874 by Hughlings Jackson (Jackson, 1958). Strictly speaking, the concept of verbalization is not identical to the concept of speech (Balkanyi, 1964). In the act of speaking, the first step is verbalization, in which the person attaches mental images of words to his inner experiences. The second step is speech itself, in which the patient attaches symbolic sounds to the mental images of words. The important differences between the capacity to verbalize and the capacity for speech are beyond the province of this book and are covered by Balkanyi (1964) and others. For this book, it is enough to simply accept the term "verbalize" (or articulate) as representing all capacities involved in the act of speaking.

A major goal of psychoanalytic psychotherapy is to understand *unconscious* meanings of conscious thoughts and feelings and manifest behavior. In order to achieve this goal, the therapist must first comprehend the *manifest* and *conscious* meanings of the patient's communications. Obviously, then, the ability to articulate becomes an important variable in assessing treatability. Just as he must overcome a resistance between the unconscious and the preconscious, the treatable patient must be capable of combatting the resistance that attempts to prevent many conscious thoughts and feelings from being verbalized.

There certainly are other necessary channels of communication between therapist and patient; for example, both therapist and patient must be able to use their bodies as means of perception (Khan, 1960).

The capacity to articulate has been reified in the psychoanalytic literature. It is safe to say, however, that in general the patient who cannot
effectively communicate verbally probably is untreatable and should
be assigned to some supportive, behavioral or environmental therapy.
The capacity to articulate, however, like intelligence and ethics, can to
some degree be influenced by the psychopathology so that, as successful
psychoanalytic psychotherapy proceeds, the defect is reduced. There is no
simple way to make this critical distinction and at this stage of our
knowledge all that helps is a large amount of clinical experience and
empathic flexibility.

Just as silence does not necessarily mean a defective ability to communicate (see Section 5.341), so does talkativeness not necessarily mean
an unusual communicative strength. Patients often unconsciously use
speech for the purpose of concealing rather than revealing (Evans, 1953).
Excessive talk characterized by evasiveness, allusiveness and vagueness in
an initial interview can be as much a harbinger of untreatability as
excessive inability to articulate.

Finally, a note of caution regarding the inadequacies of verbalizations
is in order. The inadequacy of speech as a vehicle to the unconscious
exists today as much as it did in 1952 when Kubie made the following
illuminating remarks.

> Furthermore . . . words themselves mislead us. Adult speech can
> describe only the conscious symbols into which the unconscious
> residues of the confused preverbal thoughts and feelings of childhood
> are translated. A language which can communicate these preverbal
> experiences without adultomorphic distortions is still lacking and is
> urgently needed so that we will be able to communicate better with
> the child who is within the man, so that we can understand him and
> so that his unconscious can understand us (p. 89).

5.213 PREVIOUS KNOWLEDGE AND ATTITUDES ABOUT PSYCHOTHERAPY

All patients come to therapy with some kind of previous knowledge
or attitudes and frequently after extended discussions about psychotherapy with relatives, friends and referral sources. Sometimes these
experiences tend to interfere with the therapy because of the already
established resistances and/or preformed transferences. There are times
when extraordinary expectations and demands have been encouraged by
friends, relatives or previous assessors or therapists and such expectations
may significantly contribute to untreatability.

One way that psychoanalytic psychotherapy differs from the environmental therapies or the therapies of suggestion is that psychoanalytic therapy attributes little positive value to the presence of the patient's previous knowledge about psychotherapy or expectations at the beginning of treatment. Frequently, knowledge about psychoanalytic theory or technique only serves to provide the patient with intellectualizations that are easily employed in the service of resistance. The attitudes toward therapy, excessive degree of confidence in the therapist and previous knowledge of the psychoaonalytic theory and technique, all have negligible importance in comparison to the amount of resistance and secondary gain associated with the symptoms (Freud, 1913a). If the patient shows sublime confidence in the treatment and therapist, we should probably express a gratitude to him, but warn him that such idealism will probably be shattered when we look at those parts of his mind that he avoids. To the patient who expresses profound distrust or ignorance about therapy, we should say that previous knowledge is not necessary and distrust may be a symptom of the problems leading to therapy, or may simply be a manifestation of not knowing the therapist (Freud, 1913a).

The hypothesis that previous knowledge of psychotherapy is of little importance in assessing suitability can easily be confirmed by observations of patients in psychoanalytic therapy who happen also to be mental health professionals, such as psychiatrists, psychologists, psychiatric social workers, nurses and counselors. These people are as capable of the same extreme degrees of resistance as anyone else.

> Neurosis has its roots in psychical strata to which an intellectual knowledge of analysis has not penetrated (Freud, 1913a, p. 126).

Although most therapists would agree that the patient possessing knowledge of psychoanalytic theory has no major advantages and perhaps even some disadvantages, I doubt that many therapists agree that such patients are automatically untreatable, an opinion represented by Stekel:

> A patient who comes to the analyst [psychoanalytic psychotherapist] well-equipped with analytical knowledge is a patient whose chances of benefit from analysis [psychoanalytic psychotherapy] have been spoiled. . . . [Such a patient] will simulate the cognition without really experiencing it (1940, pp. 12-13).

The best attitude for a prospective patient to have towards psychoanalytic psychotherapy is probably that of "benevolent skepticism"

(Freud, 1916-1917h, p. 244) which will, *during the course of treatment,* give way to trust in the therapist and confidence in the theoretical model from which the therapist derives the treatment.

5.214 THE DESIRE FOR LESS PSYCHIC PAIN

Although the wish to be free from psychic pain is a powerful motivation for psychoanalytic psychotherapy (Freud, 1905a), we should not overvalue the positive aspects of such motivation (Kuiper, 1968). The optimal patient is one who, during the preanalytic assessment: 1) recognizes that symptoms interfere with family, social and professional relationships; 2) recognizes that intrapsychic determinants are responsible for the symptoms; and 3) accordingly seeks self-understanding so as not only to understand the past but also to prevent reoccurrence of the symptoms.

The patient who complains the most about his symptoms is often the patient who resists the most against psychoanalytic psychotherapy (Freud, 1916-1917i). It is of historical interest to note that one of the first psychoanalytic cases, Freud's Dora (1950a), was one of those patients who was motivated by her wish for alleviation of physical and psychosomatic discomfort, although she did not want to see a psychiatrist and only did so on a direct order from her father. She originally came to Freud complaining of nervous coughs, migraine headaches, chronic dyspnea, hoarseness and aphonia. Although the transference and countertransference phenomena certainly played a part in her termination (Marcus, 1976; Muslin and Gill, 1978; Rogow, 1978), she terminated treatment when the physical symptoms subsided, only to return to treatment 15 months later complaining of facial neuralgia.

In conclusion, if the patient comes to therapy for no other reason than to experience less psychic pain or less psychosomatic pain, psychoanalytic psychotherapy frequently has less to offer than other forms of therapy such as environmental manipulation, medication or behavior modification.

5.215 PAST PERFORMANCE

The presence or absence of symptoms does not by itself tell us very much about the ego's capacity to function in the face of impairments or obstacles (see Section 5.33). Such information, however, can be obtained through close evaluation of past performance. Subjective impressions as well as empirical research (Klein, 1960; Luborsky et al., 1971) strongly suggest that most people in psychoanalytic psychotherapy have been relatively successful in school, work or play before entertaining treatment. By "success" I mean that the person has functioned at or close to what the assessor objectively considers to be his maximal capacity. A patient is not likely to succeed in psychoanalytic psychotherapy if he has consistently failed in school and work (oriented mostly on a reality principle) or in play (oriented along the pleasure principle).

The degree of success or failure in school, work or play gives us some idea of the patient's perseverance, ability to release tension in a constructive fashion, to transform fantasy life into productive sublimations (Stone, 1954), and to make internal alterations and psychic compromises in order to engender environmental change. The patient who has been successful in school, work or play is usually someone who has adjusted to unpopular but necessary "rules" of life. Psychoanalytic psychotherapy also requires perserverance and complicity to what at first might appear to be unnecessary, artificial and illogical rules authoritatively established by the therapist, such as regular and prompt attendance, relatively rigid payment schedules, free association and social abstention between patient and therapist. An assessment of past performance also facilitates an understanding of the patient's functioning in areas that are relatively stress free, and, as Hartmann (1951) and others have noted, an assessment of ego strength or mental health is incomplete without knowing how the patient functions in the absence of conflict as well as in its presence.

The success or failure of past performances in school, work or play can frequently indicate the capacity of courage and the ability to tolerate unavoidable pain and to not participate in magical demands. Success in school, work or play requires patience, the capacity for a certain amount of self-observation and self-discipline and the ability to face the truth rather than rationalize maladaptively. The same capacities are required for a successful psychoanalytic psychotherapy.

5.216 THE CAPACITY FOR PSYCHOLOGICAL MINDEDNESS AND INSIGHT

Psychological mindedness and insight are both required for a person to be treatable.

5.2161 Psychological Mindedness

Psychological mindedness is a term often bandied about in psychoanalytic literature and clinical discussions, but is rarely defined explicitly.

In fact, the term psychological mindedness does not appear in *A Glossary of Psychoanalytic Terms and Concepts* (Moore & Fine, 1968), nor does it appear in the early classical psychoanalytic literature (Appelbaum, 1973), an unfortunate absence since 25 percent of all American psychoanalytic literature on treatability focuses on the capacity for psychological mindedness (Bachrach & Leaff, 1978). For the purpose of this chapter, I suggest we follow Appelbaum's (1973) excellent paper and define psychological mindedness as a state of mind characterized by four components:

1) *Capacity to Perceive the Relationship Between Thoughts, Feelings and Actions.* This capacity requires cognition, intuition and empathy, and also requires a tendency not to externalize or project the inner self onto environmental objects. The quality of "capacity" must be emphasized. The Menninger Foundation's Psychotherapy Research Project (Kernberg et al., 1972) obtained impressive empirical data suggesting that the *preanalytic* tendency to externalize was not a significant factor in treatability, whereas the tendency to increase psychological mindedness (decrease externalizations) as psychoanalytic psychotherapy progressed was positively correlated with good clinical outcome. The treatable patient need only possess the *capacity* to think with psychological mindedness and does not necessarily have to demonstrate such thinking in preanalytic sessions.

2) *Capacity and Desire to Learn the Meanings and Causes of Experience and Behavior.* It is not enough to possess the *perceptive* cognitive and intuitive capacities; the treatable patient must also possess the capacity and desire to *understand* what causes specific thoughts, feelings or actions. This capacity is reflected in people who are simply intrigued or excited by the psychological side of human nature and find themselves often wondering why a person acted or thought in a specific way or what the meaning is with regard to some specific thought, feeling or action. In contrast, there are nonpsychologically minded people who do not care about causation and perhaps even doubt whether there is any meaning behind much of what we do. Inherent in this capacity is a humanistic concern for oneself and other people. The goal of understanding feelings as well as thoughts and actions is important in distinguishing psychological mindedness from intellectualization.

3) *Capacity to Direct Inwards, i.e. to Direct the Psychological Thinking Towards One's Own Psychic Life Rather Than Towards Other Objects.* If a person thinks psychologically but directs his thoughts only to other people, then that person would not fit Appelbaum's (1973) definition of psychological mindedness. Self-directed psychological thinking is often called "introspection" or "self-awareness."

4) *Capacity to Integrate With Psychoanalytic Process.* This component of the definition of psychological mindedness is an operational concept, is the hardest to describe briefly and, of course, cannot be preanalytically assessed. All patients have resistance to psychoanalytic psychotherapy, and all therapy involves some training on the patient's part. This capacity refers to a degree of resistance and the probability that the patient will use the above three capacities in the service of integration, synthesis and the psychoanalytic process.

Appelbaum (1973) emphasizes that although all four capacities must be present in the preanalytic patient to some degree for anyone to be psychologically minded, a deficiency in one component can be largely compensated by an excess in the other. Furthermore, although psychological mindedness is a mental state, the degree of psychological mindedness is in constant dynamic flux and subject to the variables of intrapsychic *and* environmental changes.

5.2162 *Insight*

Closely allied to the concept of psychological mindedness is the concept of insight. Psychoanalytic literature does not make clear the origin or variations (verbal, intellectual, psychological, emotional, curative) of the term and concept of insight. For the purposes of this book, insight can be broadly defined as a state of knowledge about one's own conscious and unconscious thoughts, feelings or psychic processes that is the result of deeper genetic understanding of one's behavior and a constructively altered self-perception in which new facts about oneself are learned and some old facts are perceived more beneficially. Insight is also an ideational representation (Wallerstein et al., 1956) of one's behavior and psychic processes, especially as they change in response to events such as the psychotherapy sessions.

Thus, psychological mindedness is more of a *capacity* that the patient brings to treatment whereas insight is more of a consequence of the interaction between psychological mindedness and the psychoanalytic process. It should be emphasized that, to some degree, both psychological mindedness and insight are parts of the psychoanalytic process and goals of treatment. Although these definitions of insight and psychological mindedness are brief and somewhat simplified, they are workable for the purposes of this chapter since they are directly conceptually related to the concept of treatability.

5.2163 *Some Ways to Assess Psychological Mindedness*

How can we recognize psychological mindedness when assessing treatability? Since a basic doctrine of psychoanalytic psychotherapy is that symptoms arise from intrapsychic conflict, it seems logical that one indicator of psychological mindedness is the patient's awareness at some level that symptoms arise from within oneself in response to the environmental circumstances. Marked tendencies towards generalizations, denial, projection and displacement suggest a poor probability that the capacity for psychological mindedness exists and that insight will develop in therapy (Aarons, 1962). In fact, reliable research shows that not only psychoanalytic psychotherapy, but most kinds of psychotherapy are more successful if the patients acknowledge that their problems are psychic and not somatic or environmental (Frank et al., 1957). Some patients even gain pleasure from self-awareness and self-understanding. Although the pleasure gained from self-understanding should not be the primary reason for seeking therapy, this secondary motive may constructively contribute to the overall motivation (Aarons, 1962).

The ability to recognize internal mental processes as distinguished from the external environment is one of the most reliable means by which we can assess the patient's ability to distinguish between the therapeutic alliance and transference neurosis (Zetzel, 1968). The capacity for this distinction is a prerequisite for a successful psychoanalytic therapy.

All patients in meaningful psychoanalytic psychotherapy reveal to the therapist parts of themselves that are rarely or never shown to anyone else. Such a situation tends to elicit in the therapist the false assumption that what we see in our consulting rooms is, in contrast to what is seen by the patient's friends or relatives, the real person of the patient. In point of fact, with some patients, the friends and relatives may very likely be exposed to various aspects of the patient's personality that are not manifested during the therapy session. One indicator of psychological mindedness is the patient's capacity to bring various aspects of his personality and life from outside the treatment setting into the psychotherapy session. Anna Freud (1954b) gives a case example of a psychoanalytic patient who gets angry at the therapist because the therapist only sees her in the treatment setting. The patient says:

> You analyze me all wrong. I know what you should do: you should be with me the whole day because I am a completely different person when I am here with you, when I am in school, and when I am at

home with my foster family. How can you know me if you do not see me in all these places? There is not one me there are three (p. 613).

If in treatment the patient acts in a way that is totally different from the way he is outside of treatment, then the assessor must wonder whether or not the patient has the psychological mindedness to benefit from psychoanalytic psychotherapy.

Another measure of the capacity for psychological mindedness is the degree to which the prospective patient is consciously aware of his drive levels (Dewald, 1972). In order for the therapy to be successful, the sexual and aggressive drives must to some degree be experienced cognitively, emotionally and bodily within the therapy session itself. If the patient is minimally aware of these drives, much therapeutic time and effort must be spent mobilizing the drives so that they can be experienced within the treatment session and then observed. If the patient has, as many people do, an inherent capacity to be unusually aware of his drives within the treatment session, then the therapy not only is possible but can proceed at a relatively rapid rate (Dewald, 1972).

Many patients exhibit a changed behavior in the direction of goals of therapy, but express no insight as to the reason for this change. The change may result from compliance or an attempt to please by means of a reaction formation against hostility. An important point is that compliance can be confused with psychological mindedness. The patient who readily agrees to all aspects of therapy (for example, fee, appointment times, confrontations or interpretations) may be manifesting a psychic weakness rather than a strength.

5.217 THE CAPACITY TO TOLERATE ANXIETY, DEPRESSION AND OTHER PAINFUL FEELINGS AND THOUGHTS

Clinical experience as well as empirical research (Kernberg et al., 1972) have demonstrated that psychoanalytic psychotherapy requires the capacity to tolerate frustration, anxiety, depression, guilt, shame and other painful feelings and thoughts without having to resort to action to alleviate the discomfort. This capacity can often be adequately assessed during preanalytic interviews. People who resort to drug or alcohol abuse to anesthetize their psychic pain, or people who develop psychosomatic disorders such as ulcerative colitis, are good examples of people who often are unsuitable for psychoanalytic psychotherapy because of their incapacity to bear painful feelings and thoughts and to seek psychic resolutions without acting in some way. Sometimes restless, hyperactive or very aggressive people also display this inability. A careful preanalytic history plus a detailed observation as to how the patient is relating to the stress of the preanalytic assessment interview helps to evaluate this specific capacity. Sometimes the precipitating event produces unpleasant feelings and the assessor should note carefully the prospective patient's capacity to absorb the feelings.

5.2171 *The Capacity to Tolerate Anxiety*

The capacity to tolerate anxiety may be clarified in preanalytic interviews if the assessor distinguishes between primary and secondary anxiety. Primary (sometimes called "traumatic") anxiety is the term Freud assigned to the psychic and physiological condition that results when the person is experiencing a sense of helplessness to alleviate overwhelming instinctual (sexual or aggressive) excitation. Primary anxiety is a kind of psychic panic or psychic disaster situation in which the person feels abandoned by all beneficial objects, vulnerable to attack from bad objects, and in general as if he faces total destruction. Instinctual tensions have the capacity at any time to gain the force to engender primary anxiety. There are certain periods of life such as infancy, with its weak ego, or adolescence and mid-life, with their stresses, that weaken the ego, and in turn lead to susceptibility to primary anxiety.

Secondary anxiety is defined as a defensive phenomenon in response to the ego's observation of an internal threat, such as that of primary anxiety (Freud, 1933). The development of secondary anxiety is necessary for normal psychic development. Secondary anxiety is the mind's way of warning the ego of a dangerous situation of being overwhelmed and, in fact, is often called "signal anxiety."

In our attempt to distinguish primary from secondary anxiety, it is useful to use Zetzel's (1970) analogy of two students taking examinations in which one student experiences anxiety that paralyzes performance whereas the other student experiences the anxiety as a warning of the dangers and as a motivation to prepare for the challenge. In summary then, primary anxiety is maladaptive since it leads to further impairment, whereas secondary anxiety is adaptive since it stimulates the ego to attempt increased mastery.

Zetzel (1970) postulates three stages of development of anxiety (see

FIGURE 5.1 – Zetzel's Three Developmental Stages of Anxiety

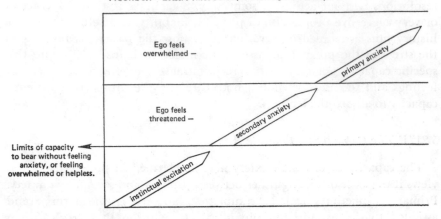

Figure 5.1). In the first stage, the instinctual excitation remains within the limits of the individual person's capacity to bear it without developing any anxiety. In the first stage the person may feel aggression or sexual desire but no anxiety. In the second stage, the sexual or aggressive tension reaches the point where the ego is threatened with being overwhelmed. At this point, *secondary anxiety* develops. The third stage occurs when the ego cannot cope, despite the warnings of secondary anxiety. The ego experiences feelings of being overwhelmed by the sexual or aggressive instinct and a helplessness to do anything about it. This now is the condition of primary (traumatic) anxiety.

It is realistically impossible to conceptually separate instinct from internalized objects. The ego may be threatened from intimidating internal objects ("paranoid anxiety," Zetzel, 1970, p. 39) or by the threat of a loss of a valued internal object ("depressive anxiety," Zetzel, 1970, p. 39). Furthermore, both types of secondary anxiety can arise from threatening external situations such as fear of an intimidating parent or a separated mother. Zetzel (1970) postulates that the inability to manifest secondary anxiety is the result of a denial of castration fear, but such theoretical speculations are beyond the province and purpose of this chapter.

Zetzel (1970) originally developed her ideas while studying British soldiers suffering from battle neuroses during World War II. These soldiers suffered from marked and painful neurotic symptoms following one specific stressful battle experience. On initial examination, most of the soldiers had a history of normal adjustment in civilian sexual and working lives, and before the present illness were functioning well, and in some cases outstandingly, in military life.

Upon further examination and subsequent treatment, despite the normality of their past, the individual soldiers manifested different patterns of secondary anxiety that were predictive of how they coped with the terrifying war experience. Those patients who had a history of experiencing little or no conscious anxiety before the stressful war incident were the patients who were *least* likely to experience anxiety in response to the horrors of war. Instead of showing conscious anxiety, these people would respond by manifesting a quick recovery to the stress and then prolonged depressive and hypochondriacal symptoms, often combined with paranoid projections of the anxiety and marked personality changes that were relatively irreversible. Such patients reacted as if, psychically, they had been completely unprepared for the fear and panic that the war situation created. Zetzel speculated that during the childhood years, these patients did not develop the capacity to cope with instinctual tension by developing adequate psychic mechanisms of secondary anxiety. Thus, when they were overwhelmed by the external situation of battle, they were unable to adequately adjust to the helplessness.

The second group of men had a previous history of experiencing normal amounts of free-floating anxiety or even phobic anxiety. These men showed a much different clinical picture following their decompensation in battle. First, these men were able to withstand more stress before the breakdown. Second, when they did eventually decompensate, their neurotic symptoms were marked by much more anxiety, their personalities were essentially unchanged, and their symptoms were far more reversible than the group discussed above. Zetzel concluded that this second group of men developed, during childhood, a more adequate warning and coping system to an accumulation of instinctual tension so that when they were overwhelmed by the war experience their egos were more prepared to adjust with secondary anxiety and the defense mechanisms that responded to secondary anxiety.

Zetzel's sample was small and highly selective, she did not apply empirical research methods to her observations, and of course her findings must be considered suggestive rather than conclusive. She herself pointed out (1970) that it is impossible to make sharp distinctions between constructive and inhibitive anxiety; most patients present some form of anxiety in which the anxiety serves as both a signal to danger and as a source of inhibiting stress.

Despite the methodological deficiencies of her report, Zetzel's work on primary and secondary anxiety is of significant value to our discussion of treatability in the following way: The development of secondary anxiety is a protection against psychic disaster and the *sine qua non* of treatability (Waldhorn, 1960; Zetzel, 1970). Through the development of secondary anxiety the person is able to minimize the appearance of the prohibiting primary anxiety. Without an adequate development of secondary anxiety there can be no defense system against the dangerous intrapsychic situations that inevitably arise in psychoanalytic psychotherapy. The patient with sufficient capacity to develop secondary anxiety can encounter the stress of psychoanalytic therapy without being overwhelmed. Any person with excessive primary anxiety is probably untreatable since the ego is too overwhelmed to do the work of therapy.

Zetzel's work is of major importance in assessing treatability since her conclusions challenge the tendency of some assessors to automatically consider the history of excessive manifest anxiety to be less indicative of treatability than a patient who has a history of little or no experience of manifest anxiety. Psychoanalytic psychotherapy is very stressful. Although Zetzel's soldier-patients were faced with life threatening stress, the stress of psychoanalytic psychotherapy can at times threaten intrapsychic equilibrium and engender a fear that is just as great as an imminent threat to one's life. One might even say that psychoanalytic psychotherapy threatens parts of the psychic life just as war combat threatens the biological life.

The patient who has shown evidence of experiencing conscious anxiety and coping with it so that it is not significantly destructive may be more treatable than a patient who reports no history of significant anxiety. In fact, since secondary anxiety is a signaling process in response to the ego observing the psychic system, we can conclude that the degree of secondary anxiety development correlates with that individual person's ego capacity for self-observation, a capacity that certainly is necessary for a successful psychoanalytic therapy (Zetzel, 1970). Conversely, the absence of secondary anxiety could indicate the absence of introspection, a condition which renders the person untreatable. A careful historical evaluation of anxiety not only helps in assessing treatability, but also may be of value in predicting the degree and types (primary or secondary) of anxiety that may emerge within the therapy sessions (Waldhorn, 1960).

5.2172 The Capacity to Tolerate Depression

In order to be treatable, a person must be able to tolerate the inevitable depression that follows real experiences of loss, frustration, sorrow, renunciation and disappointment (Zetzel, 1970). The prospective patient must be able to tolerate and master these experiences since they will be relived and occur de novo in every psychoanalytic psychotherapy.

By "depression" I mean sadness, guilt, low self-esteem and a sense of helplessness (Zetzel, 1970). By "capacity to bear," "tolerate," or similar phrases, I am referring to the following two capacities: 1) to experience the depression without significant maladaptive ego regression and/or ego disintegration and/or severe narcissistic injuries such as feelings of rejection or abandonment; and 2) to be able to utilize the secondary adaptive capacities so that the available resources are mobilized to minimize the realistically inevitable frustrations and to maximize substitutive gratifications. One way that this capacity manifests itself is that the patient can gain new available objects despite the persistent desires for the unavailable ones (Zetzel, 1970).

The lack of destructive regression, disintegration and narcissistic injuries, as well as the presence of coping abilities, must be present for the patient to be treatable. The assessor must be careful not to over-estimate the presence of one without the other.

There are, of course, enormous differences between anxiety and depression. The secondary anxiety discussed in the previous Section is a condition towards which the ego responds as if it is helpless to do anything about a loss, or threatened loss, or frustration. In depression, the ego accepts the inevitable with a sense of helplessness and low self-esteem, whereas in secondary anxiety the ego gathers together its resources and mobilizes a fight for survival (Zetzel, 1970).

The capacity to bear depression is determined developmentally by three characteristics that can, to some degree, be assessed in the pre-analytic interviews (Zetzel, 1970): 1) the capacity to develop and maintain stable, positive and trusting object relationships characterized by well-recognized delineation of ego boundaries; 2) the ability to abandon the omnipotent self-image; and 3) the capacity to accept passively the inevitable self-limitations as well as the realistic limitations of the external world and not to let oneself be dominated by fantasy. This last capacity is a prerequisite for the patient to develop coping mechanisms. Some people never develop the capacity to accept realistic limitations but are quite successful in adapting so that they accumulate apparent environmental success. Such people, however, may have responded to the inability to accept limitations by an *overdeveloped* capacity that is marked by serious vulnerability that will become increasingly apparent in the later years of life when the person faces inevitable losses and frustrations. Another way of saying the same thing is that the presence of the capacity to cope with external situations does not necessarily mean a maturely developed psychic system, unless the person also has the capacity to accept the unalterable (Zetzel, 1970).

The capacity for treatability is related to acceptance of realistic limitations. The adaptation to those limitations is directly related to the quality of the dyadic object relationships that dominate the preoedipal developmental years (Zetzel, 1970). The inevitable intrapsychic and environmental tasks of life, from birth to death, require those capacities that develop during the preoedipal period; developmental failures will have serious consequences, one of them being the incapacity to benefit from psychoanalytic psychotherapy.

The capacity to bear anxiety (see Section 5.2171) is directly related to the capacity to tolerate depression. Normal development and psychic growth involve awareness and acceptance of potential helplessness when faced with overwhelming stress and the integration of such acceptance into the perception of the intrapsychic and external world (Zetzel, 1970). If a person faced with a specific crisis has not developed the capacity to experience secondary anxiety, then that person may also develop a feeling of relative omnipotence. The belief in one's relative omnipotence interferes with the capacity to adjust to realistic limitations and to accept one's helplessness. In other words, if a person has not experienced anxiety and learned to adjust to it, then that person is not prepared to accept helplessness in the face of overwhelming inevitable stress and is therefore not prepared to tolerate the depression that follows such helplessness. Such a person, instead of accepting the underlying depression, resorts to inappropriate coping mechanisms, for example, beginning a litigious search for compensation as is sometimes seen in people with post-traumatic neurosis.

The incapacity to tolerate depression may be the result of regressive solution of the oedipal complex which is often the case in the treatable character neurosis. On the other hand, the incapacity to tolerate depression may result from pregenital deficits that have engendered relatively unalterable deficits in the capacity to develop object relationships or to accept the realistic limitations. In this latter case, the patient is untreatable (Zetzel, 1970).

5.218 THE CAPACITY TO EXPERIENCE FEELINGS WITHIN THE SESSION RATHER THAN JUST DESCRIBE THEM

Bertrand Russell points out that there are two kinds of knowledge, "knowledge by description" and "knowledge by acquaintance" (Russell, 1929; Richfield, 1954).* Knowledge by description is an awareness of a feeling, thought or object based on facts, truths, ideas or an inferential process that have been acquired by the knower through some phenomenon outside of personal experience with the feeling, thought or object. Knowledge by acquaintance is an awareness of a feeling, thought or object based on personal experience and direct relationship. Another way of saying the same thing is that a person can learn the description of a feeling, thought or object and recognize it when it appears, but have limited relationship (experience or acquaintance) with it.

And now let us apply these concepts to the discussion of treatability. As noted above, the treatable patient must be able to bear painful feelings such as anxiety and depression (see Section 5.217) and also must be able to recognize and articulate those feelings (see Section 5.212) (knowledge by description). The successful psychoanalytic psychotherapy, however, also requires *more* than an intellectual description, an awareness, or even bearing of one's own painful feelings or thoughts. Not only psychoanalytic psychotherapy patients, but *all* patients in any kind of uncovering psychotherapy must gain the knowledge by acquaintance of their feelings during the treatment session. Several authors have observed that patients who present with psychic discomfort tend to do better in therapy than those who don't (Fenichel, 1945; Singer, 1970; Weigert, 1949). Also, empirical research reports have demonstrated that the patient's capacity to experience feelings correlates positively and sig-

---

* Proponents of transcendental meditation utilize similar concepts by categorizing all "complete knowledge" into theoretical understanding and direct experience with direct experience being achieved in meditation by transcending the thinking process.

nificantly with a good clinical outcome (Gendlin et al., 1968; Tomlinson, 1967; Tomlinson & Hart, 1962; Walker et al., 1960). Luborsky et al. (1971) reviewed all work on the subject of predictability for any kind of psychotherapy and reported that the evidence strongly indicates that the patient who presents with affective symptoms is more treatable than one with little or no manifest feelings at the time of the initial assessment session. These studies, although valuable in their suggestions, are unfortunately on relatively short-term therapies, not on psychoanalytic psychotherapy. They do, however, suggest that the same principles would apply.

In essence then, based on our clinical experience and on what meager empirical research exists, it is safe to say that rational thought does not cure all. The patient who avoids experiences by talking about them is not likely to succeed in psychoanalytic psychotherapy. Psychoanalytic psychotherapy requires that the patient psychically and bodily experience feelings within the treatment sessions at the most profound and *irrational* level. The irrational experiences of feelings to the degree of occasional abreaction, and even to the degree that the patient loses the observing aspects of those experiences, is necessary for meaningful insight and for the ultimate constructive relationship with the therapist.

If the patient handles affective experiences within the therapy session through severe isolation, excessive intellectualization or other unfeeling defense mechanisms, the therapist must first focus on the defense mechanisms so that the affects eventually become available to the therapy. The therapy of a rigidly controlled patient will at best be long and arduous and could very likely be unable to achieve any degree of success. Of course, if the patient is incapable of experiencing feelings within the assessment session, the assessor cannot be sure that the patient is incapable of experiencing feelings within the treatment session, once the psychotherapy has begun. Thus, the absence of this capacity does not unequivocally indicate unsuitability; but, if the assessor observes that the patient possesses an immediate awareness of his emotions within the assessment period, then the assessor has a good piece of evidence indicating treatability. In this regard, Gendlin et al. (1968) noted that, of 38 patients studied, only five showed an increase over the course of the therapy in the ability to experience feelings, thus suggesting that in many patients this capacity remains relatively constant. The problem is, however, that the assessor has no way of knowing which patients will remain constant and which will improve during the course of the therapy.

5.219 THE CAPACITY TO REGRESS IN THE SERVICE OF THERAPY

As discussed in Section 3.6, the psychoanalytic concept of regression is quite complicated and, in fact, entails several definitions of regression, some of which are quite distinct from each other. For purposes of our discussion on treatability and regression, however, these distinctions among the various definitions are not as important as they are in other contexts. For the purpose of this chapter, regression will be conceptualized from the genetic-structural perspective (see Section 3.66) whereby the term "regression" refers to those behavioral and psychic phenomena that represent a reactive psychic process in which there is a complete, partial or symbolic return to earlier, more primitive or more irrational patterns of thoughts, feelings or behavior. This definition of regression applies to any form of behavior and to the operation of every part of the psychic apparatus, that is, all components of the id, ego and superego, with the focus on developmental aspects. *A major thesis of this Section is that maladaptive or adaptive forms of regression can occur as the above definition of regression is applied to treatability.*

The importance of understanding the concepts surrounding regression is based on two psychoanalytic presuppositions: 1) As already mentioned in Section 3.13, psychoanalytic psychotherapy presupposes that the treatment will not succeed unless critical elements in the unconscious become conscious. 2) It is assumed, based on clinical experience, that certain forms of regression greatly facilitate the making of the unconscious conscious. The basic presupposition was (according to Kris, 1952) first made by Freud in his book on jokes.

> Let us decide then to adopt the hypothesis that this is the way in which jokes are formed in the first person: *A preconscious thought is given over for a moment to unconscious revision and the outcome of this is at once grasped by conscious perception* (Freud, 1905c, p. 166, italics in the original).

Psychic growth from psychoanalytic psychotherapy cannot occur without some psychic regression. This *adaptive regression* is a phenomenon in which the regressed mechanism merges with the intact part of the mind in an attempt to master past or present unresolved and pathogenic conflicts or to gratify earlier unmet demands (Zetzel, 1965). This kind of regression may be a return to a previous failure or fixation point which is at the root of the psychopathology and, in fact, can be conceptualized as "pathognomonic regression" (Ornstein & Ornstein, 1975, p. 230). Or, the adaptive regression may be a return to an earlier successful situation (Winnicott, 1955). The desirable regression entails a reopening of intra-psychic conflicts previously sealed off by defense mechanisms that were responding to signal anxiety (Zetzel & Meissner, 1973). It is the adaptive regression that forces the necessary transference neurosis, the inter-pretation of which is a necessary step in the curative process of psycho-analytic psychotherapy.

Some clinicians propose that if the roots of the neurosis are earlier than the oedipal-genital psychosexual stage then noninvestigative psycho-analytic techniques are necessary to help the patient resolve such problems, and *then* the techniques of psychoanalytic psychotherapy are applied, when the patient is dealing with the issues of genital-oedipal regression. The so-called "noninvestigative techniques" are called dif-ferent things by different people. Eissler (1953, p. 110) refers to such techniques as "parameters" and urges the therapist never to utilize a parameter to the degree that its influence on the transference cannot be abolished by interpretation. Ornstein and Ornstein (1975, p. 231) refer to those techniques as "preparatory psychotherapy" and Glover (1960, p. 78) uses the term "rapport techniques." According to these authors, patients whose psychopathology is primarily the result of fixations earlier than the genital-oedipal stage are traditionally considered untreat-able largely because they undergo libidinal regression to pregenital (oral and anal) positions which are unmanageable and uninterpretable in therapy.

The greater the patient's capacity to develop the transference charac-terized by normal genital aims and adult love and hate, the more likely the patient is treatable (Fenichel, 1945). The greater the tendency to develop a transference characterized by pregenital defense mechanisms such as excessive incorporation, projection, denial, negation and splitting, the greater the chances are that the patient is untreatable since the more primitive modes of transference are least responsive to the psycho-analytic situation (Khan, 1960). Corwin (1974, p. 306) helps clarify these ideas by suggesting that we conceptualize the transference based on the preoedipal period as a "progressive transference" that must be handled "parametrically" until enough psychic maturation occurs within the treatment. Corwin notes that only *after* the "progressive transference neurosis" is worked through and the subsequent narcissistic alliance is formed and nurtured will the "workable transference" (i.e., the trans-ference based on oedipal issues) develop.

The aggressive drives also undergo change during transference regression. Melanie Klein (1952) was one of the first to observe that the more regressive the transference, the more unmanageable hostility will be directed towards the therapist (Greenson, 1967).

The adaptive regression, that is, the kind of regression that I am saying is required for treatability, can also be called "regression in the service of the ego" (Kris, 1952, p. 177). Schafer (1958) defines regression in the service of the ego as:

> . . . a partial, temporary controlled lowering of the level of psychic functioning to promote adaptation. Regression in the service of the ego promotes adaptation by maintaining, restoring, or improving inner balance and organization, interpersonal relations and work (p. 122).

Schafer tries to clarify these concepts by using the metaphor of the ego detouring through regression on its way towards adaptation.

Regression in the service of the ego is the kind of regression which is also seen in jokes and caricatures, and the audience's response to them; in fact, this kind of regression is required for any kind of art and symbol formation although, of course, creative activities do not always function to serve the ego.

The *maladaptive regression,* that is, the kind of regression that may render the patient untreatable, is a regression of a relatively conflict-free stage in the service of resistance as a way to avoid facing the emergence of psychic conflicts and unpleasant truths such as may be revealed during the course of psychoanalytic psychotherapy; for example, a patient may regress to anal behavior as a way of avoiding oedipal issues that arise in therapy. This particular example serves to demonstrate that the most repressed material is not always developmentally the earliest material (Alexander, 1954a).

Maladaptive regression may incapacitate previously acquired ego functions by interfering with reality testing and reducing the capacity for sustained object relationships (Zetzel, 1965; Zetzel & Meissner, 1973). The maladaptive regression also engenders an increased strictness of the superego (Greenson, 1967) and in its extreme form is the kind of regression seen in the weakened ego states of psychosis, sleep, intoxication, physical illness and exhaustion.

It is, in my opinion, an oversimplification and of no clinical value to categorize the desirable regression as "instinctual regression" and the undesirable form as "ego regression" as suggested by Zetzel and Meissner

(1973). Both adaptive and maladaptive regression require a blurring of the distinction between the psyche and external environment, a relaxation of defense mechanisms, and a sensitivity to the preconscious and unconscious stimuli (Schafer, 1958). Furthermore, both kinds of regression make very specific demands on the therapist that engender specific techniques and countertransference phenomena (Khan, 1960).

It makes some sense to view these two kinds of regression as merely different degrees of a single process. Nevertheless, it is often possible to distinguish the two types of regression, and it can be safely said that the adaptive regression is characterized by being purposive and controlled similar to the artist who experiences inspirational moments at the canvas (the "inspirational phase," Kris, 1952, p. 313) in which he is relatively engrossed in archaic content and experience, and yet can step back to observe and contemplate his work (the "elaboration phase," Kris, 1952, p. 313). In essence then, regression in the service of the ego entails a control over the discharge of energy, an ego function that can be in itself pleasurable. By making this assumption, we are applying one of the earliest and, as noted by Kris (1952), most frequently neglected thoughts of Freud (1905c), that human beings are capable of deriving pleasure from the activity itself of the mental apparatus. In contrast, the maladaptive regression is unpleasurable, destructive, lacks apparent purpose, and controls the ego rather than being controlled by the ego.

Another way of conceptualizing the distinction between adaptive and maladaptive regression is to apply the concepts of primary and secondary process thinking. *Primary process* thinking is driven by unneutralized drive energies, is regulated by the principle of tension reduction (pleasure principle), and uses the mechanisms of displacement and condensation in its constant effort to obtain immediate energy discharge. In contrast, *secondary process* thinking operates with relatively neutralized energy that is readily available for a variety of supportive ego functions. Instead of immediate gratification, the secondary process utilizes delays and detours always oriented towards objective reality (Schafer, 1958).

The adaptive regression can be conceptualized as that kind of regression in which the ego controls primary process thinking and puts it into the service of secondary process thinking. In contrast, we can conceptualize the abnormal or maladaptive regression as regression in which the primary process mode of thinking overwhelms the secondary process mode (Kris, 1952).

Many technical aspects of psychoanalytic therapy foster regression; some examples are: 1) high frequency and long duration of sessions; 2) the reduction of external stimuli; 3) the rule of free association; 4) a long course of treatment; 5) relative therapist anonymity; 6) the lack of gratification immediately derived within the treatment sessions; 7) a sleep-like state; and 8) a relative timelessness and lack of structure combined with unyielding passivity and constancy of environment and therapist behavior.

Although it is well established in the psychoanalytic literature that the security and safety of the therapeutic setting promote regression, an argument can also be made that the stress of the analytic situation also leads to regression (Macalpine, 1950). Whether regression is caused by security which allows it to emerge, or is caused by an adaptation to stress, we know that the format of psychoanalytic psychotherapy invites and facilitates the desirable kind of regression, but unfortunately also promotes the undesirable kind. The primary task in evaluating the capacity to regress as it relates to treatability is to determine the degree to which the patient is inclined towards these two types of regression (Alexander, 1956).*

The major question for the assessor to ask is: Is the patient flexible enough to undergo the adaptive regression and maintain enough ego strength, security and therapeutic alliance so that he doesn't undergo too much of the maladaptive forms of regression? Furthermore, can the patient confine to the treatment sessions most of the undesirable and desirable regression so that the therapy does not destructively impair his outside personal and professional life? This capacity is not only necessary so that the therapy will do no harm. The ability to confine the regression to therapy sessions promotes and sustains the transference neurosis. The assessor's and therapist's capacity to distinguish between the two types of regression has practical implications. For example, if a patient in treatment reveals oral regression then the therapist has to decide whether the oral manifestations are avoidance of genital issues, in which case the regression must not be reinforced, or whether oral manifestations represent significantly unresolved oral conflicts, the expression of which must then be encouraged in order to be resolved once and for all. Such a decision can only be made if the assessor has a thorough knowledge of

---

* The therapist is also constantly faced with the task of distinguishing between these two types of regression.

history and psychodynamics, the kind of detailed knowledge that rarely can be obtained by the most skillful assessor in one or two assessment sessions. This situation, then, leaves the reader with the justifiable question of whether or not it is ever possible, in a few sessions, to assess the capacity to regress as it relates to treatability. Schlessinger and Robbins (1974), Alexander (1956), and Schafer (1958) answer this question in the affirmative.

Schlessinger and Robbins (1974) propose that we can preanalytically assess the capacity to regress in the service of the ego by carefully observing the patient's capacity to engage in play and fantasy and looking for a history of sleep disturbances and decompensation in reaction to physical illness.

Alexander (1956) suggests that Freud's model of psychosexual fixation is helpful in distinguishing between the two forms of regression. If the point of fixation is cathected, then the patient probably has to regress to that point and master the conflict before he can progress in therapy. If, however, a significant fixation did not occur, then the regression can be considered an avoidance of therapy and a resistance to the unconscious. Alexander does not tell us how we can determine levels of fixation from material gathered in a few preanalytic assessment sessions.

Schlessinger and Robbins (1974) propose that we can preanalytically assessment of the capacity to regress. Schafer says that the patient will tend *not* to be able to regress in the service of the ego, that is, regress adaptively, when the process of regression has unconscious meanings that are significantly unpleasurable or unwanted, such as passivity, badness, destructiveness or defiance against authority. Schafer credits Kris (1952) with showing us that the artist traditionally is able to regress adaptively but that society's image of the artist has always been linked to either the divine or to badness, the devil and defiance against the divine (or variations such as "bohemian," "beatniks," etc.). These associations between artist and badness or the divine were explicit in ancient times but still exist, albeit less explicitly, in current times. Schafer uses these concepts to promote his proposition that the association between regression and forbidden ideas or feelings is common. Thus, there are dangers associated with regression, and for many people, the intensity of such dangers renders them incapable of regression and accordingly untreatable.

Schafer also proposes that there are factors or conditions favoring regression in the service of the ego. Schafer lists six such overlapping, but nevertheless separate, conditions that are related to ego strength and neutralization of libidinal and aggressive energy. If these conditions are placed in the negative, Schafer points out, they interfere with adaptive regression. Since the six conditions are relatively recognizable in the preanalytic assessment session, they are most relevant to our present discussion. To facilitate the reader's task, I will first list them and then briefly summarize Schafer's ideas on this subject. Schafer's six conditions are: 1) "A well-developed set of affect signals; 2) a secure sense of self; 3) a relative mastery of early trauma; 4) relative flexibility of defenses and controls; 5) a history of adequate trust and mutuality in interpersonal relations; and 6) self-awareness and personal and effective communication to others.

5.2191 *The Presence of a Well-Developed Set of Affect Signals*

In order to regress adaptively, the patient must feel relatively safe when in psychological and bodily touch with his feelings, in a way that is usually *not* seen in schizophrenics or rigid obsessionals. The patient must have enough confidence in the affective self so that he can regress with the security of knowing that should he regress to a stage where his ego may become overwhelmed by primitive thoughts or feelings, there will occur signals ("signal anxiety"—see Section 5.2171) to the ego and the appropriate ego defenses will reverse the regression. Without such a signal anxiety system, the patient is unlikely to regress adaptively.

5.2192 *A Secure Sense of Self*

Regression involves a threat to the ego. Only those patients who have a relatively secure sense of self ("ego-identity," Erikson, 1950) can take such a chance. Where there is a stable sense of self, and a secure sense of identity, the person is capable of regression and experiencing the various manifestations of regression such as primary process thinking and the transient blurring of distinction between id and ego. If there is a lack of ego identity and an insecure sense of self, then the person, out of fear of losing everything, must rigidly maintain what identity and boundaries he does have. This is one reason why psychotic people cannot adaptively regress in psychoanalytic psychotherapy.

5.2193 *A Relative Mastery of Early Trauma*

Unless the patient has achieved a relative mastery of early trauma, he will fear a return through regression to those periods of passivity, helplessness and omnipotence. In short, he will not regress to points that were so overwhelming that they have been irretrievably banished from conscious life. Only if some mastery has been achieved will the various traumas of early life not be kept from conscious experience through regression.

5.2194 *Relative Flexibility of Defenses and Controls*

The treatable patient must be able to let go of defenses. Many people are inhibited by severe anxiety or a rigid superego leading to obsessive guilt to the degree that they are unable to experience self-awareness and unable to experiment with a variety of psychic and bodily processes. In other words, they are unable to engage in a phenomenon that Schafer calls "play intrapsychically" (1958, p. 130).

5.2195 *A History of Adequate Trust and Mutuality in Interpersonal Relations*

The manifestations of adaptive regression will be observed and judged by the patient's own ego and superego, both greatly influenced by parent-child interactions. If the person did not, as a child, develop basic trust (see Section 4.221), his mistrust will lead to the assumption that regression will not be tolerated and will be punished by current object relationships. Such a person, then, is incapable of adaptive regression within the therapeutic relationship.

5.2196 *Self-Awareness and Personal and Effective Communication to Others*

A condition that favors adaptive regression is when the regression is culturally meaningful. Schafer notes that both Kris (1952) and Erikson (1950) emphasize that our tendency to be something is greatly facilitated and reinforced if that something is meaningful to our subculture and if it improves communications with other people in that subculture. A person is less likely to regress if the manifestations of his regression are phenomena that his subculture forbids or fears. Of course, the ego identity here also plays a large role. For example, Schafer points out that, in the case of the artist or the comic, both in the subculture in which he functions and the ego identity are much more compatible with a controlled ego regression than other ego identities in other professional or social settings or subcultures.

In many ways, the subcultures, past and present, of the artist are the most compatible with the capacities required to be an adequate therapist (see Section 1.5) as well as a treatable patient. Artists have, in fact, proven to be very capable of adaptively regressing as well as being appreciative and sensitive to the workings of the mind and its relationship to bodily feelings (the reader may remember the discussion in Section 3.4 where it was noted that literary artists were among the first to discover the value of free association). It is my opinion that the subcultures in which many, indeed most, psychoanalytic psychotherapists as well as potential patients live and/or have been raised and trained are subcultures in which a controlled ego regression is considered quite incompatible and unacceptable. In many ways, the subcultures in which most mental health professionals are raised, with their heavy emphasis on performance, success, formal training, proper behavior and intellectualizations, are the least desirable backgrounds for potential patients and therapists, but this subject is beyond the intent of this chapter.

5.22 External Environmental Realities

As discussed in Section 3.2, the psychoanalytic therapist presupposes that if the patient is helped to make the necessary intrapsychic changes then he (patient) will be able to make some necessary environmental adjustments that lead to less psychic pain. Sometimes, however, a potential patient may be untreatable because his environmental circumstances are so overwhelming that no amount of intrapsychic change can lead to significant adjustments (Wallerstein et al., 1956). For example, a man may be so logistically and economically dependent on his wife that no amount of psychoanalytic therapy could help him change his marital status, even if the marriage is based on severe neurotic needs. Such a person would benefit much more from some sort of supportive, cognitive or behavior therapy that would help him adjust to the spouse he will never leave. Place of employment and irreversible physical illnesses are some other common examples of relatively unchangeable environmental situations that sometimes lead to untreatability.

The assessor should not only evaluate the *existing* external situations, but also attempt to predict the outcome of a course of psychoanalytic therapy, the impact such an outcome will have on the existing external life factors, and the degree to which the predicted changed environmental factors will facilitate or obstruct the therapy (Luborsky & Schimek, 1964).

Ms. D was a 50-year-old unmarried woman who had spent the past 25 years working as an executive secretary to the president of a multi-million-dollar corporation. The patient had worked herself up to the point where she was progressively being assigned more and more tasks of an executive nature. She developed a phobia for entering the building where she worked unless accompanied by her older brother. Although the patient was not consciously aware of it, it became obvious in the first assessment interview that her superiors were asking more of her than she was capable of doing and that she was in fact failing in many aspects of her job. It also became obvious that she worked her way up to a salary that was so high that it could not be justified unless she was performing such executive functions. Finally, the assessor learned through the patient's brother that her boss, to whom she was devoted, was considering firing her and hiring a master's degree business person to take over many of her responsibilities.

This is a case where the assessor correctly felt that psychoanalytic psychotherapy was contraindicated and some other kind of supportive or environmental treatment was necessary. If the patient became aware of the meaning of her phobia, she would suffer more than she did from the psychic pain of the phobia. If she overcame the phobia and was able to go to work unaccompanied, she would soon learn that she would be fired because she was not able to keep up with the demands of the job. The loss of self-esteem would have been of more pain to her than the keeping of the phobia. Psychoanalytic treatment, in order to be successful, has to deal with the revelation of the truth, and such an experience would be of no help to this patient. She did not have the capacity or the skills to do the work, so it wasn't as if her neurosis was preventing her from functioning on the job. She was already quite secure financially, so there was no need for her to keep the job.

By maintaining this very circumscribed phobia limited only to this specific job, the patient could receive a medical disability and termination from her job which would give her benefits and pension that were well earned and would maintain her self-esteem while not interfering in other areas of her life. The assessor correctly concluded that the treatment should be of a supportive nature with the therapist advising that she resign her position because of her psychological problems. The assessor suggested that perhaps, when she is feeling better, she could look for some other job of a different nature where she would be appreciated.

5.221 AGE

5.2211 *The Aged Patient*

The contemporary psychoanalytic therapist tends to favor patients in their twenties and thirties. In a survey by the American Psychoanalytic Association of 3,019 patients in psychoanalytic psychotherapy, 46% were between the ages of 26 and 35 and only 8% were older than 45 (Hamburg et al., 1967). It is unclear, however, whether the contemporary therapists' favoring the younger age groups is for the same reasons given by Freud (see Section 5.11) since contemporary therapists certainly observe patients living longer and enjoying sexual activity at a later age.

Abraham (1919) was the first to report success in administering psychoanalytic psychotherapy to patients who were older than the age that Freud considered treatable. Abraham described four patients in their forties and fifties who showed a very favorable response to psychoanalytic psychotherapy and concluded that the age of the neurotic symptoms is far more indicative of treatability than is the age of the patient.

Many contemporary analytic therapists believe that successful psychoanalytic psychotherapy with an aged patient is "rarely possible" (Goldfarb, 1962, p. 114). Furthermore, the empirical research shows that younger adults tend to have a better prognosis than older adults (Luborsky et al., 1971). On the other hand, there is another group of psychoanalytic therapists who, for years, have proposed that, although some special problems and unique issues of countertransference occur, it makes no clinical sense to withhold psychoanalytic therapy from the elderly (Berezin, 1977; Berezin & Fern, 1967; Blau, 1967; Blau & Berezin, 1975; Brooks, 1969; Da Silva, 1967; Gitelson, 1965; Grotjahn, 1955; Hauser, 1968; Kahana, 1979; Meerloo, 1961; Pfeiffer, 1971; Rechtschaffen, 1959; Rockwell, 1956; Segal, 1958; Wayne, 1953; Zarsky & Blau, 1970). There are case histories of successful psychoanalytic psychotherapy in patients over the age of 50, such as those of Jones (1920), Kaufman (1937), and Segal (1958). A report was recently published of a successful psychoanalytic psychotherapy in a patient who began treatment at age 58 and successfully completed the treatment at age 66 (Sandler, 1978). There is even a report of successful psychoanalytic therapy of a 71-year-old man with some signs of senile dementia (Grotjahn, 1940).

No matter what the age, in order for the patient to be treatable by these methods, he must not be so set in his ways that personality and behavioral changes are impossible or impractical. More specifically, if the patient is not capable of libidinal and narcissistic gratifications, then all the psychoanalytic therapy can offer is a frustrating awareness of past failures and helplessness to make up for them (Fenichel, 1945).

5.2212 *The Young Patient*

Regarding a minimum age limit, the patient must be old enough to achieve

> . . .insight into the trouble . . . confidence in the analyst [therapist], and turning the decision for analysis [psychoanalytic psychotherapy] from one taken by others into its [patient's] own (A. Freud, 1946, p. 6).

Of course, children are much more dependent on their environment. Furthermore, the real relationship and transference are more inextricable than with adults. Thus, the treatment of children requires some very special techniques and some very unique aspects of the therapeutic relationship and of the external situation (A. Freud, 1946). For example, children do not free associate well and the therapist must be skilled at obtaining clinical material in other ways, such as observing drawings or general behavior or engaging in the "play therapy" originated by Hug-Hellmuth in Vienna and Melanie Klein in Berlin and London (A. Freud, 1946). Despite these special circumstances, children as young as six years old have been shown to be treatable by psychoanalytic therapy (A. Freud, 1946) and most therapists would agree with Freud that

> . . . youthful persons under the age of adolescence are often exceedingly amenable to influence [of psychoanalytic psychotherapy] (1905b, p. 264).

Before a young person is referred for treatment, if at all clinically possible, he should first have an opportunity to experiment with the world. With every patient, but especially adolescents and children, the preanalytic assessor should consider whether or not some environmental manipulation may be employed that would remove the obstacle to normal growth and allow the child or adolescent to grow on his own and make psychoanalytic therapy unnecessary. Children and adolescents are especially susceptible to misperceptions about seeing a "head doctor" and are especially susceptible to misunderstanding and even ridicule from peers and family. The assessor or therapist may best serve the patient if he helps remove the external obstacle to psychic growth and simply tells the patient that therapy is a possibility if it is needed at a later date. Frequently, the obstacle that interferes with the psychic growth of the child or adolescent is the psychological illness of a family member such as a parent or sibling or a disturbance in a family system, for example a troubled marriage.*

5.222 Fee and Time Commitment

The issue of fee has often been discussed in the literature (Brody, 1949; Chodoff, 1964, 1978; Eissler, 1974; Fingert, 1952; Gedo, 1962; Haak, 1957; Hilles, 1971; Koren & Joyce, 1953; Lievano, 1967; Lorand & Console, 1958; Meyers, 1976).** Despite the large amount of writing about fees, the issue is rarely discussed in relationship to treatability.

It is critical for the issue of fees to be considered in preanalytic assessment sessions. Much can be learned about a person's psychic life if we observe how he handles money. Not only is money a means of self-preservation and power, but important developmental relationships exist between the adult handling of money and the early infantile, especially anal, experiences (Freud, 1908). Furthermore, many people treat money with the same reticence, inconsistency, prudishness and hypocrisy with which they handle sexual matters (Freud, 1913a). If the assessor does not talk openly and candidly about the fee and the patient's ability to pay it, the assessor reinforces through indirect suggestion the patient's tendency not to share private and shameful thoughts and feelings.

As mentioned above (see Section 5.11), Freud advised against gratuitous treatment. Freud's conviction can be seriously challenged. Of course, free treatment will undoubtedly engender some specific transference, countertransference and real relationship problems, as discussed in some detail by Lorand and Console (1958), who report their observations of 59 analysands over a 6½ year period at the Psychoanalytic Clinic of the

---

*Melanie Klein and her followers would disagree with this view and suggest psychoanalytic psychotherapy not only as a way to alleviate a neurotic child's symptoms, but as a valid means of facilitating the development of a normal child.

**For a recent publication of this issue, the reader is referred to DiBella, G. A. W., Mastering money issues that complicate treatment: The last taboo. *The American Journal of Psychotherapy,* 34(4):510-522, 1980.

New York State University Medical Center, the first clinic in America with an extensive experience of free psychoanalytic psychotherapy. Despite the unique problems, however, it is my opinion and the opinion of others (e.g., Lorand & Console, 1958) that it is inaccurate to adopt a general rule that gratuitous psychoanalytic psychotherapy is destined to fail. Gratuitous therapy, like everything else, must be closely assessed with regard to the individual patient and psychoanalytic situation. With many, perhaps most patients, the charging of a fee is for the therapist's benefit and any impression to the contrary is pretentious and may provoke in the patient justifiable mistrust.

Regarding the patient's complaint that the therapy costs too much, the assessor of treatability should weigh the cost of psychoanalytic psychotherapy against the cost of the illness in terms of the decreased earning capacity, not only for the patient, but for other members of the family who are negatively influenced. The recovered patient may manifest a productivity that makes psychoanalytic psychotherapy, in retrospect, a very good bargain from a purely financial perspective. If the cost of the psychoanalytic psychotherapy seems minor in comparison to the cost of the illness, then perhaps the patient's complaints about money are motivated in part in the service of resistance (Freud, 1913a).

The way in which the patient handles the arrangement of specific times of therapy sessions can also be an indicator of treatability. The degree of motivation and resistance may be reflected by the flexibility that the patient shows when appointment times are being arranged. Just as with the fee, the assessor and therapist are obligated never to give any false pretenses about the specific arrangements being mostly for the patient's benefit.

It is well known that many and perhaps most patients initially seek psychological help with the expectation that the treatment will be a brief experience (Gurman, 1978). It has been shown that this is especially true if the patient is from a lower socioeconomic or educational group (Lorion, 1973, 1974). Furthermore, most clinicians have observed that many psychotherapeutic contacts turn out to be brief experiences whether or not they are initially planned to be (Gurman, 1978).

Introducing a patient to psychoanalytic psychotherapy is quite different from other medical treatments. For example, when talking to a prospective surgical patient, the surgeon tends to minimize the pain and cost and maximize the chances of a favorable outcome. This approach is often in the patient's best interests since overoptimism on the part of the surgical patient may alleviate anxiety, facilitate a good clinical outcome and usually does not interfere with the treatment.

Most prospective psychoanalytic therapy patients are similar to the surgical patient in that they wish for a guarantee of cure and no pain of treatment. The assessor does not want to frighten the patient by exaggerating the money or time required. On the other hand, in contrast to the surgeon, the assessor must always be totally frank with the patient in explaining that psychoanalytic psychotherapy is an unavoidably costly, long and sometimes painful treatment with no shortcuts and no promises of cure. (Freud often said that the best way to shorten the length of a course of psychoanalytic psychotherapy was for the patient and analyst to do it skillfully [1898, 1904]). If the assessor underestimates the severity of the problem or the length of the treatment, when the patient learns the truth he may be left with a shaken confidence in the therapist that could interfere with the progress of therapy (Fromm-Reichmann, 1950). The patient may use the fact that he was deprived of the truth as an instrument of resistance and negative transference (Freud, 1916-1917c).

Many therapists (e.g., Glover, 1928) suggest that the assessor not provide the prospective patient with an estimate of the length of psychotherapy, and that if the patient specifically asks, the best response is to say gently, "I don't know." It is my opinion, however, that the patient deserves more than mere guidance during the assessment, so I prefer informing patients requiring therapy that they should not expect the treatment to end in less than two years and it could be three or more years.

With regard to the chances of cure, the assessor or therapist should state quite concretely that he cannot promise a cure but that he knows of no other treatment that is more appropriate for the patient's specific problems. This is a safe statement to say since, as mentioned in Section 5.36, if there is a treatment that is more likely to help the patient, then the patient should not be seeing the psychoanalytic therapist in the first place. If it can be said honestly, the assessor may comment that he has seen patients in the past with similar problems who have gotten significant help from this kind of treatment, but of course each patient is an individual and there are no guarantees.

I might add at this point that most contemporary psychoanalytic therapists do not follow Freud's (and his early followers, e.g., Fenichel, 1945) practice of a trial period for a variety of reasons, the most significant reason being the common belief that the decision not to recommend psychoanalytic psychotherapy after the "trial" is very likely to cause the patient psychic trauma and result in the patient's feeling defective, rejected and hostile towards any form of psychotherapy (Gitelson, 1952; Glover, 1928). There are, however, still some contemporary therapists (e.g., Bak, 1970; Greenson, 1967; Loewenstein, 1964) who favor a trial psychoanalytic psychotherapy and question whether treatability in most neurotic patients can ever be adequately evaluated without a trial period.

If, for whatever reasons, the patient does not want to make the investment of time and money nor put up with the discomfort, then he is untreatable. This should be known at the outset. Of course, there is no way of knowing whether or not the patient will honor a verbal commitment. On the other hand, by knowing the negative aspects of the treatment, the patient at least has a more realistic option to refuse.

5.223 GEOGRAPHIC STATUS AND PLANS

It is surprising how often assessors fail to inquire during preanalytic interviews about geographic status and plans in assessing treatability. (Bachrach and Leaf's [1978] treatability literature review discloses that demographic factors "tend to be mentioned the least" [p. 886].) Psychoanalytic psychotherapy is hard enough without making it even more difficult by recommending a therapist whose office, for example, is 45 minutes away on the other side of town, when an equally appropriate therapist has an office only 10 minutes away from the patient's home or place of employment. Furthermore, some therapists' offices are on buslines and others are not and some patients have cars and others do not. The inconvenience of travel may contribute to the service of resistance and may be avoided by a few simple questions.

Another aspect of geographic status is the patient's plans for the future. Many prospective patients honestly do not realize that psychoanalytic psychotherapy may take two or more years. The assessor may refer a patient for psychoanalytic psychotherapy when in fact that patient has already planned a move to another city in a few months. Of course, all these issues are usually multidetermined and may be directly related to the ambivalence about entering therapy.

Ms. U was a 30-year-old business woman, married and divorced twice, who came to psychotherapy because of a long history of inability to get close to people. The few relationships in which she allowed herself to feel intimacy resulted in her, one way or another, arranging for them to end. She showed many strengths that indicated that she was an ideal candidate for psychoanalytic psychotherapy and she began twice-weekly sessions. A few months after beginning treatment, while therapy was progressing quite well, she informed the therapist that she had moved to a city about 50 miles away. She reassured the therapist that she would still keep attending her sessions. Her therapist did not pursue the matter any further.

After a few weeks it became quite clear that with the traffic, bad weather, problems with her car, problems with getting out of work early or coming into work late and a variety of other logistical problems, it was realistically impossible to continue the treatment. Both therapist and patient terminated with the retrospective awareness that she had acted out the negative side of her ambivalence about treatment by moving to a nearby city. It became clear just before termination that she had preconsciously been planning such a move even when she began the treatment. A likely hypothesis is that she could only allow herself to get close to the therapist knowing that she was going to move. All of this might have been worked through had the assessor who found her treatable and referred her to treatment, or had the therapist himself, explored her geographic plans in more detail at the very beginning of treatment.

The assessor should not be too quick to rule out psychoanalytic psychotherapy, even if the patient lives hours away from the nearest available therapist. There are various options which all must be weighed against the inconvenience of the psychological problems and the probability that therapy will help. The patient may consider moving in order to be closer to the therapist or the patient could arrange something like traveling the distance, having a double session one night and another double session the next morning or some such combination. Potential patients are often willing to make such sacrifices but are reluctant to suggest the idea to the assessor. The assessor has the responsibility to the patient to be creative in considering all options.

5.224 PREVIOUS SOCIAL ACQUAINTANCE WITH THE ASSESSOR OR THERAPIST

The importance of a previous social relationship with a psychoanalytic therapist is an issue of some controversy if supportive psychotherapy or crisis intervention is being considered. When it comes to the assessment or delivery of psychoanalytic psychotherapy, however, there is practically unanimity that there should be no previous or current social relationship. Some clinicians feel strongly that the therapist cannot remain objective and will let his own emotions interfere with the therapy if he has had a previous social relationship with the patient. The main issue regarding previous relationships, however, centers around the priority placed on the role of the transference neurosis and the therapeutic setting. If the patient has already established a relationship with the therapist, then the therapist has the extra task of understanding the preformed transference instead of the more desirable situation of observing from the beginning the growth and development of the transference into the transference neurosis (Freud, 1913a).

Of course, there is always some degree of preformed transference that arises from what the patient has heard or read about therapists or the assessor personally (Greenson, 1970b). Ideally speaking, it is easier for the assessor or therapist to be objective if he is not "personally" involved with the patient. Furthermore, it is always best to keep the preformed transference at a minimum. Nevertheless, there may be times when it is appropriate to do the assessment or even therapy of a friend or relative of a friend because the alternatives are less desirable clinically. If the assessor or therapist has had a previous social relationship with the patient and if the *unusual situation occurs where there is no clinically appropriate alternative,* the therapist must be willing and prepared to lose the friendship in the best interests of the patient (Freud, 1913a), and the assessor must be instrumental in referring the patient to that therapy.

It is not uncommon for an assessor or therapist, when faced with no acceptable alternatives, to withhold even supportive types of therapy or withhold the preanalytic assessment itself on the premise that the previous relationship precludes any type of professional intervention. *Of course, every effort should be made to find an acceptable alternative.* However, the assessor or therapist must heed the warnings of Szasz (1963) and not use psychological theories about the *therapeutic alliance* or *transference neurosis* as a way to rationalize the assessor's or therapist's response to the *real relationship.* This rationalization may be a consequence of the assessor's or therapist's interpersonal deficits rather than what is in the best interest of the patient.

Mr. and Mrs. C were long-time personal friends of the assessor. For the past several years the assessor had little social contact with Mr. and Mrs. C, but they still remained good friends, and whenever the assessor was in town he was sure to visit them. One day Mrs. C made a serious suicide attempt, and the couple said that they would speak to nobody but the assessor as he was the only therapist they knew and the only one that they would trust. After trying in vain to get them to see another therapist, the assessor-friend agreed to a series of individual meetings and finally a few couples sessions in an attempt to find out what the problems were and what the best disposition would be.

In the assessment sessions the couple revealed things about their sexual life, their marriage and their extramarital affairs that the assessor had no idea about when he interacted with them socially. After five sessions, the couple had become familiar with talking about their problems and were less threatened with the painful ideas and feelings. They readily accepted the assessor's recommendation for prolonged individual psychoanalytic therapy for each one of them by separate therapists, neither one being the assessor. Both Mr. and Mrs. C entered treatment and were able to make constructive and therapeutic changes in their marital relationship. The friendship with the assessor, however, wasn't quite the same, as there appeared to be a certain amount of wish for distance on the part of all three people.

5.225 Current Somatic Illness

Somatic illness, by itself, may render a patient unsuitable for psychoanalytic psychotherapy. The illness may cause the patient to be unable to focus his energies on intrapsychic problems, or the illness may cause frequent interruptions of the therapy. Patients with significant organic brain disease interfering with their ability to remember or to form abstract conceptualizations are usually excluded, but not necessarily so.

5.226 Attitude of Family Towards Therapy

The responsibility of the assessor is not limited to an assessment of the patient. The attitudes towards therapy held by those people closest to the patient can be a critical factor in contributing to the success or failure of a course of psychoanalytic psychotherapy, especially if the family member is contributing to the payment of the fee. The reasons for the family member's resentment towards psychoanalytic psychotherapy may reflect relatively uncomplicated factors such as fear that the therapist will become aware of intimacies of their lives, or jealousy that someone may help where the family member has failed. Or, the reasons may be much more complex and involve fear of some change in the relationship that will flush out the family member's neurosis. Either directly by meeting with the family member, or indirectly through the patient being assessed, the assessor should encourage treatment for any disturbed family member. If the disturbed family member has a destructive impact on the patient, treatment of the family member may be a prerequisite for the patient being assessed to be found treatable.

The optimal treatment situation is one in which a significant other, such as a spouse, is essentially healthy, supportive and capable of adjusting to the personality change that is bound to result in the patient if the psychoanalytic psychotherapy is successful. Ideally, the family member should be able to offer realistic satisfactions to the patient in exchange for the patient's abandonment of neurotic symptoms and wishes (Dewald, 1972).

Mrs. S was a 34-year-old schoolteacher in twice-weekly psychoanalytic psychotherapy with the chief complaint of insomnia, excessive anxiety and unexplained periodic sadness. Mrs. S was married to Mr. S, a 36-year-old engineer, and the couple had three children. The marriage was successful, there were never any serious marital problems, and the couple liked each other.

Up to the beginning of psychotherapy, both Mrs. and Mr. S were people who significantly repressed body awareness and sexual feelings. They did not have any sexual problems partly because neither one of them enjoyed sex and neither one of them was dissatisfied with the infrequency and rigidity of their sexual life. As the therapy progressed, Mrs. S became very much aware of the excessive degree to which she repressed her sexual urges, bodily feelings, and in general any aspect of excitement. By the third year of therapy, Mrs. S began to experience bodily feelings that had not been conscious since her adolescence. She also became involved in dancing, lost weight, took more pride in her body, and found that she would frequently wish for a more satisfactory sexual life. As Mrs. S's sexual urges became more conscious, both within and outside of the psychotherapy sessions, she found herself progressively dissatisfied with her husband's sexual rigidity and repression. Her reawakened sexual urges, combined with her husband's status quo, led to a serious marital problem that was a direct result of the psychoanalytic psychotherapy. Mrs. S no longer had insomnia, her periods of sadness were markedly reduced, and in general she was feeling significantly better as a result of her psychotherapy. She now had, however, a problem that she did not foresee, namely dissatisfaction with her husband that seriously threatened her marriage and her home life.

Mr. S was left with a difficult decision. He either had to adjust to Mrs. S's sexual urges or risk losing his wife. Mr. S valued his wife and his marriage, took a hard look at himself as a result of her changed behavior, and elected to go into psychotherapy himself as a way of becoming more aware of his own repressed sexuality. Mr. S's psychotherapy was very successful and the marriage was not only saved, but both partners reached a level of bodily pleasure that they had previously denied themselves. If Mr. S were inflexibly neurotic so that any change in Mrs. S threatened the neurotic interaction, he would have most likely, in some way, attempted to prevent or abort his wife's therapy, either overtly and consciously or in subtle and unconscious ways.

If the patient changes, but the significant family member does not, an environmental change frequently results. For example, the environmental change may be a divorce if the significant member is a spouse, or, if the patient is the offspring of neurotic parents, the patient may drastically decrease interaction. Sometimes patients being assessed will ask what psychoanalytic therapy will do to their marriage. When clinically indicated, I often respond by saying that a successful therapy will strengthen a healthy marriage and lead to the termination of an unhealthy marriage.

The availability of a parent during the patient's psychoanalytic psychotherapy is a complicated issue that relates to treatability and, as with all other items, must be assessed with regard to each individual patient. It is, to some extent, impossible to reconstruct, in abstentia, the total truth about the parent's personality if the parent is unavailable to the patient during the therapy. A live and available parent is usually a major advantage since the patient has the opportunity to use the psychoanalytic psychotherapy to resolve the childhood neurotic distortions, and then to reality test the new perceptions. Once the intrapsychic conflicts are resolved, the patient can observe the parents as they really are as opposed to the deceased parent enshrined in distorted recollections. Of course, the opposite can occur. Some patients cannot deal in psychoanalytic psychotherapy with certain positive and negative feelings toward the parents if they have to interact with them outside of the session. The feelings are simply too frightening and too intense. The absence of the parents may make such a patient feel freer to experience strong feelings in the treatment session.

5.227 FAMILY OR ENVIRONMENTAL CRISES

In the assessment of current family or environmental crises, three important technical guidelines must be kept in mind. First, psychoanalytic psychotherapy is not indicated if the external crisis overwhelms the patient to the point of ego disintegration. Second, the patient must have some distance from the crisis in order to form a therapeutic alliance. If the ego is so invested in the painful reality of the current or past crisis, then the patient will usually be incapable of exploring the underlying psychic events (Freud, 1937).

Third, the patient has inherent capacities to correct or at least alleviate or adjust to many external situations if the neurotic impediments are removed. All people have enormous adaptive capacities and the overall goal of any psychoanalytic psychotherapy can be considered as achieving the ability to change the changeable and adjust to the unchangeable. The Menninger Foundation's 20-year psychotherapy research study included the examination of 21 patients in psychoanalytic psychotherapy and empirically concluded that, provided that the ego is intact, "initial stress" was not a factor in determining clinical outcome (Kernberg et al., 1972). Thus, the evidence suggests that, if the ego is intact and able to observe itself, no external stress should contraindicate psychoanalytic psychotherapy.

Frequently, people seem preoccupied with the external stress and show only minimal signs of some of the strengths required for psychoanalytic psychotherapy, such as psychological mindedness. However, the assessor must not be fooled by these preoccupations and must assess the degree of ego strength rather than the seriousness of the crisis.

> We [psychoanalytic therapists] do not deal with the happenings in the external world as such, but with their repercussions in the mind (A. Freud quoted by Aarons, 1962, p. 522).

Resistance exerts its influence from the very first moment of the initial interview. Although the patient may not have caused the crisis, reaction to the crisis can be multidetermined, and a preoccupation with the crisis may serve to help the patient avoid looking at those parts of himself which he avoids. Furthermore, external problems such as an unhappy marriage or physical illness often satisfy neurotic needs for psychic pain so that the patient does not have as much need for neurotic symptoms (Freud, 1919).

Since most patients come to therapy following some crisis or "eye opening" experience, it is frequently very difficult to distinguish the patient with a major developmental ego defect that renders him untreatable from the more treatable patient who is experiencing a temporary situational regression. Frequently, in order to make this distinction an extended assessment is necessary (Zetzel, 1968), or the judgment must await the psychoanalytic psychotherapy itself.

Finally, when faced with a crisis which is serving as the immediate precipitant for seeking therapy, the assessor must be very careful to avoid, if possible, being drawn into the role of advisor, reassurer, premature interpreter or intellectualizer. The prospective patient, often quite ambivalent about a commitment to therapy, may be quick to observe critically any signs of weakness or falseness in the assessor's attitude. A well-meaning assessor may reassure, advise and even praise a patient who already has had too many promises that could not be kept, too much advice that he was unable to follow or too much paternalistic praise. The assessor's reassurance, advice or praise may serve only to weaken the already fragile trust and confidence that the patient has in the assessor as a person or in psychoanalytic psychotherapy as a treatment modality. In fact, the patient may even unconsciously arrange a trap in which the assessor gives reassurance, advice or praise so that the patient can criticize or disapprove of it (Greenacre, 1952).

Premature interpretation or overeager intellectualizations by the assessor can be as destructive as misguided or invalid reassurance or praise. If the assessor hurls complicated psychodynamic theories at the patient, the assessor indirectly reinforces the patient's intellectualization. Since intellectualization is a powerful defense against the revelation of the inner self, any reinforcement of intellectualization may interfere with the assessment and subsequent psychoanalytic therapy.

The assessor best serves the patient if he displays a quiet attitude of knowing his business and never forgets that his most reassuring and enlightening role is not sympathy, but is empathically resonating to the problem so that the patient knows the assessor has a realistic assessment of the situation. An empathic, realistic assessment, combined with a recommendation for therapy, is in itself reassuring since the implicit message is, "I see how bad things really are but there is a way for you to alleviate the pain."

There are, of course, times when the patient will present with a situation or somehow arrange the interaction so that the assessor is faced with the choice of either giving some advice or facing the strong probability that the patient will become more symptomatic or engage in some destructive act to *prove* his need for advice. When this is the case, the assessor should respond by restating the possible decisions that the patient has already outlined, perhaps emphasizing the most reasonable choice, but always leaving the patient with the attitude that the final decision is his. Of course, any patient who behaves in this way is offering provisional evidence for untreatability.

5.23 *The Issue of Morality*

Freud referred to morality and ethics but never expanded on the subject.

> Furthermore, a certain measure of natural intelligence and ethical development are required; if a physician has to deal with a worthless character, he soon loses the interest which makes it possible for him to enter profoundly into the patient's life (Freud, 1904, p. 253).

One year later Freud again revealed his conviction on this matter when he said:

> Those patients who do not possess a reasonable degree of education and a fairly reliable character should be refused for psychoanalysis [psychoanalytic psychotherapy]. It must not be forgotten that there are healthy people as well as unhealthy ones who are good for nothing in life, and ascribe to their illness everything that incapacitates them, if they show any signs of neurosis (Freud, 1905b, p. 263).

The fact of the matter is that sometimes people manifest "immoral" or "unethical" behavior that can be directly related to the psychological problem for which they seek psychoanalytic therapy, whereas at other times their immoral or unethical behavior is only peripherally or indirectly related to such symptoms. Of equal, if not more, importance than the presence of unethical behavior is the response that such behavior elicits in the assessor or eventual therapist. If the assessor for some reason finds the patient's behavior repulsive, then he may unconsciously label the patient as "untreatable" as a way of expressing this hostility. An adequate assessment or therapy cannot be done unless the assessor or therapist genuinely likes the patient as a person no matter what the patient says or does (in this context Rogers uses the term "unconditional positive regard" [1957, p. 98]).

It is hard to imagine how a therapist can deliver effective psychoanalytic therapy if he is repulsed by the patient's behavior. If the patient's behavior is of the kind that elicits strong negative reactions in some people, then it is the responsibility of the assessor to try to make some judgment as to what kind of therapist and perhaps which specific therapist ought to treat that given patient. If the behavior is one that is very likely to elicit a negative response in the therapist, the assessor should go so far as to call the potential therapist and ask if he would be willing to treat this patient and if he could handle listening to the clinical material. Such a course of action is especially important for certain behavioral disorders such as sexual perversions and crimes such as child or spouse abuse, theft and chemical abuse.

5.24 Personality and Attitudes of Assessor and Therapist

It is not enough for the assessor to answer the questions of who is being treated for what. The assessment should also involve a thorough consideration of the personality and attitude of the therapist and the patient-therapist fit.* Since any one person has a personal response to any other person (including a therapist), with whom he closely relates, the assessor should attempt some judgment of what kind of personality would best fit, or would best be avoided, with the specific prospective patient. In fact, when assessing a prospective patient, the assessment is grossly incomplete unless the assessor asks the patient what kind of person and personality would he prefer in a therapist. The prospective patient may have a previous therapist to use as a basis for comparison, but either way, the patient should be encouraged to give free reign to his fantasies

---

* A note of caution: Although the various aspects of the patient-therapist fit are of the utmost importance, clinicians must be careful not to swing too far in the other direction and use the patient-therapist fit as a screen behind which we hide technical errors, unresolved transferences and countertransferences, and even professional incompetence.

and to be as specific as possible in his answer. The answer to this question often is far more important in finding the appropriate therapist than the biographical or mental status details.

Most assessors agree in theory that, next to the patient, the personality of the therapist and the therapist's willingness to get therapeutically involved with the patient and to bear the ensuing feelings are the most critical determinants behind the therapeutic success (Bugental, 1964; Frank, 1974; Rosenzweig, 1936). In fact, in all of medicine, no other form of therapy is so influenced by the personality, thoughts and feelings of the person delivering the treatment. And yet, it is strangely and unfortunately true that many assessors do not evaluate the appearance, personality, attitude or affective characteristics of the therapist as to their fit with the potential patient. Regarding the patient-therapist fit issue, the psychoanalytic literature has not improved much since 1938 when Clara Thompson wrote:

> One seldom finds an account of anything that suggests the differences in personality of various psychoanalysts [psychoanalytic therapists] or the significant entering of the analyst's [psychoanalytic therapist's] personality anywhere in the whole protracted process [psychoanalytic process] (p. 205).

As Lipton (1977) notes, Freud himself excluded from discussions on "technique" his personal relationship with the patient. Among many assessors, the personality of the potential therapist is not only neglected, it is actively avoided as an issue for consideration. Unfortunately, many assessors act as if the potential therapist's personality and emotional makeup are privileged areas which are of no business to the assessor, despite the fact that subjective impressions (e.g., Kohut, 1971; Pollock, 1960) and even some empirical evidence (Howard et al., 1969, 1970; Luborsky et al., 1971) offer convincing evidence that good clinical outcome is highly correlated with certain therapist factors, such as similarity, interest and empathy for the patient. Contemporary therapists would no doubt agree that their patient population is the result of some sort of natural selection of patients whom they most enjoy treating, which makes it even more puzzling why the personality of the therapist is so often disregarded in assessing and referring the patient for psychoanalytic psychotherapy. My concern is certainly not original and, in fact, this issue is the subject of some literature that attempts to clarify the complex subject of the role of the person of the therapist in psychoanalytic therapy, such as the outstanding book edited by Kenneth Frank in which he says:

> The paucity of such material in the psychoanalytic literature is, I believe, the result of a phobic attitude toward the inner life of the analyst as he functions professionally, resulting in a failure to address the human dimension in psychoanalytic practice (1977, p. 2).

The failure to consider the personality of the therapist can lead to serious consequences that may irreversibly harm the patient. Guntrip (1975) eloquently describes how his analyses with Fairbairn and Winnicott were greatly dependent on the different personalities of the two analysts. Fenichel (1945) makes a general warning that the treatment may fail with some cases if the therapist's real personality is too similar to that of the patient's parent. Bibring (1936) and Greenson (1967) give clinical examples in which the psychoanalytic therapist so closely resembled the hated parent in speech and personality that the symptoms and the resistance intensified to the degree that the psychoanalytic psychotherapy had to be terminated, in Bibring's examples, and was marginally successful, in Greenson's case. The patients resumed psychoanalytic psychotherapy with different therapists and were able to complete a successful course of treatment.

Shapiro (1973) describes a patient who experienced the difference in the personalities of two therapists. The first therapist was an open, warm person who treated the patient in a totally accepting manner that fostered the patient's regression to the point of halting therapeutic progress. The second therapist was less open and warm, was more interested in setting limits for the patient, was far less threatened by the anal clinical material and, in fact, even encouraged the patient to experiment behaviorally outside of the sessions with her anal fantasies. The patient had a very favorable therapeutic outcome with the second therapist, and, as Shapiro points out, it was clearly the difference in personalities of therapists that accounted for the patient's failure with one therapist and success with another.

Although most assessors verbally agree that no therapist can completely avoid countertransference problems, no matter how successful his own therapy has been, the same assessors, by their avoidance of the therapist's personality and its fit to the prospective patient, behave as if the therapist is liberated from all unconscious bias, is ready to handle any situation and is essentially the perfectly treated therapist, a phenomenon that, of course, exists only in our omnipotent fantasies. An avoidance of the therapist's personality is especially unrealistic when we consider that many therapists have chosen their profession largely because of their own painful experiences with mental conflict (Glover, 1928; Guntrip, 1975). In fact, it is well known that Freud himself used intense self-examination of his own neurotic struggles as a vehicle to obtain much of the clinical material upon which he based his revolutionary theories and techniques.

The assessor should not only consider the prospective therapist's personality, but also must pay some attention to the relationship between the preanalytic assessor and the prospective therapist. If, for example, there are conscious or unconscious psychological or philosophical conflicts or bondages between the assessor and the prospective therapist, then the patient may begin psychoanalytic psychotherapy in an atmosphere of disagreement, therapist's anxieties or positive feelings which could very well interfere with the treatment.

5.3 GROUP TWO CATEGORIES—POSTANALYTIC ASSESSMENT

As mentioned in the Introduction to this chapter (see Section 5.1), the second major classification of categories by which we can approach the subject of treatability is that group of variables which, although essential for treatability, cannot be adequately assessed until after the patient has been in psychoanalytic psychotherapy. Again, I want to emphasize, as I did in Section 5.1, that the postanalytic categories may, for some patients, be adequately evaluated in preanalytic assessment sessions. The assignment of a category to a postanalytic group is based on a tendency, as a general rule, to be inaccessible to adequate evaluation in the pretreatment assessment sessions. I also want to emphasize that, despite the need to defer judgment on these items, the assessor must still begin evaluating these items in the initial assessment sessions.

There are six major subcategories of postanalytic assessment: 1) motivation for psychoanalytic psychotherapy and the role of secondary gain; 2) a history of past trauma; 3) degree and quality of symptoms; 4) patient strengths; 5) treatment goals of patient and assessor; and 6) the capacity to develop and maintain the therapeutic relationship.

5.31 *Motivation for Psychoanalytic Psychotherapy and the Role of Secondary Gain*

"Motivation" is a term used loosely in psychoanalytic literature and rarely defined in the papers and seminars in which it is discussed. For example, for some authors, motivation seems to be equivalent to what I am calling "psychological mindedness" (see Section 5.216); for others motivation is used to mean what I am calling "therapeutic alliance" (see Section 4.21). In this chapter I am using the term motivation to refer to the collection of variables responsible for the *desire for some specifically defined change* and *decision to make the initial appointment with the assessor*. This restricted use of the term motivation should be distinguished from those forces keeping the patient in treatment once the treatment has begun. In this Section, I will propose that the relationship between motivation and treatability is far too complex to be understood within the initial assessment sessions and should not be used as the basis of a preanalytic judgment of treatability. The apparent immediate reason for seeking treatment must be explored by the assessor but it is not always the most important and, in fact, is often very misleading. There may very well be a deeper and more total commitment to engaging in therapy than was at first thought of by patient and assessor and that was not discovered until treatment had begun.

5.311 NEUROTIC VERSUS HEALTHY MOTIVATION

A healthy motivation for psychoanalytic psychotherapy arises out of a strong and sincere wish for intrapsychic change which includes insight, less psychic pain and more psychic growth. Not all motivation for therapy arises out of a wish for mental health and less psychic pain than the patient currently experiences. Some motivation may stem from neurosis. Neurotic motivation is based on a wish that reinforces rather than alleviates the neurosis. For example, a person may seek therapy so as to achieve a neurotic wish for exceptional professional success. Or, a person may seem well motivated and capable of tolerating the pain of therapy, when what the patient is actually doing is fulfilling his masochistic wish for additional punishment. If such a patient were in treatment, his masochism might not allow him to make therapeutic progress. At the time when the therapist might expect him to be showing alleviation of symptoms, the patient might show an exacerbation of symptoms, a phenomenon labeled by Freud as a "negative therapeutic reaction" (1923b, p. 49), and described clinically in the "Wolf Man" case history (Freud, 1918). It was, in fact, the concept of negative therapeutic reaction that eventually served as the foundation for Freud's discovery of the superego and structural theory (Bergmann & Hartman, 1976;

Freud, 1923b), and it was considered by Freud to be the ". . . most frequent cause of failure in psychoanalytic psychotherapy" (Freud, quoted by Bergmann & Hartman, 1976, p. 33). Glover (1928) explains the negative therapeutic reaction as an expression of an ego-superego conflict whereby the need for punishment continues to support painful symptoms and prevents resolution of intrapsychic conflict.

Psychoanalytic psychotherapy is an experience that can be attractive for other unhealthy reasons that will only reveal themselves after psychoanalytic psychotherapy has begun. For example, a patient may be motivated by an urge to confess or to be granted absolution; a need to alleviate anxiety by talking; a narcissistic need to have someone totally devoted to listening and being with him; a desire to find someone who can take his side against a spouse; or a wish to avoid responsibility (Gill et al., 1954; Waldhorn, 1960).

Greenson proposes that no person is treatable unless he sees himself as a "patient":

> People who seek psychoanalysis [psychoanalytic psychotherapy] for research purposes, or professional advancement, training, or for curiosity should be considered as resistant and in need of preparatory psychotherapy (1967, p. 360).

Some empirical research (Luborsky et al., 1971) as well as our intuitive judgment makes it tempting for us to believe that the poorly motivated patient is less likely than the highly motivated patient to have a favorable clinical outcome. Nevertheless, in contrast to Greenson's quotation in the previous paragraph, it is my opinion that the assessor should not jump to the conclusion of untreatable merely because the prospective patient appears poorly motivated. The assessor must approach the prospective patient by remembering that *all* people possess natural or intrinsic strivings towards emotional growth and mental normality just as they have basic drives towards food, water and sex. All people, no matter how apparently uninterested they appear about being a "patient," can be considered as possessing some degree of constructive motivation towards treatment.

I disagree with Greenson and others who propose that the people seeking treatment because of curiosity, professional reasons, research, etc. should be immediately ruled out without a trial period in which the deeper motivational forces may emerge. The very presence of a patient seeking help to any degree indicates the patient's recognition of the need for help and an *active* attempt by the patient to do something about his psychological problems. The primary issue is not whether or not the patient is motivated to be a patient; the primary issue is the *degree* to which the prospective patient has the capacities to do the work of psychoanalytic therapy.

After the postanalytic judgment is made, the degree of motivation can still be considered a relatively weak variable in determining treatability. Levin (1962) reports a small but quite revealing study. Levin surveyed six psychoanalytic therapists, all practicing for at least six years. These therapists, in their collective practices, reported 16 patients whom they had found treatable, put into psychoanalytic therapy, and then discovered were untreatable. Of these 16 patients, only one was *not* highly motivated to continue psychoanalytic psychotherapy at the time that they were, by their behavior or mental status, showing evidence that they were untreatable and had to terminate the treatment.* Levin's (1962) observations are supported by the final report of the Menninger Foundation's extensive research project which also concludes that in psychoanalytic psychotherapy, given sufficiently high ego strength, motivation is not a statistically significant variable towards a favorable clinical outcome (Kernberg et al., 1972). Another relevant study is that of Sashin et al. (1975) who report 122 cases in psychoanalytic therapy and conclude that preanalytic motivation is not a discriminating factor in predicting clinical outcome. It is of interest to note that these recent empirical reports support the subjective statement made in 1926 by Nunberg:

> We can never calculate the probable duration and success of analytic treatment from the conscious wish to get well. . . . The motives which impel neurotics towards recovery are as manifold as the motives of their illness itself (p. 64-67).

It appears, then, that motivation to begin or continue psychoanalytic psychotherapy by itself is of little value in assessing treatability, and we can conclude that preanalytic motivation is of little assessment value. The drive towards mental health, however, should not be underestimated by the *postanalytic* assessor (therapist). Motivation represents a portion

---

* This approach is in direct opposition with the Hungarian school, originated by Ferenczi, that recommends, as a general rule, that the patient should be treated as long as the patient still wants to be treated (Bak, 1970).

of ego energy committed towards a specific goal or task (Wheelis, 1956). This commitment of psychic energy can be either ally or enemy of the treatment depending on the underlying dynamics. The postanalytic assessor is faced with the task of not only assessing the degree of motivation to continue psychoanalytic psychotherapy, but assessing why such motivation exists, that is, why does the patient choose to continue in treatment? The postanalytic assessor must clearly distinguish between the desire to achieve constructive psychic change and the desire to remain in treatment for unconstructive reasons. When these questions are postanalytically answered for a given patient, then an accurate assessment of the relationships between treatability and motivation can be made.

5.312 PRIMARY AND SECONDARY GAIN

All symptoms have a *primary gain* and most symptoms have a significant *secondary gain*. The primary gain can be defined as the homostatic balance to the psychic apparatus that the symptom manages to achieve. The primary gain of the symptom prevents conscious awareness of certain unconscious psychic conflicts and elements. Being an internal mentalistic phenomenon, the primary gain is very difficult to assess in the initial few interviews (Glover, 1956).

The definition of secondary gain is often unclear in the literature. For the purpose of this book, I will define secondary gain as a favored environmental or intrapsychic situation that is a consequence of the symptoms or the treatment. Secondary gain is usually more recognizable in the first few sessions than the primary gain and can become so profoundly favored as to significantly contribute to untreatability (Glover, 1956). Secondary gain may be associated with many symptoms, even those that cause great psychic suffering.

Mrs. Z was a 34-year-old air traffic controller who was awarded a medical retirement because of excessive anxiety and depression which a federal commission considered directly caused by her job. She received her full salary as a retirement pension and all that was required of her was to be seen by a government psychiatrist every six months so that the government could be assured that she was still "totally disabled."

Mr. C was a 26-year-old father of one who presented with symptoms of excessive anxiety, insomnia and suicidal thoughts. He desperately wanted his wife not to carry through with her threat of divorce and was told by her that as long as he was in psychotherapy she would not leave him.

Needless to say, the secondary gain factors are critical in the assessment of these two patients. If Mrs. Z achieved an alleviation of her anxiety and depression, which were genuinely distressing her, she would also lose a salary which was above anything which she could have earned since her old job was no longer available. Likewise with Mr. C, although his symptoms were real, it appeared that he was seeking treatment in order to please his wife.

The cases of Mrs. Z and Mr. C serve as excellent examples of how a very obvious secondary gain should not necessarily imply unsuitability. In fact, in both these cases, although the assessor was well aware of the secondary gains of the illness (Mrs. Z) and of the treatment (Mr. C), the patients were found treatable and referred for psychoanalytic therapy. A one-year follow-up revealed that the secondary gain of the neurosis was not an insurmountable obstruction to treatment for Mrs. Z. Furthermore, in the case of Mr. C, the secondary gain of the treatment was used by the therapist as an avenue by which the narcissistic and therapeutic alliances (see Sections 4.2 and 4.3) were facilitated.

The cases of Mrs. Z and Mr. C are examples of secondary gains or losses that are external and quite obvious. Often, the secondary gains are more subtle, more on a purely psychic level so that the symptoms have not yet engendered an amount of pain that is greater than the subtle narcissistic pleasure gained from the neurosis. Two not uncommon examples are: 1) the satisfaction gained from a professional success that is the result of an obsessive compulsive need to succeed professionally in order to overcome low self-esteem; and 2) the satisfaction gained from a perversion that has not yet caused serious social conflicts.

5.32 *A History of Past Trauma*

The importance of past traumatic events to treatability tends to vary more with the different assessors than with the nature of the events themselves. When the patient relates a trauma during the initial interview, the assessor is usually not able fully to grasp the developmental aspects, the emotional impact nor the amount of discharge of affect that occurred at the time of the trauma.

The traumatic event by itself is of relatively little importance in comparison to the manner in which the traumatic event is handled by the patient and by significant others such as parents, spouse or children. The response and the personalities, in general, of the significant others (such as parents) and the patient's ego strengths are critical in helping the person integrate the traumatic event so that it does not become a pathogenic experience (Kohut, 1971). This hypothesis has been supported by Vaillant (1974) who reports on the study of 95 college sophomores who were originally selected for psychological *health* and then closely and regularly followed and evaluated over the next 30 years. Vaillant reports that the capacity to deal with trauma in an organized and practical manner was far more predictive of psychological health than the frequency and severity of early or recent traumatic events. For example, regarding the trauma of losing a parent, Vaillant writes:

> It is not the sudden loss of a parent as much as the continued presence of a disturbed parent, and it was not a disturbed relationship with one parent as much as it was a globally disturbed childhood that affected adult adjustment (1974, p. 21).

Anna Freud (1958) provides another example that supports the exhortation not to oversimplify traumatic events. She observed that some parents tended to report the loss of a grandparent as a major trauma in the life of their child. Analysis of the child, however, frequently showed that the death itself was relatively ignored by the child. Instead it was the parents' sadness, depression or emotional retreat that the child experienced as traumatic.

Another Anna Freud (1958) example that is relevant to our discussion is as follows: An adult patient reported that at the age of four she observed a fight between parents in which the mother was murdered by the father. The traumatic event was reported by the patient during the initial interview, but it was not until the patient had been in therapy for a considerable amount of time that the therapist learned that the major trauma was not the killing of the mother. During the fight, the mother yelled at the child, "Get out," and this was perceived by the child as total rejection. It was the rejection that was most traumatic.

In essence, then, the capacity to adapt or the overall underlying environmental pathology is a more important determinant of psychological illness than the *frequency* or *quality* of specific traumatic events. The same thing can be said about historical trauma as it relates to treatability. The capacity to adapt and the overall pathology of the environment are much more important in assessing treatability than individual trauma, no matter how severe that trauma may be. Furthermore, if the ego maladjusts to the traumatic event, we can conclude that the trauma in some way interacted with previous unconscious intrapsychic conflicts (Semrad, 1967; Zetzel, 1970). We must conclude, then, that the impact of a traumatic event cannot be assessed until the patient has undergone a significant amount of therapy. The patient should not be considered untreatable preanalytically because of any single trauma or series of traumatic events.

5.33 Degree and Quality of Symptoms

The degree and quality of symptoms are important categories in any discussion on treatability (see Section 3.12 for a definition and discussion of the psychoanalytic concept of "symptom"). The issue of symptom degree and quality as it relates to treatability can be approached from two sides: 1) the tendency to *overestimate* the severity of symptoms as they relate to the *needs* for treatment; and 2) the relationship between the severity of symptoms and the treatability itself.

5.331 THE OVERESTIMATION OF SEVERITY OF SYMPTOMS AS THEY RELATE TO THE NEED FOR TREATMENT

A fact that is sometimes neglected by assessors of treatability is that the patient may be treatable but may not be in *need* of psychoanalytic therapy, unless of course the need is considered an essential component of the definition of "treatable." A condition of unhappiness is not equivalent to psychological symptoms. Indeed, most of our intrapsychic problems are resolved or at least alleviated by large dosages of old fashioned intelligence, common sense, courage, faith in ourselves and others, environmental manipulations, emotional strength, and support from friends and relatives (Stone, 1954). A successful psychoanalytic therapy requires significant sacrifices of time, money and psychic and physical energy. Before any such sacrifice is made, the assessor must give serious thought as to whether or not the psychic symptoms are causing enough problems to warrant this expensive and time-consuming treatment. Included in this assessment is an attempt to evaluate whether or not the sacrifices of therapy are in correct proportion to the desirable and realistic potential results of therapy. Inherent in such an assessment is the evaluation as to whether or not the symptoms are transitional and represent recent environmental change towards which the patient will soon adjust without the help of psychoanalytic therapy.

In essence then, the assessor must evaluate the potential patient's capacity to alter the unacceptable internal *and* external situations. Most of us in the mental health field are well aware of the destructiveness of psychological problems and the pain that they inflict on their victims. We must remember, however, that the psychologically abnormal position from which the patient presents to the assessor may be the last and only position which the patient can relatively master. We must keep an open mind as to the possibility that, in any given case, the best solution to the specific problems being faced may indeed be the psychic disorder itself.

Ms. K was a 22-year-old second-year medical school student who had always enjoyed success academically and interpersonally. She had come from a family in which both parents were highly educated and professionally successful, and her four siblings had all attended the best of colleges and graduate schools and were enjoying professional success. She had never been pressured to succeed or to work hard but the work ethic in the family was unmistakable. About halfway through her sophomore year in medical school, she showed an uncharacteristic withdrawal, insomnia, sadness, irritability, and progressive low self-esteem. She began to fail in courses in which previously she would get A's, and her condition was brought to the attention of the dean of the medical school who recommended psychiatric consultation. The patient told the psychiatrist that she had never experienced psychiatric symptoms before but that she was now feeling very depressed. The psychiatrist recommended twice-a-week psychoanalytic psychotherapy. The patient began the therapy but shortly terminated, objecting to the recommendation for psychoanalytic therapy when, in her opinion, her major problem was that she did not want to be a doctor but did not know how to break the news to her parents since she did not want her parents to see her as a failure. After abruptly quitting therapy the patient dropped out of medical school, moved to another city, got a job that she liked, and enrolled in night school taking courses that she enjoyed. Her significant depression diminished within weeks of leaving medical school. Once she was out of medical school she no longer felt like a failure and she no longer felt the intrapsychic conflicts that existed previously. At one-year and two-year follow-ups, although she received no therapy, she showed no signs of clinical depression and she was functioning at her premedical school high level of social and professional satisfaction.

5.332 THE RELATIONSHIP BETWEEN THE SEVERITY OF
       SYMPTOMS AND TREATABILITY

> At the beginning of analysis [psychoanalytic psychotherapy], before we have insight into the structure of a neurosis, it is impossible to predict how the patient will respond to treatment. There is no guarantee that two individuals with the same symptomatology will react similarly to the same technical procedure (A. Freud, 1954a, quoted by Tyson & Sandler, 1971, p. 214).

A major thesis of this chapter is that the severity, in terms of quality and degree, of symptoms is generally an unreliable guide in assessing treatability and almost never an indication that the patient is untreatable (e.g., Aarons, 1962; Bachrach & Leaff, 1978; Bak, 1970; Brenner, 1976; A. Freud, 1954a; Huxster et al., 1975; Kubie, 1948; Kuiper, 1968; Levin, 1960, 1962; Rogers, 1957; Stone, 1954; Tyson & Sandler, 1971; Waldhorn, 1960). In fact, the severity of the symptoms often serves the opposite effect since, although the symptoms provide substitutive satisfactions, they simultaneously provide neurotic misery that can be a powerful constructive force sustaining the psychoanalytic therapy.

Of course, clinical and research literature (e.g., a review of the empirical research by Luborsky et al., 1971) strongly supports the hypothesis that more serious disorders such as chronic psychotic and schizophrenic patients will respond less to just about any kind of psychotherapy than will the neurotic groups. The overwhelming empirical and subjective evidence favoring neurotics should, however, only serve as a major guideline in assessing treatability and should not lead to the sanctification of diagnoses and categorical statements such as the following:

> The psychoanalytic process . . . simply cannot be effective for abnormalities other than the transference neuroses—hysterias, phobias, and obsessional neuroses or characterological phenomena which stem directly from these symptoms (Guttman, 1968, p. 254).

Within the neurotic groups, I submit that the diagnostic labels are by themselves of no value in assessing treatability and I disagree with

Fenichel (1945), Glover (1956), Nacht and Lebovici (1959) and others who place great prognostic emphasis on diagnoses in assessing neurotics. Such oversimplified proposals do psychoanalytic therapy a disservice. There is no empirical or, for that matter, theoretical evidence that supports dogmatic propositions such as that of Karasu (as reported by Guttman, 1960) who proposed that *content* of phobias indicates the degree of treatability, so that a patient who fears motion is more treatable than one who fears dirt. In essence then, the quality and degree of the symptoms must be seen as analogous to the manifest content of dreams and the revelation of deeper meanings must await a course of psychotherapy. There are, of course, exceptions to these generalizations about symptoms. For example, Freud (1904) long ago pointed out that psychoanalytic therapy is not the treatment of choice when for some somatic reason there is need for rapid remission of a symptom, for example severe anorexia nervosa.

Regarding treatability, symptoms must be assessed in a functional relationship to the psychic apparatus. For example, if the ego is strong and not excessively vulnerable to the superego or id, capacities for reintegration and reality testing remain intact regardless of the symptom choice or severity. It is not the quality or degree of symptoms that the assessor must evaluate so much as the dynamic capacity of the ego not to be overwhelmed by the symptoms (Aarons, 1962; Zetzel, 1966). If the ego is overwhelmed and disintegrates, defective reality testing (psychosis) may result, in which case the patient most likely is untreatable. Sometimes the ego is not overwhelmed to the point of overt psychosis, but the person resorts to abnormal reliance on the primitive defense mechanisms of denial, projection, distortion and magical thinking, in which case the patient is most likely untreatable. Sometimes, however, the most severe symptoms exist in patients who are quite adaptable. For example, a severely obsessive compulsive patient may be very successful professionally, despite the application of enormous amounts of psychic energy in the service of troublesome compulsions (Aarons, 1962).

Ego strength may be hard to evaluate with the patient sitting up since the face-to-face, question-answer, structured setting between prospective patient and assessor creates a supportive situation for the patient. The patient finds the situation supportive because the assessor usually asks direct questions in an empathic and visibly caring and active manner that leaves little time for fantasies that may lead to painful thoughts or feelings. This supportive interaction promotes ego synthesis and defense

mechanisms such as avoidance, denial and other forms of concealment that may mask ego weaknesses which, if observed by the assessor, might lead to a finding of untreatability. In this regard, some authors (e.g., Deutsch, 1949; Knight, 1953; Stekel, 1940) have employed a free association interview or "associative anamnesis" in which no direct questions are asked and the patient is simply requested to say whatever comes to his mind. Sometimes this technique is employed by asking the patient to lie on a couch; whether sitting or lying, the patient, by the demands of free association, is often stripped of defensive adaptive mechanisms and is thus more likely to show the force of his symptoms.

Any patient who finds that the associative anamnesis is unbearably painful should not be unequivocally labeled untreatable since many patients gradually learn to free associate relatively comfortably as the therapy progresses, the narcissistic alliance develops, and the trust and faith in the therapy increase. Of course, good judgment must be used in deciding how far the assessor should allow a patient to verbalize in the stress situation.

In summary, it is invalid to automatically label as untreatable any person for no other reason than because that person was once, but is no longer, psychotic; or is suffering from "characterological" rather than "neurotic" illness; or is exhibiting certain unusual or bizarre symptoms. Such mechanical conclusions are simply not supported by any well-controlled empirical research. Until such research is conducted, diagnostic labels should not automatically indicate untreatability, and the symptoms have to be assessed individually in a postanalytic situation.

5.34 Patient Strengths

As mentioned in Section 5.2, a useful way to approach treatability is to assess patient strengths. In this section I will discuss some strengths that are needed for treatability, although their existence cannot be determined adequately until therapy is underway.

5.341 THE CAPACITY TO DEAL WITH SILENCE

Silence is, in some ways, the overt opposite of verbalizations (see Section 5.212). On the other hand, silence, whether belonging to the patient, the assessor or the therapist, should not be automatically construed as meaning not listening or having nothing meaningful to say. The most accurate and useful way for the clinician to assess the patient's silence is to conceptualize silence as an *active* process, something that occurs *despite* the patient having something to say, and something that elicits a response just as an active verbal intervention elicits a response (Lipton, 1977). When a patient becomes silent, the assessor or therapist, instead of asking "What are you thinking?" may ask "What stopped you from talking?"

There can be many reasons for silence that are *not* indications of untreatability and will only be learned after psychoanalytic psychotherapy has begun. The patient may be silent because he does not consciously or preconsciously wish to give certain material verbal expression in the presence of a person that he has only known for a short time; the silence may represent embarrassment or shame that will decrease once the treatment progresses; the silence may simply reflect the fact that the patient never learned to communicate well but is capable of learning such social skills. Some patients feel very comfortable in the assessor's office and the silence may exist because the patient is feeling a trust and relief since he does not have to talk to cover up anxiety or insecurities. In this regard, Fromm-Reichmann (1950) quotes the son of dominating parents who, when reflecting upon his silence during a session, expressed his gratitude at:

> The happiness to dare to breathe and vegetate and just to be, in the presence of another person who does not interfere (p. 138).

Not only is silence not necessarily a manifestation of weakness, it may even reflect strength, a fact often overshadowed by the expediency of words in psychoanalytic psychotherapy. Patients may be silent for long periods of time because they are expressing thoughts or feelings that represent constructive reflection precipitated by the interaction with the assessor or therapist. Certain feelings or thoughts, such as body awareness, can be most meaningfully experienced during periods of silence rather than periods of talking or listening (Nacht, 1964). During such periods, the patient may talk as a way to resist the full force of the feelings.

> Words often give shape to affects which are by themselves extremely fluid, and force them to harden into forms which do not correspond with essential truth. . . . We could almost say that in analysis [psychoanalytic psychotherapy], language has no better assistant than

silence, because in silence its full significance and deep efficaciousness is best realized (Nacht, 1964, p. 302).

Just as silence is an active process, receptivity must also be considered an activity. The inexperienced assessor who feels uncomfortable with silence may try to alleviate his own anxiety by breaking the silence, thereby interfering with his effectiveness as a listener. Sometimes a silent patient becomes uncomfortable with the silence and this progressive discomfort is enough to break the silence. The assessor who rushes into interrupting the silence hinders the patient's spontaneous effort to terminate his own silence. Of course, the preanalytic assessor has a limited amount of time in which to collect data to make the judgment of treatability and so he must weigh the risk of interrupting silence against the need to gather the necessary data. Nevertheless, the assessor must beware that his own silence or reluctance to interrupt silence is not a reflection of his own anxiety, hostility or passive-aggression. If the assessor inappropriately interrupts the silence he may create an artificial or superficial dialogue which, paradoxically, may result in a form of meaningless inactivity. Finally, a close observation of the patient's response to the assessor's interruption of the silence may also give us some idea of the patient's ability to respond constructively to a therapist's intervention. (See Loomie, 1961, for a review of the psychoanalytic literature on the subject of the silent patient.)

5.342 THE CAPACITY TO FREE ASSOCIATE

In order for a patient to succeed in psychoanalytic psychotherapy, the patient must be able to free associate during the treatment session (see Section 3.4 for a definition and discussion of free association). The process of free association requires the capacity to reduce external perceptions and cognitive activity, focus on intrapsychic stimuli, suspend secondary process and the usual judgmental censoring of verbalizations, and allow primary process modes of thinking to emerge such as condensation, expression of opposites and an absence of referents in causality, time, place and situation (Bellak, 1961).

The capacity to free associate does not by itself tell us much about treatability. The free associations must be combined with a variety of other requirements for treatability such as regression in the service of the ego and the capacity for psychic integration and increased acuity. These combined capacities can be termed "ego oscillating functions"

(Bellak, 1961, p. 17). Without an "ego oscillating function" the patient could easily slip into mechanical processes of free association referred to by Bellak (1961, p. 16) as an "internal travelogue" or "narcissistic reverie."

Each patient has his own capacity to free associate which is directly related to what free associating means to that specific patient. The patient's responses to these meanings often determine his methods of resistance and reveal parts of his character development and neurosis (Abraham, 1919). For many patients, free associating requires a sacrifice of some narcissism. For some patients free associating requires the capacity for secondary trust (see Section 4.225), since giving oneself over to free association means losing a certain amount of control over the analytic situation and means trusting that, in some ways, the therapist knows more about the psychoanalytic process than the patient. For some patients free association has been noted to have meaning associated with flatus or emptying the bowels with all of the stigma on the one hand and desire to please on the other hand that are associated with those activities from infancy and childhood. For some patients there may be a pleasurable or dreaded voyeuristic meaning to freely associating. Some patients, with little fear of oral passivity, may find that free associating is an enjoyable experience of letting ideas flow from the mind to the mouth to the therapist. Other patients may be terrified of passivity, linking the process of free association to an oral or anal invasion of their body (Bellak, 1961).

As originally noted by Eissler (1958), free associations require the capacity for relative shifting of influence and reciprocity among the macrostructures (id, ego, superego) of the mind. If one of the macrostructures is in absolute control, then free associations are meaningless and monotonous. For example, if a person's superego is excessively deficient, then free associations may yield unproductive id material. Or, if the superego is in complete control, then free associations may reveal nothing but isolated self-criticisms (Bergmann & Hartman, 1976).

The role of the preanalytic assessor and that of the postanalytic assessor (therapist) are somewhat different with regard to free association. For the therapist, free associations are clinical material which lead to the unconscious. If the substitutes of associations are only slight distortions of the unconscious, then the therapist may be able to employ clarification to reveal the unconscious idea. If the free associations are major distortions of the unconscious, that is, if there is strong resistance, then the therapist uses interpretation both to reveal the resistances and to infer the meaning of the association. The therapist's interpretations certainly do not depend only on the free associations. The therapist must also consider the circumstances of the associations, their relationships to what is currently occurring within the therapeutic relationship, and all aspects of the patient's behavior before and after the associative material (Kanzer, 1961).

It would be very useful if the preanalytic assessor were able to decide the degree to which the free associations are substitutions of the unconscious material. Such knowledge would allow the assessor to gain some awareness of the degree to which the patient resists the unconscious. Realistically speaking, however, the preanalytic assessor does not have the time to make such determinations. To assess treatability preanalytically as it relates to the capacity to free associate, all that the assessor can do is simply observe the degree to which the patient free associates, especially in response to silences during the assessment session.

Although the capacity to free associate is of the utmost importance (see Section 3.4), the many variables in the preanalytic assessment period may inhibit the free associations which will freely flow once the patient is in treatment. Thus, the patient who free associates during the assessment period is providing significant evidence that he is treatable, whereas the inability to free associate during the preanalytic assessment period should not by itself balance the judgment towards untreatability.

5.343 THE CAPACITY TO TRANSFORM INSIGHT INTO ADAPTIVE BEHAVIOR

The ultimate goal of psychoanalytic therapy is to transform insight into adaptive behavior so that there is an alleviation of psychological impairments to work and love. The capacity to make such a transformation is a critical requirement which sometimes can be assessed by careful history but usually cannot be evaluated until the psychoanalytic psychotherapy is underway, especially since constructive insight can only be achieved in gradual stages and only when associated with a meaningful affective experience.

Alexander (1944, p. 328; Alexander & French, 1946, p. 98) suggests that "trial interpretations" should be given in preanalytic assessment interviews and then the patient's response to interpretation be assessed as an indicator of the capacity to transform insight into adaptive behavior. Alexander (1944) gives a case history in which the patient responds with hostility to the trial interpretation, showing his inability to cope with the awareness of the psychic truth.

One must be very careful, however, not to jump to conclusions when observing the responses to trial interpretation during a preanalytic assessment session (Eissler, 1950). Such interpretations are made without the benefit of a solid therapeutic relationship and the necessary meaningful affective component that would exist in a successful ongoing psychoanalytic psychotherapy. Furthermore, there are serious risks associated with preanalytic trial interpretations. The untimely interpretation may engender a negative reaction that could interfere with the therapy should the patient be referred to psychoanalytic psychotherapy.

5.344 THE CAPACITY TO MINIMIZE RESISTANCE

> It is easy then to accept the fact shown by daily experience that the outcome of an analytic treatment [psychoanalytic psychotherapy] depends essentially on the strength and on the depth of root of these resistances that bring about an alteration of the ego (Freud, 1937, p. 239).

The degree of potential resistance is one of the most difficult factors to assess, but if accurately assessed is perhaps the most predictive of treatability since the success of the psychoanalytic psychotherapy parallels the success in overcoming the resistance (see Section 3.5 for a discussion of the concept of resistance). The assessor must never underestimate the potential of a given patient for resistance no matter what the apparent high degree of motivation.

> No stronger impression arises from the resistance during the work of analysis [psychoanalytic psychotherapy] than of there being a force which is defending itself by every possible means against recovery and which is absolutely resolved to hold onto illness and suffering (Freud, 1937, p. 242).

Most of what is usually called psychological mindedness is *not* an accurate indicator of potential for resistance. Only by closely examining the defense mechanisms can we predict resistance to treatment. Some defense mechanisms such as rationalization and sublimation are less suggestive of serious resistance than are mechanisms such as denial or projection (Aarons, 1962).

Whereas resistance is broken down by a skillful therapist, it also grows with therapy. In some ways, resistance is at a minimum in the initial interview, since the patient is relatively naive about therapy, and the forces of resistance have not been mobilized by the probing aspects of therapy. The transference is especially involved in this process, a fact reflected in the term "transference resistance," since as the transference becomes more intense, the libidinal and aggressive impulses become stronger, thereby engendering increased resistance. Freud recognized a similar phenomenon in his study of dreams.

> The more that the patient has learned of the practice of dream interpretation, the more obscure do his later dreams as a rule become. All the knowledge acquired [by the patient] about dreams serves only to put dream constructing process on its guard (Freud, 1911b, p. 95).

5.345 THE CAPACITY TO NOT "ACT OUT"

There is a consensus of opinion among psychoanalytic psychotherapists that the capacity to verbalize without "acting out" is a major prerequisite for psychoanalytic psychotherapy. Beyond this generalization, however, there is a wide divergence of opinion among clinicians as to what is meant by acting out and how we can assess this capacity. For the purposes of this book, acting out will be defined as any behavior, in or out of the session, that is the direct result of feelings and thoughts that have arisen as a result of the therapy. Since acting out is a consequence of the psychoanalytic therapy itself, it seems logical to conclude that this capacity cannot be adequately assessed preanalytically. Even if there is a history of a previous course of therapy in which acting out occurred, it is almost impossible to make valid assumptions of what will occur in a new situation or with a different therapist. Furthermore, a certain amount of acting out of transference or of other manifestations of the therapy occurs to some degree in every patient (Brenner, 1976).

Thus, when we discuss acting out as an indication of treatability, what we are really talking about in an abbreviated form is the capacity to minimize acting out so that the therapy and the patient's welfare are not seriously endangered by the patient's behavior. In fact, most clinicians use the term acting out only when referring to behavior that interferes with the progress of therapy, or behavior that is unanalyzable or unmanageable, and assign other labels (for example "psychic growth" or "transference cure") to behavior that arises from the therapeutic relationship but is not an obstacle to the progress of therapy.

As the therapy becomes more intense, there is a progressive urge to act out sexual or aggressive drives or impulses and to seek immediate gratification of those drives. Also, as Freud long ago noted, acting out often takes the form of repeating earlier patterns as a way to resist against remembering and against psychically reexperiencing painful forgotten moments such as those of abandonment, intense loneliness and murderous rage (Freud, 1914a).

The force of this urge to seek gratification or act out resistance should be assessed in relationship to the ego's capacity to keep the urges at an affective or verbal level. If the person's ego is not able to tolerate these urges, or if the ego's strengths are being depleted by preventing other forms of decompensation, the patient may be unsuitable and require some form of supportive treatment (Knight, 1952).

The technique of interpretation makes the unconscious conscious. When this happens "genetic" and "instinctual" regression often occurs and the patient experiences libidinal and aggressive urges demanding relief through action instead of the therapeutic goal of self-understanding. The acting out of reemerged drives may take the form of sexual hyperactivity of the normal or perverted variety, sudden outbursts of feelings, violence towards self or others, or excessive inhibition as a reaction formation to the barely controllable urges (Waldhorn, 1960).

The urge to act out requires some patients to resort to primitive defense mechanisms such as projection, psychotic denial or distortion, which could easily render the patient untreatable. One parameter by which we can assess the capacity not to act out reawakened urges is to evaluate the patient's ability to employ *mature* defense mechanisms such as sublimation or intellectualization to achieve instinctual gratification. In order to make this assessment, we must first be able to categorize defense mechanisms along a developmental hierarchy such as suggested by Vaillant (1971) (see Section 3.6614). This assessment is well worth the effort since, if the patient yields to temptations of these liberated primitive drives, not only his therapy but private and professional circumstances could be directly endangered.

Frequently the urge to act out is a response to an interpretation. Such a response suggests that the urge represents resistance not only to newly conscious material but to thoughts and feelings not yet conscious (Aarons, 1962). Thus, the degree to which the impulsivity is or is not a contraindication to psychoanalytic psychotherapy is a difficult matter. Poor impulse control may suggest a decreased ability to benefit from psychoanalytic psychotherapy or could suggest that the current psychoanalytic psychotherapy is doing more harm than good. On the other hand, the poor impulse control during the preanalytic assessment period or during the course of the therapy could be a resistance to unconscious material and therefore an indication for further interpretive work by the therapist.

The appropriateness or inappropriateness of action over words is not always easy to judge, and the assessor must be very careful not to quickly label someone as untreatable because the person is action oriented. In fact, it is because the tendency to act out is so complicated and poorly understood that I have chosen to place this capacity in the postanalytic assessment category.

It is, in my opinion, impossible to isolate verbal from nonverbal behavior within the psychoanalytic treatment experience. Certain acting out behavior may be a necessary precursor to the patient's acceptance of certain verbal interpretations and meaningful insight. In fact, for many, perhaps all, patients there are certain memories, thoughts or feelings that can never be fully understood, appreciated and resolved unless they are acted out. The goal of psychoanalytic psychotherapy is to liberate the patient from neurotic impulses so that he is free to *choose* behavior. Frequently people cannot choose which behavior they prefer until they have actually performed the action in question. Thus, if a person chooses a "wrong" behavior, it does not necessarily imply poor impulse control or inability to delay gratification.

The tendency to act out is especially prominent among normal and disturbed adolescents. For such patients, knowing is doing, and impulsivity must be seen as an indication for therapy and not a contraindication. Furthermore, since the impulsivity serves a psychic function, it is hard for the patient to give up these tendencies. Thus, again, the assessor is left in the difficult position of deciding whether or not a particular characteristic indicates a need for a therapy or represents evidence suggesting untreatability.

5.35 Treatment Goals of Patient and Assessor

The psychotherapist must always bear in mind the distinction between "treatment goals" and "life goals." As suggested by Ticho (1972), despite overlap, the treatment goals can be distinguished from life goals in that life goals represent the goals that the patient would seek to attain if he could make full use of all of his potential, whereas treatment goals entail the removal of those psychological obstacles to the patient's discovery and utilization of those potentialities that he does possess. If the therapist and patient are not aware of the difference between treatment goals and life goals, they are likely to overestimate what can be achieved in therapy and find themselves continually dissatisfied with the outcome of treatment.*

It is frequently assumed by the uninitiated that insight (see Section 5.2162 for a definition of insight) per se is the treatment goal of psychoanalytic psychotherapy. This assumption is an oversimplification of the curative processes in psychoanalytic psychotherapy and is frequently the "straw man" that is set up and then attacked by critics who demonstrate the clinical ineffectiveness of psychoanalytic treatment (Dewald, 1972). Insight *alone* is not clinically effective, although the potential for insight is a necessary predecessor for the patient to benefit from analytic therapy. The oversimplification regarding insight stems in part from the psychoanalytic topographical perspective (see Section 3.61) which asserts that all that is necessary for cure is to make the unconscious conscious.

The assessor must be aware of the treatment goals achievable by the treatment modality for which the patient is being assessed. Although this question of treatment goals is very complicated, it can be approached from a variety of perspectives, for example, behavioral, environmental, intrapsychic, interpersonal, subjective or metapsychological. Of course, goals of therapy vary with each patient since each person has his own special combination of psychic conflicts. Nevertheless, some generalizations can be made that apply to all patients. Psychoanalytic therapy, by definition (see Section 2.23 and 2.5), always has the goal of an alleviation of intrapsychic conflict both at a conscious and unconscious level. It is expected that symptomatic relief, improved loving and working relationships and psychic growth will soon follow the resolution of intrapsychic conflict (Brenner, 1976).

It should be noted that, regardless of the therapist's orientation, from the "mindlessness" of the behaviorist to the most mentalistic of classical psychoanalysts, all successful therapy results in some eventual changed

---

* For an excellent review of the classical psychoanalytic literature on the subject of treatment goals, see Wallerstein (1965).

external behavior. If the psychic changes engendered by psychotherapy are not reinforced by action, it is unlikely that the therapy has had a meaningful impact.

Although it is essential for the assessor to be aware of the treatment goals *achievable* by psychoanalytic therapy, the assessor or therapist should try to avoid the situation whereby he must decide the degree or quality of environmental or intrapsychic change that is desirable for a given patient. Such treatment goal selection is too directive and can only serve to interfere with the progress of the treatment.* Psychoanalytic psychotherapy is most effective if the assessor or therapist maintains total respect for the patient's right and clinical need to select his own ultimate treatment goals. No one but the patient can ever be fully aware of his intrapsychic struggles nor assimilate the insights achieved in therapy. Thus, ideally speaking, the most treatable situation is one in which only the patient decides what should or should not be accomplished in therapy. The therapist's goal is to help the patient gain freedom from the intrapsychic conflicts that interfere with the patient's capacity to freely choose his goals and behavior. As soon as the assessor or therapist selects the treatment or life goals for the patient, then that very selection has already limited the independence that is necessary for a successful clinical outcome to be achieved.

Carl Rogers (1942), although far from a psychoanalytic therapist, is a constant proponent of this view regarding goals:

> One prominent therapist has stated in a professional meeting that he does not wish to adjust his clients to the status quo—instead he leaves them "healthy rebels." The fact that he regarded it as his prerogative to decide where they should be "left" seems completely to have escaped his notice (1947, p. 113).

Another example of excessive direction of goals is given by Stone in his description of assessing a patient for "brief interpretive psychotherapy":

> One must depend on one's initial interpretations of the entire case more than is necessary in psychoanalysis. As with the working diagnosis of general medicine, it is important to decide which of the

---

* It is not always possible for the assessor to avoid taking an active role in goal selection. For example, see the case history in Section 5.22 where the assessor chose to avoid the investigation of the patient's phobias to save her self-esteem and to prevent her from learning that she would be fired.

patient's dynamic problems are crucial, those whose alteration is most likely to affect the dynamics of his personality and illness and to act on that selection (1951, p. 227).

Although Stone goes on in the next sentence to admonish the reader that, "One should avoid interfering with the patient's way of life unless it is unequivocably pathological . . . ," it seems to me that the assessor cannot help but "interfere" with the patient's autonomy if he takes it upon himself to ". . . decide which of the patient's dynamic problems are crucial."

Psychoanalytic therapy requires that the patient's strengths, not the therapist's, be explored and enhanced. The overall goal of psychoanalytic psychotherapy is to facilitate self-exploration, self-awareness and emotional growth so that the patient will fully understand the workings of his thoughts and feelings and is, accordingly, more able to constructively adjust to the realities of his intrapsychic and external life. On this specific point, there is a considerable degree of agreement between the client-centered, nondirective *goals* of Rogerian counseling (Rogers, 1942, 1947) and the goals of psychoanalytic psychotherapy although, of course, the paths taken vary enormously. Both Rogers and Freud would agree that we can best understand our patients through the patient's intrapsychic frame of reference, that is, through the patient's own eyes.

In conclusion, since we give the responsibility of goal selection to the patient, and since the process of cure is unknown (see Section 3.7 for a brief discussion of cure theory), it seems logical to conclude that, regarding the relationship between goals and treatability, the most the assessor needs to know is whether or not there is some probability that the patient's goals are realistic. In most cases, such an assessment cannot be preanalytically determined.

5.36 *The Capacity to Develop and Maintain the Therapeutic Relationship*

In Chapter 4 we discussed the various aspects of the therapeutic relationship by dividing a therapeutic relationship into four components: transference, therapeutic alliance, narcissistic alliance and real relationship. In this Section we will take a closer look at how the therapeutic relationship is related to treatability, and again, for expository purposes, we will divide the discussion into the four components of the therapeutic relationship.

One of the most frequent criticisms of psychoanalytic psychotherapy is that the treatment demands a relationship with the therapist that many patients are incapable of sustaining, since it is the lack of these very interpersonal capacities that have led the patient to seek the psychological treatment in the first place. This is a valid criticism in that a constructive therapeutic relationship requires psychological and interpersonal strengths, many of which are discussed in this chapter, that many people do not have and, thus, they are not candidates for this kind of treatment. The criticism, however, is often carried to an incorrect extreme by equating the psychological and interpersonal capacities required for treatability with mental health. These critics of psychoanalytic therapy claim that the capacities for treatability are so demanding that the most intensive and expensive treatment is given to the healthiest patients. Such a conclusion is a gross oversimplification and does psychoanalytic psychotherapy a disservice. What I would like to make absolutely clear in this chapter is that the treatable patient must possess certain capacities (some of which can be preanalytically assessed) *and* must be in clinical need of the treatment. The determination of "clinical need," by definition, assumes that the patient is in psychic pain *and* that there is no treatment that would be equally effective, less expensive, less painful or less time-consuming.

Despite what has been said in this chapter (for example in Sections 5.31 and 5.33) about the forces that lead the patient to seek treatment, it is the relationship to the therapist that provides the patient with the strongest motivation to collaborate in psychoanalytic psychotherapy and to withstand the inevitable stress of a successful treatment. In order for the patient to be treatable, he must be able to recognize fully and utilize actively the relationship with the therapist along the four dimensions of the therapeutic relationship: 1) therapeutic alliance, 2) narcissistic alliance, 3) transference neurosis, and 4) real relationship. What makes treatability so demanding is that these four relationships, although requiring antithetical ego functions, must be consistently alternated and blended so that there is a balance that insures the dominance of the observing autonomous ego (Namnum, 1968).

How then are we to expect the patient to participate in the cure, especially if deficiencies in these ego capacities are what have led to the neurosis in the first place? Of course, there is no simple answer to this question, but a partial answer is that we expect the patient to have more ego strengths in the conflict-free spheres than in the areas around which the neurosis has evolved (Greenson, 1967; Hartmann, 1951). The treatable patient will have the capacity to perform the antithetical ego functions as long as those functions do not come too close too quickly to the issues of neurotic conflict. When the various ego functions impinge on the areas of neurotic conflict, there is a reduced elasticity of ego function and a reduced capacity to do the work of psychoanalytic psychotherapy. For example, a patient may be able to treat the therapist in a father transference manner until some issue of oedipal conflict arises, in which case the anxiety of the transference becomes frightening and the patient resorts to a real relationship and resists against the transference neurosis (Greenson, 1967).

5.361 INITIAL REACTION TO THE ASSESSOR

The subjective clinical impressions as well as the empirical research (for example, The Menninger Psychotherapy Research Study [Kernberg et al., 1972]) have demonstrated that the quality of interpersonal relationships is highly correlated with treatability. With some patients, the capacity to develop a therapeutic relationship with the therapist can be preanalytically assessed by closely scrutinizing the way the patient relates and reacts to the preanalytic assessor in the initial few sessions. In fact, if the preanalytic assessor has only a few interviews in which to do the assessment, the patient's relationship to that assessor can be considered current observable fact and may be more reliable than any historical data about past or current relationships. The trust in the assessor and the warmth and intensity of the relationship, although perhaps only a few minutes old, can give the assessor an idea of how much the patient is capable of relating to the therapist. If the patient manifests a significant aloofness, mistrust and other defenses against establishing a meaningful relationship, then he may very likely repeat these patterns towards his therapist and be unable to establish the constructive therapeutic alliance.

Despite the fact that the initial preanalytic assessment sessions may offer valuable data regarding this capacity, I have chosen to consider it in the postanalytic assessment category. Psychoanalytic psychotherapy is a relationship unlike any other. The capacity required to utilize the transference neurosis, therapeutic and narcissistic alliance and real relationship is, in my opinion, for most patients far too complex and cast in far too relatively abstract terms to be adequately evaluated until there is the significant experience within the treatment itself.

5.362 TRANSFERENCE NEUROSIS

The transference neurosis is an "inevitable necessity" (Freud, 1905b, p. 116) in any successful psychoanalytic psychotherapy. As noted by Macalpine (1950), the development of a transference neurosis in psychoanalytic psychotherapy is similar in some ways (although of course more prolonged and gradual) to the state of hypnosis that develops between hypnotist and subject.* In hypnosis the suggestive stimulus fosters regression; in psychoanalytic psychotherapy, it is the infantile analytic setting that the therapist perceptibly and imperceptibly, consciously and unconsciously, establishes. By following this logic, we can assume that one way to assess the capacity to form the transference neurosis is to assess the degree of suggestibility possessed by the patient. The more suggestive the patient, the more likely the patient will regress within the analytic setting so that the person of the therapist begins to be associated with early images (Macalpine, 1950). Suggestibility within the analytic setting is impossible to evaluate preanalytically, although most patients will reveal these phenomena early in the course of treatment.

Another major task of the postanalytic assessor is to distinguish between the patient who transforms from the patient who transfers. The patient who transforms attempts (unconsciously) to change the therapist into someone else in his past or present life. The patient who transfers uses a variety of defense mechanisms including displacement and projection in order to perceive the therapist *as if* he were a significant person in the patient's life, usually a person from early life such as an original love object. Thus, the transformer makes the therapist into another person whereas the transferer knows the therapist is not someone else but still treats him as if he were. The problem for the assessor, however, is that the capacities for transformation and transference take time to express themselves and usually cannot be accurately assessed in a few initial interviews. Nevertheless, the concepts are critical in understanding the psychoanalytic process and at least an attempt should be made to assess their contribution to treatability.

Finally, the reader is referred to our previous discussion of basic trust (Sections 4.221-4.224). As was emphasized in these Sections, it is basic

---

* Acknowledging the similarity to suggestion does not mean agreement with Macalpine's (1950) assertions that transference is an artifically evolved form of regression, idiosyncratic to the psychoanalytic situation (see Section 4.1 for further discussion).

trust that is responsible for the transference being a neurotic (transference neurosis) rather than psychotic (transference psychosis) experience.

5.363 THERAPEUTIC ALLIANCE

As I have already mentioned, no psychoanalytic therapy can succeed unless the patient has the capacity for a therapeutic alliance.

As discussed in Section 4.22, the therapeutic alliance requires the capacity for basis trust *and* secondary trust. Basic trust is necessary for the existence of the transference neurosis, whereas secondary trust is necessary for the transference neurosis to be workable within the therapeutic relationship. The failure to develop secondary trust means that there has occurred premature closure and solidification of internal archaic parental objects. This closed system does not allow for the structural modifications (for example, superego) necessary for development of the therapeutic alliance and resolution of the transference neurosis. The capacities for both basic trust and secondary trust usually cannot be assessed in preanalytic sessions except in those cases where deficiencies are most blatant.

5.3631 *Basic Trust*

Basic trust is essential to treatability since it is only through basic trust that the patient is able to establish and maintain the distinction between transference phenomena and reality.

As mentioned in Section 4.222, basic trust requires successful resolution of preoedipal developmental stages. Many oedipal issues engender a revival and repetition of the dyadic issues. Thus, the successful resolution of the oedipal conflict (age four-five) is, in part, the result of the degree of frustration and anxiety associated with the dyadic preoedipal stage of psychosexual development. If relatively mature object relationships are not first achieved during the pregenital (preoedipal) stage, the psychoanalytic psychotherapy may produce fruitless regression to dyadic issues.

The capacity for basic trust can be postanalytically assessed by observing the patient's willingness to allow himself to relax censoring so as to free associate; to agree to abandon the usual expectations of regular, verbal and perceptual feedback; to accept certain rules of therapy that may at first appear to be illogical or incomprehensible; to accept the limitations of reality; and to distinguish between the mature and primitive aspects of psychic life. Also, the capacity for basic trust can be postanalytically assessed by observing the patient's willingness to separate his wishes from needs; to accept the fact that the therapeutic relationship is in some ways not reciprocal; and to acept the fact that the therapy is unavoidably painful and embarrassing and will not provide immediate gratification.

5.3632 Object Constancy

Clinical observations have repeatedly shown that adults who lack positive mothering in childhood will often be found to be lacking in basic trust and unable to internalize the mothering aspects of the therapeutic relationship. Such patients often are lacking object constancy (see Section 4.223) and are left with a feeling that the therapist has been annihilated or does not exist. People with this kind of past history often not only lack the internalized "good mother" but are incapable of feeling reassured that the therapist and/or external environment will provide what is absent (Adler, 1979; Buie & Adler, 1972).

5.3633 Evocative Memory Capacity

In addition to object constancy, another capacity essential to the existence of basic trust is evocative memory (see Section 4.224). If a patient does not have a stable evocative memory capacity, he will be unable, when under stress, to draw on cathected memories and to be gratified by those memories. Such a patient is left relatively alone with inevitable psychic pain such as that which is engendered by psychoanalytic psychotherapy. Such a person is untreatable.

5.3634 Secondary Trust

In Section 4.221, 4.222, 4.225 and 4.226 we discussed the definitions and ontogeny of basic trust and secondary trust. We can now relate these concepts to treatability.

One of the purposes of the following discussion on secondary trust as it relates to treatability is to help the reader understand what some of the dynamics may be in the following clinical situation, which represents a pattern that I am sure is a very familiar one to all experienced psychoanalytic therapists.

The patient is preanalytically assessed to be an excellent candidate for psychoanalytic psychotherapy. The patient begins treatment, seems to make use of the treatment and even makes constructive changes to alleviate the problems which precipitated the seeking of treatment. Around this time, which may vary from a few months to a few years, the patient seems less involved in the treatment and less willing to do the work of therapy. The patient informs the therapist that things are going much better in his life, he has gained much from the treatment, but he now wishes to terminate and "try it on my own." The therapist reluctantly agrees, realizing that the patient's external situation and symptoms have indeed improved, but yet feeling that the patient never really got involved in the treatment. The therapist feels that the patient never developed a transference neurosis; never really experienced the therapeutic relationship to its fullest extent; never really placed his psychic self in the hands of the therapist. In essence, although the preanalytic assessment that the patient had the capacity for basic trust was an accurate assessment, the patient never really displayed the capacity for secondary trust so that when the time came for the patient to move into this phase of treatment, the patient chose to terminate.

The above clinical situation is one in which the patient shows object constancy, evocative memory and other aspects of object relationships that are characteristic of basic trust. Such patients also manifest, however, a pseudo-alliance in that they are usually performance oriented during the session, often relinquish secrets only so that others are retained, and even often cautiously withhold information. The dominant characteristic of such patients is that they are limited in the degree to which they will transfer or yield control over to other people, including their closest relationships. In essence, these patients lack the capacity for secondary trust.

The therapeutic alliance is a relationship that requires mature ego capacities derived from a relatively later stage in life and is not a function of *only* preoedipal object relationships, that is, the primitive introjections that represent basic trust. If the patient, as a child, closes off the internalized, archaic, parental images, that person is deprived of the capacity to modify those internalized object relationships. Such modifications are necessary for a therapeutic alliance to develop. The patient who insists on primitive parental object relationships will be unable to engage in the relatively mature interpersonal characteristics necessary for the therapeutic alliance since the capacities for a therapeutic alliance develop at a later stage than the development of the primitive parental introjections. To put it in different words, a premature closure of parenting encapsulates the primitive, archaic, parental images, prevents their modifications, obstructs the development of the therapeutic alliance and renders the patient untreatable.

The reader can see from the above discussion that, by our very definition of secondary trust, the therapist cannot preanalytically assess the patient's capacity to develop secondary trust with the therapist until the patient has been in therapy for enough time to overcome the normal reservations that any person may show towards another person whom they have just met. In other words, secondary trust cannot be preanalytically assessed. One of the major problems with the assessment of secondary trust as a capacity of treatability is that many patients, especially the obsessive compulsive types, are people who may strengthen their capacity for secondary trust as a *consequence* of therapy. In fact, many patients seek psychoanalytic therapy because their inability for secondary trust interferes with object relationships and leaves them lonely and dissatisfied (Mehlman, 1976, 1977). Another way of saying the same thing is that such people have developed relatively good primary object relationships based on their capacity for basic trust, but at the same time possess defective secondary object relationships. Thus, the postanalytic assessor (therapist) is in a very difficult situation. If the patient shows deficiencies in the capacity for secondary trust, the therapist has to make the very difficult decision as to what degree that deficiency indicates untreatability or represents an indication for treatment. Of course, what is crucial to this decision is the degree to which the patient possesses the other capacities for treatability which may serve as allies in overcoming the secondary trust deficiencies. There is no simple answer to these problems, and all that can be expected is that the therapist give the patient every benefit of doubt. The therapist should not become impatient with the patient's incapacity to display the secondary trust, but rather realize that whatever capacities the patient may have for secondary trust may take months or years to develop within the therapeutic relationship. It should also be remembered that, if the patient improves his capacities for secondary trust within the therapeutic relationship, there is a tendency for this improved capacity to generalize to object relations outside of the therapeutic relationship. If some generalization occurs, the patient can benefit greatly from the therapeutic situation.

5.3635 *Narcissism and the Therapeutic Alliance*

When a patient seeks treatment, he frequently is feeling the full force of symptoms and is thus more likely to be maximally preoccupied with himself and his narcissistic needs. An attempt should still be made, however, to assess the quality and degree of *premorbid* narcissistic preoccupation, and its relationships to the capacity to utilize the therapeutic relationship. For example, if a woman comes to therapy for a depression precipitated by discovering her husband is having an affair, she may be able to respect her husband and look at what role she has taken in the marital problem. Prospective patients who seem irritated because they cannot get an appointment immediately, or who seek immediate relief from medications or from compulsions such as overeating or overdrinking, should lead us to suspect that they cannot tolerate the inevitable frustration encountered in the relationship with the therapist. Sometimes the presence of empathy, creativity or the acceptance of the finiteness of life are useful parameters indicating a lack of severely pathological narcissism (Schlessinger & Robbins, 1974).

Although we must always be very careful about generalizations in the science and philosophy of human behavior, it is probably safe to say that people who live by the self-centered code of "I have the right to have what I want when I want it" are the same people who most likely lack the capacity for a constructive patient-therapist relationship (Levin, 1960). Such a patient is likely to see psychoanalytic psychotherapy as an experience that is largely characterized by getting something from the therapist instead of the more desirable conceptualization of psychoanalytic psychotherapy as an experience whereby the therapist and patient experience a therapeutic relationship that helps the patient gain something for himself.

The preceding idea is strangely paradoxical. Psychoanalytic psychotherapy is in many ways a very unrealistically self-centered experience, unmatched by any other relationships that the patient has had including those with people who love him most. The therapist tries to *always* put the patient's best interests first and accepts the patient for what he is no matter how repulsive his symptoms, thoughts or feelings may be to other people, and no matter what personal thoughts, feelings or problems the therapist may be experiencing at that time. Furthermore, the therapist is willing to devote hundreds of hours and many years towards helping and empathically understanding the patient. Yet, those patients who are pathologically narcissistic are, in general, the least likely to be satisfied with the treatment, an unfortunate phenomenon since the pathological narcissism is a source of great psychic pain for the patient and is often the consequence of deeper pathogenic elements such as profound guilt and masochism which will not allow the patient to relinquish the punishment of the symptoms (Freud, 1923b; Murray, 1964).

As has been noted many times (e.g., Levin, 1960; Murray, 1964; Stone, 1954), it is not the inability to develop a relationship with the therapist that precludes treatability among the severely narcissistic patients; it is the extremes to which these people relate. At one extreme, these patients exhibit pathetically little investment in their therapist. People lacking the capacity for intense object relationships are unable to be constructively influenced in psychoanalytic psychotherapy (Freud, 1916-1917j).

Narcissistic patients who withdraw libido are relatively less difficult to detect preanalytically. It is much more difficult to assess the narcissistic patient who manifests his disorder at the other extreme, that is, the non-psychotic patient (often called "borderline") who develops an intense primitive and ambivalent relationship with the therapist which then frightens the patient and prevents the patient from further developing or constructively using the alliance, transference or real relationship. These patients may at first glance appear to have the capacity to develop mature object relationships because their history indicates that they have reached out towards other people and actively relate. A course of psychoanalytic psychotherapy, however, may show that such patients relate to other people in a way that is solely for the purpose of satisfying their own narcissistic needs. Once the psychoanalytic psychotherapy is underway, the therapist may discover that the patient is, in fact, not as successful in relating to other people as at first appeared since he often uses primitive defense mechanisms such as denial, devaluation, splitting and projective identification. Patients who use these kinds of defense mechanisms often fail at satisfying relationships with friends, family or therapist because they attribute to other people rejected aspects of themselves, thus depriving the relationship of any supportive value (Adler, 1979; Kernberg, 1967).

5.3636 *Some Concluding Remarks on Therapeutic Alliance*

It should be emphasized that a therapeutic alliance is a consequence as well as a requirement for successful psychoanalytic psychotherapy. If the therapy is progressing successfully, it makes sense that the patient will develop more hopefulness and will solidify the verbal and nonverbal pact made with the therapist. If, on the other hand, the patient does not find the ongoing therapy helpful, in any practical way, it is unreasonable to expect the patient to continue the commitment to the pact made with the therapist. Patients are in treatment in order to achieve more peace of mind and should not be expected to want to engage in the process per se.

Finally, I would like to conclude the discussion on therapeutic alliance by emphasizing my exhortation that, until we know more about the relationships between therapeutic alliance and treatability, the assessor should never reach a judgment of untreatability based on a patient showing no capacity to form a therapeutic alliance with the assessor in the preanalytic assessment sessions. The therapeutic alliance requires secondary trust, a condition that is always, to some degree, a function of the length of a relationship and cannot be expected to develop towards an assessor if that patient has had no previous contact. Adler (1979) proposes that with "primitive" ("borderline") patients, the therapist must help the patient progress through a "developmental sequence" starting first with the establishment of sustaining self-object transference, then to a progressively increasing capacity to appreciate the therapist as a separate and real person, and finally, to a therapeutic alliance as defined in Section 4.21. I submit that this or some other, as yet not understood, developmental sequence also has to occur in all treatable patients.

5.364 *Narcissistic Alliance*

As discussed in Sections 4.2 and 5.363, the therapeutic alliance requires the capacity for both basic trust and secondary trust. The capacity to recognize and utilize the narcissistic alliance does not tell the assessor much about the patient's ability to utilize secondary trust, but does reveal significant information about the patient's capacity for basic trust. In fact, the assessor of treatability can, in the absence of historical data, assume with a relative degree of certainty that if the patient is capable of developing a narcissistic alliance, then that patient has achieved the pregenital developmental tasks necessary for basic trust (Mehlman, 1976).

As mentioned in Section 4.34, the transference neurosis evolves out of the narcissistic alliance, the latter being a necessary precursor to the former. This means that we can logically assume that the capacity to develop a transference neurosis requires the capacity to develop the narcissistic alliance. Also, as mentioned in Section 4.3, a patient develops the narcissistic alliance by relaxing narcissistic defenses and allowing an increase in dependence, closeness and hypercathexis towards the therapist so that, in essence, the narcissistic devices are replaced by the bodily presence of the therapist. Patients who cannot allow such abrogation of narcissistic defenses and replacement by the bodily presence of the therapist are incapable of developing the narcissistic alliance and thus, in turn, incapable of developing the transference neurosis. Such patients can be considered untreatable. Patients, such as overt psychotics, who demonstrate highly developed preformed transferences, or patients with firmly developed narcissistic defenses which will not allow replacement, are people who can be considered untreatable since they are incapable of developing the narcissistic alliance.

In essence then, the patient is not treatable if unable to form a narcissistic alliance. Since the transference neurosis is an essential ingredient of a successful psychoanalytic psychotherapy, and since the transference neurosis evolves out of the narcissistic alliance, the patient must not only have the capacity to develop the narcissistic alliance, but must also have the capacity to convert the primitive narcissitic alliance into the less primitive transference neurosis (Mehlman, 1976).

Before leaving this Section, I would like to repeat what has already been said in Section 4.3. From a practical perspective, one of the most important lessons for the assessor or therapist to learn from our discussions of narcissistic alliance is that the predominant existence of a narcissistic alliance with a preanalytic or postanalytic patient should not lead the assessor or therapist to label the patient "untreatable." Instead, the existence of the narcissistic alliance should be expected, and allowed to flourish, until a significant therapeutic alliance develops (Corwin, 1974). Of course, the longer it takes for the therapeutic alliance and the transference neurosis to evolve out of the narcissistic alliance, the greater the probability of an unworkable therapeutic relationship (Greenson, 1967; Mehlman, 1976; Zetzel, 1965).

5.365 The Real Relationship

Most therapists no longer consider that the only meaningful relationship between patient and therapist is the transference and that the only important interventions are interpretations of the transference neurosis. Nevertheless, many contemporary assessors and therapists still tend to underestimate the capacity to recognize fully and to utilize the real relationship as a means to promote psychic growth within the psychoanalytic situation. The contemporary neglect of the real relationship is reminiscent of Freud's early neglect of the value of the transference and countertransference, a neglect he partially corrected with his publication of the Dora case (Freud, 1905a; Marcus, 1976; Muslin & Gill, 1978; Rogow, 1978).

It is unclear why contemporary assessors and therapists neglect the real relationship. Or, perhaps it is because Freud himself, despite volumes of writings, never published a description of how he incorporated himself as a real person into the psychoanalytic situation. Despite this lack, Freud certainly did recognize the existence of the real relationship:

> Furthermore . . . not every good relation between an analyst and his subject during and after analysis was to be regarded as the transference; there were also friendly relations which were based on reality and which proved to be valuable (1937, p. 222).

We also learn from Freud's patients that he was far from a "mirror" to them, but rather related to them realistically, personably and with warmth (Blanton, 1971; Kardiner, 1977; Racker, 1968).

An underestimation of the capacity to form a real relationship is especially unfortunate because, without the capacity to fully recognize and utilize the real relationship, the patient is unable to form the therapeutic alliance and to benefit from the transference neurosis (Greenson, 1965, 1967, 1970b, 1971, 1972; Greenson & Wexler, 1969, 1970; Dewald, 1976).

The assessor must strictly bear in mind the different components of the therapeutic relationship (transference neurosis, therapeutic alliance, narcissistic alliance and real relationship) and not mistake one for the other. Some patients can form a meaningful real relationship and transference neurosis, but do not have the ego and superego strength to develop a constructive therapeutic alliance. Other patients have the ability to relate meaningfully in the real relationship and even some capacity for a beginning therapeutic alliance but are terrified to even partially and transiently abandon reality testing and experience a transference neurosis.

Both these groups are untreatable, an idea introduced by Freud when he tried to distinguish between the treatable "transference neuroses" and untreatable "narcissistic neuroses" as diagnostic entities (Greenson, 1967, p. 207).

REFERENCES

AARONS, Z. A. (1962), Indications for analysis and problems of analyzability (with a discussion by Sidney Levin). *Psychoanalytic Quarterly*, 31:514-531.

ABRAHAM, K. (1919), The applicability of psychoanalytic treatment to patients at an advanced age. In: *Selected Papers On Psychoanalysis*. London: Hogarth Press, 1927.

ADLER, G. (1979), The myth of the alliance with borderline patients. *American Journal of Psychiatry*, 136 (5):642-646.

AICHHORN, A. (1935), *Wayward Youth*. New York: Viking Press.

AINSLIE, G. (1975), Specious rewards: A behavioral theory of impulsiveness and impulse control. *Psychological Bulletin*, 82:463-486.

AINSLIE, G. & SCHAEFER, E. (1981), The application of economic concepts to the motivational conflict in alcoholism. In: Gottheil, E., McLellan, A. T. and Druley, K. (Eds.), *Patient Needs and Treatment Methods*. New York: Pergamon Press.

ALEXANDER, F. G. (1944), The indications for psychoanalytic therapy. *Bulletin of the New York Academy of Medicine*, 20:319-332.

——— (1953), Current views on psychotherapy. *Psychiatry*, 16:113-122.

——— (1954a), Some quantitative aspects of psychoanalytic technique. *Journal of the American Psychoanalytic Association*, 2:685-701.

——— (1954b), Psychoanalysis and psychotherapy. *Journal of the American Psychoanalytic Association*, 2:722-733.

——— (1956), Two forms of regression and their therapeutic implications. *Psychoanalytic Quarterly*, 25:178-196.

ALEXANDER, F. G. & FRENCH, T. M. (1946), *Psychoanalytic Therapy, Principles and Application*. New York: Ronald Press.

ANDERSSON, O. (1962), *Studies in the prehistory of psychoanalysis. The etiology of psychoneurosis and some related themes in Sigmund Freud's writings and letters, 1886-1896*. Stockholm: Svenska Bokforlaget/Norstedts Bonniers, pp. VIII + 237.

APPEL, K. E., LHAMON, W. T., MYERS, J. M., & HARVEY, W. A. (1953), Long-term psychotherapy. *Proceedings Association for Research in Nervous and Mental Disease*, 31:21-34.

APPELBAUM, S. A. (1973), Psychological mindedness: Word, concept and essence. *International Journal of Psychoanalysis*, 54:35-46.

ARLOW, J. A. & BRENNER, C. (1964), Psychoanalytic concepts and the structural theory. *Journal of the American Psychoanalytic Association*, Monograph Series No. 3. New York: International Universities Press.

BACHRACH, H. M. & LEAFF, L. A. (1978), "Analyzability": A systematic review of the clinical and quantitative literature. *Journal of the American Psychoanalytic Association*, 26 (4):881-920.

BAK, R. C. (1970), Psychoanalysis today. *Journal of the American Psychoanalytic Association*, 18:3-23.

BALINT, A. & BALINT, M. (1939), On transference and countertransference. *International Journal of Psycho-Analysis*, 20 (3&4):223-230.

221

BALKANYI, C. (1964), On verbalization. *International Journal of Psycho-Analysis,* 45:64-74.

BASESCU, S. (1977), Anxieties in the analyst. In: K. Frank (Ed.), *The Human Dimension in Psychoanalytic Practice.* New York: Grune & Stratton.

BELLAK, L. (1961), Free association: Conceptual and clinical aspects. *International Journal of Psycho-Analysis,* 42:9-20.

BENEDEK, T., as reported by Ludwig, O. (1954), IV. Psychoanalysis and psychotherapy: Dynamic criteria for treatment choice. *Journal of the American Psychoanalytic Association,* 2:346-350.

BENJAMIN, J. D. (1947), Psychoanalysis and nonanalytic psychotherapy. *Psychoanalytic Quarterly,* 16:169-176.

BEREZIN, M. A. (1977), Normal psychology of the aging process revisited—II. The fate of narcissism in old age: Clinical case reports. *Journal of Geriatric Psychiatry,* X (1):9-26.

———— (1978), The elderly person. In: A. M. Nicholi (Ed.), *The Harvard Guide to Modern Psychiatry.* Cambridge, MA and London, England: The Belknap Press of Harvard University Press, pp. 541-549.

BEREZIN, M. A. & CATH, S. H., eds. (1965), *Geriatric Psychiatry.* New York: International Universities Press.

BEREZIN, M. A. & FERN, D. J. (1967), Persistence of early emotional problems in a seventy-year-old woman. *Journal of Geriatric Psychiatry,* 1:45-60.

BERGMANN, M. S. & HARTMAN, F. R., eds. (1976), *The Evolution of Psychoanalytic Technique.* New York: Basic Books.

BERLINER, B. (1941), Short psychoanalytic psychotherapy: Its possibilities and its limitations. *Bulletin of the Menninger Clinic,* 5:204-213.

BERNHEIM, H. (1886), *De la suggestion et de ses applications à la thérapeutique.* Paris: Octave Doin.

BIBRING, E. (1936), A contribution to the subject of transference-resistance. *International Journal of Psycho-Analysis,* 17:181-189.

———— (1937), Symposium on the theory of the therapeutic results of psychoanalysis. *International Journal of Psycho-Analysis,* 18:170-189.

———— (1954), Psychoanalysis and the dynamic psychotherapies. *Journal of the American Psychoanalytic Association,* 2:745-770.

BIRD, B. (1972), Notes on transference: Universal phenomenon and hardest part of analysis. *Journal of the American Psychoanalytic Association,* 20:267-301.

BLAIS, A. & GEORGES, J. (1969), Psychiatric emergencies in a general hospital outpatient department. *Canadian Psychiatric Association Journal,* 14:23-133.

BLANTON, S. (1971), *Diary of My Analysis with Sigmund Freud.* New York: Hawthorn.

BLAU, D. (1967), The loneliness and death of an old man: Three years of psychotherapy of an eighty-one-year-old depressed patient: Discussion. *Journal of Geriatric Psychiatry,* 1:38-40.

BLAU, D. & BEREZIN, M. A. (1975), Neurosis and character disorders. In: J. Howells (Ed.), *Modern Perspectives in the Psychiatry of Old Age.* New York: Brunner/Mazel.

BLUM, H. (1971), On the conceptions and development of the transference neurosis. *Journal of the American Psychoanalytic Association,* 19:41-53.

BLUM, R. (1966), Psychoanalytic views of alcoholism. *Quarterly Journal of Studies on Alcohol,* 27:259-299.

BONAPARTE, M. (1952), Some biopsychical aspects of sado-masochism. *International Journal of Psycho-Analysis,* 33:373-384.

BORING, E. G. (1950), *A History of Experimental Psychology,* Second Edition. New York: Appleton-Century Crofts.

BOUVET, M. (1958), Technical variation and the concept of distance. *International Journal of Psycho-Analysis,* 39:211-221.

BRENNER, C. (1976), *Psychoanalytic Technique and Psychic Conflict.* New York: International Universities Press.

BREUER, J. & FREUD, S. (1893), On the psychical mechanism of hysterical phenomena: Preliminary communication. *Standard Edition,* 2:1-19. London: Hogarth Press, 1955.

———— (1895), Studies on Hysteria. *Standard Edition,* 2:1-310. London: Hogarth Press, 1955.

BRODY, C. (1949), Fee charging—A dynamic in the casework process. *Social Casework,* 30:65-71.

BROMBERG, W. (1975), *From Shaman to Psychotherapist: A History of the Treatment of Mental Illness.* Chicago: Henry Reginery Company.

BROOKS, L. (1969), A case of eroticized transference in a 73-year-old woman. *Journal of Geriatric Psychiatry,* 2:150-162.

BROWN, J. & KOSTERLITZ, N. (1964), Selection and treatment of psychiatric outpatients. *Archives of General Psychiatry,* 11:425-437.

BUGENTAL, J. F. T. (1964), The person who is the psychotherapist. *Journal of Consulting Psychology,* 28 (3):272-277.

BUIE, D. H. & ADLER, G. (1972), The uses of confrontation with borderline patients. *International Journal of Psychoanalytic Psychotherapy,* 1 (3):90-108.

CARKHUFF, R. & PIERCE, R. (1967), Differential effects of therapist race and social class upon depth of self-exploration in the initial clinical interview. *Journal of Consulting Psychology,* 31:632-634.

CHASSELL, J. O. (1949), Psychoanalysis and psychotherapy. *Bulletin of the American Psychoanalytic Association,* 5 (3):60-64.

———— as reported by English, O. S. (1953), The essentials of psychotherapy as viewed by the psychoanalyst. *Journal of the American Psychoanalytic Association,* 1:550-561.

CHODOFF, P. (1964), Psychoanalysis and fees. *Comprehensive Psychiatry,* 5:137-145.

———— (1978), Psychiatry and the fiscal third party. *American Journal of Psychiatry,* 135:10, 1141-1147.

CORWIN, H. A. (1972), The scope of therapeutic confrontation from routine to heroic. *International Journal of Psychoanalytic Psychotherapy,* 1:68-89.

———— (1974), The narcissistic alliance and progressive transference neurosis in serious regressive states. *International Journal of Psychoanalytic Psychotherapy,* 3:299-316.

COUCH, A. S. (1979), *Therapeutic Functions of the Real Relationship in Analysis.* Paper presented at the Scientific Meeting, Boston Psychoanalytic Society and Institute, Inc., January 10, 1979.

DA SILVA, G. (1967), The loneliness and death of an old man: Three year's psychotherapy of an eighty-one-year-old depressed patient. *Journal of Geriatric Psychiatry,* 1:5-27.

DEUTSCH, F. (1949), *Applied Psychoanalysis: Selected Objectives of Psychotherapy.* New York: Grune & Stratton.

DEWALD, P. A. (1972), *The Psychoanalytic Process.* New York: Basic Books.

———— (1976), Transference regression and real experience in the psychoanalytic process. *Psychoanalytic Quarterly,* 45:213-230.

DIATKINE, R. (1968), Indications and contraindications for psychoanalytical treatment. *International Journal of Psycho-Analysis,* 29:266-270.

EISSLER, K. R. (1950), The Chicago institute of psychoanalysis and the sixth period of the development of psychoanalytic technique. *Journal of General Psychology,* 42:103-157.

——— (1953), The effect of the structure of the ego on psychoanalytic technique. *Journal of the American Psychoanalytic Association,* 1:104-143.

——— (1958), Notes on problems of technique in psychoanalytic treatment of adolescents with some remarks on perversions. *The Psychoanalytic Study of the Child,* 13:223-254. New York: International Universities Press.

——— (1974), On some theoretical and technical problems regarding the payment of fees for psychoanalytical treatment. *International Review of Psychoanalysis* 1:73-101.

EKSTEIN, R. (1956), Psychoanalytic techniques. In: D. Brower and L. Abt (Eds.), *Progress in Clinical Psychology.* New York: Grune & Stratton, 2:79-97.

ELLENBERGER, H. (1970), *The Discovery of the Unconscious: The History and Evolution of Dynamic Psychiatry.* New York: Basic Books.

ENGEL, G. L. (1962), *Psychological Development in Health and Disease.* Philadelphia: W. B. Saunders.

——— (1968), Some obstacles to the development of research in psychoanalysis. *Journal of the American Psychoanalytic Association,* 16:195-204.

ENGLISH, O. S. (1953), The essentials of psychotherapy as viewed by the psychoanalyst. *Journal of the American Psychoanalytic Association,* 1:550-561.

ERIKSON, E. H. (1950), *Childhood and Society.* New York: W. W. Norton.

——— ed. (1978), *Adulthood.* New York: W. W. Norton.

ERLE, J. B. & GOLDBERG, D. A. (1979), Problems in the assessment of analyzability. *Psychoanalytic Quarterly,* Jan., 48-84.

EVANS, W. N. (1953), Evasive speech as a form of resistance. *Psychoanalytic Quarterly,* 22:548-560.

FEATHER, B. W. & RHOADS, J. M. (1972), Psychodynamic behavior therapy I and II. *Archives of General Psychiatry,* 26:496-511.

FELDMAN, D. (1968), Results of psychoanalysis in clinical case assignments. *Journal of the American Psychoanalytic Association,* 16:274-300.

FENICHEL, O. (1941), *Problems of Psychoanalytic Technique.* Albany, New York: The Psychoanalytic Quarterly.

——— (1945), *The Psychoanalytic Theory of Neurosis.* New York: W. W. Norton.

——— (1954), Brief psychotherapy. In *Collected Papers,* second series. New York: W. W. Norton and Co.

FERENCZI, S. (1919), Abuse of free association. In: *Selected papers of Sandor Ferenczi, M.D. Vol. 2. Further contributions to the theory and technique of psychoanalysis.* New York: Basic Books, pp. 177-189.

FERENCZI, S. & RANK, O. (1925), *The Development of Psychoanalysis.* New York and Washington: Nervous and Mental Disease Publishing Company.

FINE, R. (1979), *A History of Psychoanalysis.* New York: Columbia University Press.

FINGERT, H. H. (1952), Comments on the psychoanalytic significance of the fee. *Bulletin of the Menninger Clinic,* 16:98-104.

FLEMING, J. (1975), Some observations on object constancy in the psychoanalysis of adults. *Journal of the American Psychoanalytic Association,* 23:743-759.

FRAIBERG, S. (1969), Libidinal object constancy and mental representation. *The Psychoanalytic Study of the Child,* 24:9-47. New York: International Universities Press.

FRANK, J. D. (1971), Therapeutic factors in psychotherapy. *American Journal of Psychotherapy,* 25:350-361.

——— (1974), How psychotherapy heals. *Henry Ford Hospital Medical Journal,* 22 (2): 71-79.

FRANK, J. D., GLIEDMAN, L. H., IMBER, S. D., NASH, E. H., & STONE, A. R. (1957), Why patients leave psychotherapy. *American Medical Association Archives of Neurology and Psychiatry*, 77:283-299.

FRANK, K. ed. (1977), *The Human Dimension in Psychoanalytic Practice*. New York: Grune & Stratton.

FREUD, A. (1936), *The Ego and the Mechanisms of Defense*. London: Hogarth Press, 1937.

——— (1946), *The Psychoanalytical Treatment of Children*. New York: International Universities Press.

——— (1951), Observations on child development. *The Psychoanalytic Study of the Child*, 6:18-30. New York: International Universities Press.

——— (1954a), Problems of technique in adult analysis. In: *Indications for Child Analysis*. London: Hogarth Press, 1969.

——— (1954b), The widening scope of indications for psychoanalysis. *Journal of the American Psychoanalytic Association*, 2:607-620.

——— (1958), Child observation and prediction of development: A memorial lecture in honor of Ernst Kris. *The Psychoanalytic Study of the Child*, 13:92-116. New York: International Universities Press.

——— (1960), Discussion of grief and mourning in infancy, by John Bowlby. In: *The Psychoanalytic Study of the Child*, Vol. XV. New York: International Universities Press.

——— (1963), Regression as a principle in mental development. *Bulletin of the Menninger Clinic*, 27:126-139.

FREUD, S. (1888), Preface to the Translation of Bernheim's Suggestion. *Standard Edition*, 1:71-86. London: Hogarth Press, 1966.

——— (1894), The neuro-psychoses of defense. *Standard Edition*, 3:41-62. London: Hogarth Press, 1953.

——— (1895), Project for a scientific psychology. *Standard Edition*, 7:1-123. London: Hogarth Press, 1953.

——— (1897), Letter of October 27, 1897. *Standard Edition*, 1:266. London: Hogarth Press, 1966.

——— (1898), Sexuality in the aetiology of the neuroses. *Standard Edition*, 3:261-286. London: Hogarth Press, 1962.

——— (1900), The interpretation of dreams. *Standard Edition*, 4 & 5. London: Hogarth Press, 1953.

——— (1904), Freud's psychoanalytic procedure. *Standard Edition*, 7:247-254. London: Hogarth Press, 1953.

——— (1905a), Fragment of an analysis of a case of hysteria. *Standard Edition*, 7:1-122. London: Hogarth Press, 1953.

——— (1905b), On psychotherapy. *Standard Edition*, 7:255-269. London: Hogarth Press, 1953.

——— (1905c), Jokes and their relation to the unconscious. *Standard Edition*, 8:1-247. London: Hogarth Press, 1960.

——— (1908), Character and anal erotism. *Standard Edition*, 9:167-177. London: Hogarth Press, 1959.

——— (1910), Five lectures on psycho-analysis. *Standard Edition*, 2:1-56. London: Hogarth Press, 1955.

——— (1911a), Psycho-analytic notes on an autobiographical account of a case of paranoia. *Standard Edition*, 12:3-84. London: Hogarth Press, 1958.

——— (1911b), The handling of dream interpretation in psychoanalysis. *Standard Edition*, 12:89-97. London: Hogarth Press, 1958.

────── (1912), The dynamics of transference. *Standard Edition*, 12:97-108. London: Hogarth Press, 1958.

────── (1913a), On beginning the treatment (Further recommendations on the technique of psycho-analysis, I). *Standard Edition*, 12:121-144. London: Hogarth Press, 1958.

────── (1913b), Totem and taboo. *Standard Edition*, 13:1-161. London: Hogarth Press, 1955.

────── (1914a), Remembering, repeating and working-through (Further recommendations on the technique of psycho-analysis, II). *Standard Edition*, 12:145-157. London: Hogarth Press, 1958.

────── (1914b), On narcissism: An introduction. *Standard Edition*, 14:67-105. London: Hogarth Press, 1957.

────── (1914c), On the history of the psycho-analytic movement. *Standard Edition*, 14:1-67. London: Hogarth Press, 1957.

────── (1915a), Instincts and their vicissitudes. *Standard Edition*, 14:111-140. London: Hogarth Press, 1957.

────── (1915b), Observations on transference-love (Further recommendations on the technique of psycho-analysis III). *Standard Edition*, 12:157-172. London: Hogarth Press, 1958.

────── (1915c), Repression. *Standard Edition*, 14:141-158. London: Hogarth Press, 1957.

────── (1915d), Thoughts for the times on war and death. *Standard Edition*, 14:273-301. London: Hogarth Press, 1957.

────── (1916-1917a), Resistance and repression. *Standard Edition*, 16:286-303. London: Hogarth Press, 1963.

────── (1916-1917b), Some thoughts on development and regression-aetiology. *Standard Edition*, 16:339-358. London: Hogarth Press, 1963.

────── (1916-1917c), Introductory lecture on psycho-analysis. Part I, Lecture I. Introduction. *Standard Edition*, 15:15-24. London: Hogarth Press, 1961.

────── (1916-1917d), Introductory lectures on psycho-analysis, Part I, Lecture VII, The manifest content of dreams and the latent dream-thoughts. *Standard Edition*, 15:113-126. London: Hogarth Press, 1961.

────── (1916-1917e), Introductory lectures on psycho-analysis, Part II, Lecture XIV, Wish fulfillment. *Standard Edition*, 15:213-228. London: Hogarth Press, 1961.

────── (1916-1917f), Introductory Lectures on psycho-analysis, Part II, Lecture XIII, The archaic features and infantilism of dreams. *Standard Edition*, 15:199-213. London: Hogarth Press, 1961.

────── (1916-1917g), Introductory lectures on psycho-analysis, Part II, lecture XXIII, The paths to the formation of symptoms. *Standard Edition*, 16:358-378. London: Hogarth Press.

────── (1916-1917h), Introductory lectures on psycho-analysis, Part III, Lecture XVI. Psycho-analysis and psychiatry. *Standard Edition*, 16:234-256. London: Hogarth Press, 1963.

────── (1916-1917i), Introductory lectures on psycho-analysis. Part III. Lecture XXIV. The common neurotic state. *Standard Edition*, 16:378-391. London: Hogarth Press, 1963.

────── (1916-1917j), Introductory lectures on psycho-analysis. Part III, Lecture XXVII, Transference. *Standard Edition*, 16:431-447. London: Hogarth Press, 1963.

────── (1916-1917k). Introductory lectures on psycho-analysis. Part III, Lecture XXVIII, Analytic therapy. *Standard Edition*, 16:448-463.

────── (1917), Mourning and melancholia. *Standard Edition*, 14:237-259. London: Hogarth Press, 1957.

——— (1918), From the history of an infantile neurosis. *Standard Edition,* 17:1-123. London: Hogarth Press.

——— (1919), Lines of advance in psycho-analytic therapy. *Standard Edition,* 17:157-168. London: Hogarth Press, 1955.

——— (1920a), Beyond the pleasure principle. *Standard Edition,* 18:1-65. London: Hogarth Press, 1955.

——— (1920b), A note on the prehistory of the technique of analysis. *Standard Edition,* 18:263-266. London: Hogarth Press, 1955.

——— (1921), Group psychology and the analysis of the ego. *Standard Edition,* 18:65-145. London: Hogarth Press, 1955.

——— (1923a), Two encyclopedia articles. *Standard Edition,* 18:235-263. London: Hogarth Press, 1955.

——— (1923b), The ego and the id. *Standard Edition,* 19:1-60. London: Hogarth Press, 1961.

——— (1925a), An autobiographical study. *Standard Edition,* 20:1-71. London: Hogarth Press, 1959.

——— (1925b), Negation. *Standard Edition,* 19:235-241. London: Hogarth Press, 1961.

——— (1926a), Inhibitions, symptoms and anxiety. *Standard Edition,* 20:75-173. London: Hogarth Press, 1959.

——— (1926b), Question of lay analysis. *Standard Edition,* 20:177-250. London: Hogarth Press, 1959.

——— (1933), New Introductory lectures on psycho-analysis. *Standard Edition,* 22:5-249. London: Hogarth Press, 1964.

——— (1937), Analysis terminable and interminable. *Standard Edition,* 22:209-255. London: Hogarth Press, 1964.

——— (1938), An outline of psycho-analysis. *Standard Edition,* 23:139-205. London: Hogarth Press, 1964.

——— (1939), Moses and monotheism: Three essays. *Standard Edition,* 23:1-139. London: Hogarth Press, 1964.

——— (1940), An outline of psychoanalysis. *Standard Edition,* 23:139-209. London: Hogarth Press, 1964.

FRIEDMAN, L. (1969), The therapeutic alliance. *International Journal of Psycho-Analysis,* 50:139-153.

FROMM-REICHMANN, F. (1950), *Principles of Intensive Psychotherapy.* Chicago: University of Chicago Press.

——— (1954), Psychoanalytic and general dynamic conceptions of theory and of therapy. Differences and similarities. *Journal of the American Psychoanalytic Association,* 2:711-721.

FUERST, R. A. (1938), Problems of short time psychotherapy. *American Journal of Orthopsychiatry,* 8:260-264.

GALTON, F. (1879), Psychometric experiments. *Brain,* II (July):151.

GEDO, J. (1962), A note on nonpayment of psychiatric fees. *International Journal of Psycho-Analysis,* 44:368-371.

GENDLIN, E. T., BEEBE, J., CASSENS, J., KLEIN, M., & OBERLANDER, M. (1968), Focusing ability in psychotherapy, personality and creativity. In: J. M. Schlein (Ed.), *Research in Psychotherapy.* Washington, D.C.: American Psychological Association, 3:217-241.

GERSON, S. & BASSUK, E. (1980), Psychiatric emergencies: An overview. *The American Journal of Psychiatry,* 137:1-11.

GILL, M. M. (1951), Ego psychology and psychotherapy. *Psychoanalytic Quarterly,* 20:62-71.

—— as reported by English, O. S. (1953), The essentials of psychotherapy as viewed by the psychoanalyst. *Journal of the American Psychoanalytic Association,* 1:550-561.

—— (1954), Psychoanalysis and exploratory psychotherapy. *Journal of the American Psychoanalytic Association,* 2:771-797.

—— (1980), Psychoanalysis and psychotherapy: 1954-1979. Unpublished manuscript. A revised version is currently being submitted to *Psychoanalytic Quarterly.*

GILL, M. & BRENMAN, M. (1961), *Hypnosis and Related States.* New York: International Universities Press.

GILL, M. M. NEWMAN, R., & REDLICH, F. (1954), *The Initial Interview in Psychiatric Practice.* New York: International Universities Press.

GITELSON, M. (1951), Psychoanalysis and dynamic psychiatry. *Archives of Neurology and Psychiatry,* 66:280-288.

—— (1952), The emotional position of the analyst in the psychoanalytic situation. *International Journal of Psycho-Analysis,* 33:1-2.

—— (1965), A transference reaction in a sixty-year-old woman. In: M. A. Berezin and S. H. Cath (Eds.), *Geriatric Psychiatry: Grief, Loss, and Emotional Disorders in the Aging Process.* New York: International Universities Press.

GLOVER, E. (1928), *The Technique of Psychoanalysis.* London: Bailliere, Tindall & Cox.

—— (1931), The therapeutic effect of inexact interpretation: A contribution to the theory of suggestion. *International Journal of Psycho-Analysis,* 12:397-411.

—— (1937), Symposium theory on the therapeutic results of psychoanalysis. *International Journal of Psycho-Analysis,* 18(1-3):25-192.

—— (1956), The indications for psychoanalysis. In: *On the Early Development of the Mind.* New York: International Universities Press, pp. 406-420.

—— (1960), Psychoanalysis and psychotherapy. *British Journal of Medical Psychology,* 33:73-82.

GOLDFARB, A. I. (1962), The psychotherapy of elderly patients. In: H. T. Blumenthal (Ed.), *Medical and Clinical Aspects of Aging.* New York: Columbia University Press.

GOULD, R. (1972), The phases of adult life: A study in development psychology. *American Journal of Psychiatry,* 129(5):33-43.

GREENACRE, P. (1952), *Trauma, Growth and Personality.* London: Hogarth Press. New York: International Universities Press, 1969.

—— (1954), The role of transference. Practical considerations in relation to psychoanalytic therapy. *Journal of the American Psychoanalytic Association,* 2:671-684.

—— (1959), Certain technical problems in the transference relationship. *Journal of the American Psychoanalytic Association,* 7:484-502.

GREENSON, R. R. (1965), The working alliance and the transference neurosis. *Psychoanalytic Quarterly,* 34:155-181.

—— (1966), That "impossible" profession. *Journal of the American Psychoanalytic Association,* 14(1):9-27.

—— (1967), *The Technique and Practice of Psychoanalysis,* Vol. 1. New York: International Universities Press.

—— (1970a), Plenary Session of the 26th International Psycho-Analytical Congress, Rome, 28 July 1969 Discussion of the 'Non-Transference Relationship in the Psychoanalytic Situation'. *International Journal of Psycho-Analysis,* 51:143-150.

—— (1970b), The non-transference relationship in the psychoanalytic situation. *International Journal of Psycho-Analysis,* 51:143-145, 147-150. (Discussion paper)

—— (1971), The real relationship between patient and psychoanalyst. In: M. Kanzer

(Ed.), *The Unconscious Today*. New York: International Universities Press, pp. 213-232.

——— (1972), Beyond transference and interpretation. *International Journal of Psycho-Analysis*, 53:213-217.

GREENSON, R. R. & WEXLER, M. (1969), The non-transference relationship in the psychoanalytic situation. *International Journal of Psycho-Analysis*, 50:27-39.

——— (1970), Discussion of "the non-transference relationship in the psychoanalytic situation." *International Journal of Psycho-Analysis*, 51:143-150.

GREENSPAN, S. & CULLANDER, C. (1973), A systematic metapsychological assessment of the personality—Its application to the problem of analyzability. *Journal of the American Psychoanalytic Association*, 21:303-327.

GROTJAHN, M. (1940), Psychoanalytic investigation of a seventy-one-year-old man with senile dementia. *Psychoanalytic Quarterly*, 9:80-97.

——— (1955), Analytic psychotherapy with the elderly, I. The sociological background of aging in America. *Psychoanalytic Review*, 42:419-427.

GUNTRIP, H. (1975), My experience of analysis with Fairbairn and Winnicott. (How complete a result does psychoanalytic therapy achieve?) *International Review of Psychoanalysis*, 2:145-156.

GURMAN, A. S. (1978), Contemporary marital therapies: A critique and comparative analysis of psychoanalytic, behavioral and systems theory approaches. In: T. J. Paolino, Jr. and B. S. McCrady (Eds.), *Marriage and Marital Therapy: Psychoanalytic, Behavioral and Systems Theory Perspectives*. New York: Brunner/Mazel, 445-566.

GUTHEIL, T. G. & HAVENS, L. L. (1979), The therapeutic alliance: Contemporary meanings and confusions. *International Review of Psychoanalysis*, 6:467-481.

GUTMANN, D. (1975), Parenthood: A key to the comparative psychology of the life cycle. In: N. Datan and L. Ginsberg (Eds.), *Life-Span Development Psychology*. New York: Academic Press.

GUTTMAN, S. (1960), Scientific proceedings. Panel reports. Criteria for analyzability. *Journal of the American Psychoanalytic Association*, 8:141-151.

——— (1968), Indications and contraindications for psychoanalytic treatment. *International Journal of Psycho-Analysis*, 49:254-255.

HAAK, N. (1957), Comments in the analytical situation. *International Journal of Psycho-Analysis*, 38:183-195.

HAMBURG, D. A., BIBRING, G. L., FISHER, C., STANTON, A. II., WALLERSTEIN, R. S., WEINSTOCK, H. I., & HAGGARD, E. (1967), Report of ad hoc committee on central fact gathering data of the American Psychoanalytic Association. *Journal of the American Psychoanalytic Association*, 15:841-861.

HARTMANN, H. (1939), *Ego Psychology and the Problem of Adaption*. New York: International Universities Press, 1958.

——— (1950), Comments on the psychoanalytic theory of the ego. *The Psychoanalytic Study of the Child*, 5:74-96. New York: International Universities Press.

——— (1951), Technical implications of ego psychology. *Psychoanalytic Quarterly*, 20:31-43.

——— (1952), The mutual influences in the development of the ego and the id. In: *Essays on Ego Psychology*. New York: International Universities Press, 1964.

——— (1956), Development of the ego concept in Freud's work. *International Journal of Psycho-Analysis*, 37:425-438.

——— (1958), Comments on the scientific aspects of psychoanalysis. *The Psychoanalytic Study of the Child*, 13:127-146. New York: International Universities Press.

—— (1964), Technical implications of ego psychology. In: *Essays on Ego Psychology*. New York: International Universities Press.

HAUSER, S. T. (1968), The psychotherapy of a depressed aged woman. *Journal of Geriatric Psychiatry*, 2:62-87.

HEIMAN, M. as reported by English, O. S. (1953), The essentials of psychotherapy as viewed by the psychoanalyst. *Journal of the American Psychoanalytic Association*, 1:550-561.

HELLMAN, I. (1954), Some observations on mothers of children with intellectual inhibitions. *The Psychoanalytic Study of the Child*, 9:259-274. New York: International Universities Press.

HENDRICK, I. (1958), *Facts and Theories of Psychoanalysis*. New York: Alfred A. Knopf.

HILLES, L. (1971), The clinical management of the nonpaying patient: A case study. *Bulletin of the Menninger Clinic*, 35:2, 98-112.

HOLLINGSHEAD, A. & REDLICH, F. (1958), *Social Class and Mental Illness*. New York: John Wiley & Sons.

HORNEY, K. (1939), *New Ways in Psychoanalysis*. New York: W. W. Norton.

HOWARD, K. I., KRAUSE, M. S., & ORLINSKY, D. E. (1969), Direction of affective influence in psychotherapy. *Journal of Consulting and Clinical Psychology*, 33(5):614-620.

HOWARD, K. I., ORLINSKY, D. E., & HILL, J. A. (1970), Affective experience in psychotherapy. *Journal of Abnormal Psychology*, 75:267-275.

HUNT, G. M. & AZRIN, N. H. (1973), A community-reinforcement approach to alcoholism. *Behavior Research and Therapy*, 2:91-104.

HUXSTER, H., LOWER, R., & ESCOLL, P. (1975), Some pitfalls in the assessment of analyzability in a psychoanalytic clinic. *Journal of the American Psychoanalytic Association*, 23:90-106.

JACKEL, M. N. (1966), Transference and psychotherapy. *The Psychiatric Quarterly*, 40:43-58.

JACKSON, H. (1958), *Selected Writings of John Hughlings Jackson*, J. Taylor (Ed.), Vol. II. London: Staples.

JOHNSON, A. as reported by English O. S. (1953), The essentials of psychotherapy as viewed by the psychoanalyst. *Journal of the American Psychoanalytic Association*, 1:550-561.

JONES, E. (1920), *Treatment of the Neuroses*. London: Bailliere, Tindall & Cox.

—— (1953), *The Life and Work of Sigmund Freud* (Vol. 1). New York: Basic Books.

KAHANA, R. (1979), Strategies of dynamic psychotherapies with the wide range of older individuals. *Journal of Geriatric Psychiatry*, 12 (1):71-100.

—— (1980), Psychotherapy with elderly patients. In: T. B. Karasu and L. Bellak (Eds.), *Specialized Techniques in Individual Therapy*. New York: Brunner/Mazel.

KANDEL, D. (1966), Status homophily, social context and, participation in psychotherapy. *American Journal of Sociology*, 71:640-650.

KANTROWITZ, J. L., SINGER, J. G., & KNAPP, P. H. (1975), Methodology for a prospective study of suitability for psychoanalysis: The role of psychological tests. *Psychoanalytic Quarterly*, 44:371-391.

KANZER, M. (1961), Verbal and nonverbal aspects of free association. *Psychoanalytic Quarterly*, 30:327-350.

KARASU, T. B. (1977), Psychotherapies: An overview. *American Journal of Psychiatry*, 134:851-863.

KARDINER, A. (1977), *My Analysis with Freud: Reminiscences*. New York: Harper & Row.

KAUFMAN, M. R. (1937), Psychoanalysis in late life depressions. *Psychoanalytic Quarterly*, 6:308-335.

KEPECS, J. G. (1966), Theories of transference neurosis. *Psychoanalytic Quarterly*, 35:497-521.

KERNBERG, O. F. (1967), Borderline personality organization. *Journal of the American Psychoanalytic Association*, 14:641-685.

——— (1968), The treatment of patients with borderline personality organization. *International Journal of Psycho-Analysis*, 49:600-619.

KERNBERG, O. F., BURNSTEIN, E. D., COYNE, L., APPELBAUM, A., HOROWITZ, L., & VOTH, H. (1972), Psychotherapy and psychoanalysis: Final report of the Menninger Foundation psychotherapy research project. *Bulletin of the Menninger Clinic*, 36:3-275.

KHAN, M. M. R. (1960), Regression and integration in the analytic setting: A clinical essay on the transference and countertransference aspects of these phenomena. *International Journal of Psycho-Analysis*, 41:130-146.

KLEIN, H. A. (1960), A study of changes occurring in patients during and after psycho-analytic treatment. In: P. Hoch and J. Zubin (Eds.), *Current Approaches to Psychoanalysis*. New York: Grune & Stratton.

KLEIN, M. (1931), Contribution to the theory of intellectual inhibition. *International Journal of Psycho-Analysis*, 12:206-218.

——— (1952), The origins of transference. *International Journal of Psycho-Analysis*, 33:433-438.

KNAPP, P., LEVIN, S., McCARTER, R., WERMER, H., & ZETZEL, E. (1960), Suitability for psychoanalysis: A review of one hundred supervised analytic cases. *Psychoanalytic Quarterly*, 29:459-477.

KNIGHT, R. P. (1941-42), Evaluation of the results of psychoanalytic therapy. *American Journal of Psychiatry*, 98:434-446.

——— (1948), Psychoanalytically oriented psychotherapy. Panel on psychoanalysis and psychotherapy. *Bulletin of the American Psychoanalytic Association*, 4(3):36-39.

——— (1949), A critique of the present status of the psychotherapies. *Bulletin of the New York Academy of Medicine*, 25:100-114.

——— (1952), An evaluation of psychotherapeutic techniques. *Bulletin of the Menninger Clinic*, 16:113-124.

——— (1953), Borderline states. *Bulletin of the Menninger Clinic*, 17:1012.

KOHUT, H. (1971), *The Analysis of the Self*. New York: International Universities Press.

KOLB, L. C. & MONTGOMERY, J. (1958), An explanation for transference cure, its occurrence in psychoanalysis and psychotherapy. *American Journal of Psychiatry*, 115:414-421.

KOREN, L. & JOYCE, J. (1953), The treatment implications of payment of fees in a clinic setting. *American Journal of Orthopsychiatry*, 23:350-357.

KRIS, E. (1952), *Psychoanalytic Explorations in Art*. New York: International Universities Press.

KUBIE, L. S. (1947), The fallacious use of quantitative concepts in dynamic psychology. *Psychoanalytic Quarterly*, 16(4):507-518.

——— (1948), Symposium on the evaluation of therapeutic results. *International Journal of Psycho-Analysis*, 29:7-23.

——— (1952), Problems and techniques on psychoanalytic validation and progress. In: E. Pumpian-Mindlin (Ed.), *Psychoanalysis as Science: The Hixon Lectures on the Scientific Status of Psychoanalysis*. Stanford, Ca: Stanford University Press.

KUIPER, P. C. (1968), Indications and contraindications for psychoanalytic treatment: A symposium. *International Journal of Psycho-Analysis*, 49:261-264.

LAGACHE, D. (1953), Some aspects of transference. *International Journal of Psycho-Analysis*, 34:1-10.

LANGS, R. (1973), *The Technique of Psychoanalytic Psychotherapy*, Vol. 1. New York: Jason Aronson.

—— (1974), *The Technique of Psychoanalytic Psychotherapy*, Vol. 2. New York: Jason Aaronson.

LAPLANCHE, J. & PONTALIS, J. B. (1973), *The Language of Psychoanalysis*. New York: W. W. Norton.

LEWIN, B. D. (1950), *The Psychoanalysis of Elation*. New York: W. W. Norton.

LEWIN, K. K. (1973-74), Dora revisited. *Psychoanalytic Review*, 60:519-532.

LEVIN, S. (1960), Problems in the evaluation of patient for psychoanalysis. *Bulletin of the Philadelphia Association of Psychoanalysis*, 10:86-95.

—— (1962), Indications for analysis and the problems of analyzability: Discussion. *Psychoanalytic Quarterly*, 31:528-531.

LEVINSON, D. (1978), *The Seasons of a Man's Life*. New York: Knopf.

LIEVANO, J. (1967), Observations about payment of psychotherapy fees. *Psychiatric Quarterly*, 41:324-338.

LIMENTANI, A. (1972), The assessment of analyzability: A major hazard in selection for psychoanalysis. *International Journal of Psycho-Analysis*, 53:351-361.

LIPTON, S. (1977), The advantages of Freud's technique as shown in his analysis of the rat man. *International Journal of Psycho-Analysis*, 58(3):255-273.

LOEWALD, H. (1960), On the therapeutic action of psychoanalysis. *International Journal of Psycho-Analysis*, 41:16-33.

—— (1971), The transference neurosis: Comments on the concept and the phenomenon. *Journal of the American Psychoanalytic Association*, 19:54-66.

LOEWENSTEIN, R. M. (1956), Some remarks on the role of speech in psychoanalytic technique. *International Journal of Psycho-Analysis*, 37:460-468.

—— (1963), Some considerations on free association. *Journal of the American Psychoanalytic Association*, 11:451-473.

—— (1964), As reported by Altman. Panel report: Theory of psychoanalytic therapy. *Journal of the American Psychoanalytic Association*, 12:620-631.

LOOMIE, L. S. (1961), Some ego considerations in the silent patient. *Journal of the American Psychoanalytic Association*, 9:56-78.

LORAND, S. & CONSOLE, W. A. (1958), Therapeutic results in psycho-analytic treatment without fee: Observation on therapeutic results. *International Journal of Psycho-Analysis*, 39:59-65.

LORION, R. P. (1973), Socioeconomic status and traditional treatment approaches reconsidered. *Psychological Bulletin*, 79:263-270.

—— (1974), Patient and therapist variables in the treatment of low-income patients. *Psychological Bulletin*, 81:344-354.

LOWER, R. B., ESCOLL, P. J., & HUXSTER, H. K. (1972), Basis for judgments of analyzability. *Journal of the American Psychoanalytic Association*, 20:610-621.

LUBORSKY, L., CHANDLER, M., AUERBACH, A. H., COHEN, J., & BACHRACH, H. M. (1971), Factors influencing the outcome of psychotherapy: A review of quantitative research. *Psychological Bulletin*, 75(3):145-185.

LUBORSKY, L. & SCHIMEK, J. (1964), Psychoanalytic theories of therapeutic and developmental change: Implications for assessment. In: P. Worchel & D. Byrne (Eds.), *Personality Change*. New York: Wiley.

LUBORSKY, L., SINGER, B., & LUBORSKY, L. (1975), Comparative studies of psychotherapies: Is it true that "everyone has won and all must have prizes?" *Archives of General Psychiatry*, 32:995-1008.

MACALPINE, I. (1950), The development of the transference. *Psychoanalytic Quarterly*, 19:501-539.

MAHLER-SCHOENBERGER, M. (1942), Pseudo-imbecility: A magic cap of invisibility. *Psychoanalytic Quarterly*, 11:149-164.

MANN, J. & SEMRAD, E. V. (1959), Conversion as process and conversion as symptom in psychosis: In: Felix Deutsch (Ed.), *On the Mysterious Leap from the Mind to the Body*. New York: International Universities Press.

MARCUS, S. (1976), Freud and Dora: Story, history, case history. In: *Representations: Essays on Literature and Society*. New York: Random House, pp. 247-310.

MARGOLIN, S. as reported by English, O. S. (1953), The essentials of psychotherapy as viewed by the psychoanalyst. *Journal of the American Psychoanalytic Association*, 1:550-561.

MARMOR, J. (1962), A re-evaluation of certain aspects of psychoanalytic theory and practice. In: *Modern Concepts of Psychoanalysis*. New York: Citadel Press.

McLEAN, H. V. (1948), Treatment of the neuroses. *Cincinnati Journal of Medicine*, 29:545-555.

MEERLOO, J. A. M. (1961), Modes of psychotherapy in the aged. *Journal of American Geriatric Society*, 9:225-234.

MEHLMAN, R. D. (1976), *Transference Mobilization, Transference Resolution, and the Narcissistic Alliance*. Paper presented at the Scientific meeting of the Boston Psychoanalytic Society and Institute, February 25, 1976.

——— (1977), Narcissistic alliance. *International Encyclopedia of Psychiatry, Psychology, Psychoanalysis and Neurology*, 7:439-441. New York: Aesculapius Publishers.

MENNINGER, K. (1963), *The Vital Balance*. New York: Common Viking Press.

MEYERS, B. S. (1976), Attitudes of psychiatric residents toward payment of psychotherapy fees. *American Journal of Psychiatry*, 133(12):1460-1462.

MODELL, A. H. (1975), A narcissistic defense against affects and the illusion of self-sufficiency. *International Journal of Psycho-Analysis*, 56:275-282.

MOORE, B. E. & FINE, B. D. (1968), *A Glossary of Psychoanalytic Terms and Concepts* (2nd Edition). New York: American Psychoanalytic Association.

MUNROE, R. L. (1955), *Schools of Psychoanalytic Thought*. New York: Dryden.

MURRAY, J. M. (1964), Narcissism and the ego ideal. *Journal of the American Psychoanalytic Association*, 12:477-511.

MUSLIN, H. & GILL, M. (1978), Transference in the Dora case. *Journal of the American Psychoanalytic Association*, 26(2):311-328.

MYERSON, P. (1973), The establishment and disruption of the psychoanalytic modus vivendi. *International Journal of Psycho-Analysis*, 54(1):133-142.

NACHT, S. (1964), Silence as an integrative factor. *International Journal of Psycho-Analysis*, 45:299-303.

NACHT, S. & LEBOVICI, S. (1959), Indications and contraindications for psychoanalysis of adults. In: S. Nacht (Ed.), *Psychoanalysis of Today*. London & New York: Grune & Stratton.

NAMNUM, A. (1968), The problem of analyzability and the autonomous ego. *International Journal of Psycho-Analysis*, 49:271-275.

NEUGARTEN, B. (1964), *Personality in Middle and Late Life*. New York: Atherton Press.

——— (1979), Time, age and the life cycle. *The American Journal of Psychiatry*, 136:7, 887-894.

NUNBERG, H. (1926), The will to recovery. *International Journal of Psycho-Analysis*, 7:64-78.

────── (1928), Problems of therapy. In: *Practice and Theory of Psychoanalysis*. New York: Nervous and Mental Disease Monographs, 1948.

────── (1933), The theoretical basis of psychoanalytic therapy. In: S. Lorand (Ed.), *Psychoanalysis Today: Its Scope and Function*. New York: Covici Friede.

────── (1951), Transference and reality. *International Journal of Psycho-Analysis*, 32:1-9.

────── (1955), *Principles of Psychoanalysis*. New York: International Universities Press.

OBERNDORF, C. P. (1942), Factors in psychoanalytic therapy. *American Journal of Psychiatry*, 98:750-756.

────── (1946), Constant elements in psychotherapy. *Psychoanalytic Quarterly*, 15:435-449.

────── (1950), Unsatisfactory results of psychoanalytic therapy. *Psychoanalytic Quarterly*, 19:393-407.

OLSEN, P. (1977), Recognitions of the soul. In: K. Frank (Ed.), *The Human Dimension in Psychoanalytic Practice*. New York: Grune & Stratton.

OREMLAND, J. D. (1972), Transference cure and flight into health. *International Journal of Psychoanalytic Psychotherapy*, 1:61-75.

ORNSTEIN, P. H. & ORNSTEIN, A. (1975), On the interpretive process in psychoanalysis. *International Journal of Psychoanalytic Psychotherapy*, 4:219-271.

ORR, D. W. (1954), Transference and countertransference: A historical survey. *Journal of the American Psychoanalytic Association*, 2:621-670.

PANEL DISCUSSION (1956), Problems of transference. *International Journal of Psycho-Analysis*, 37:367-395. (Waelder, Zetzel, Hoffer, Spitz, Winnicott, Crapf, Servadio).

PAOLINO, T. J. JR. & McCRADY, B. S., Eds. (1977), *The Alcoholic Marriage: Alternative Perspectives*. New York: Grune & Stratton.

────── Eds. (1978), *Marriage and Marital Therapy: Psychoanalytic, Behavioral and Systems Theory Perspectives*. New York: Brunner/Mazel.

PETERFREUND, P. (1975), How does the analyst listen? On models and strategies in the psychoanalytic process. In: D. Spence (Ed.), *Psychoanalysis and Contemporary Science*. New York: International Universities Press.

PFEFFER, A. Z. (1963), The meaning of the analyst after analysis: A contribution to the theory of therapeutic results. *Journal of the American Psychoanalytic Association*, 11:229-244.

PFEIFFER, E. (1971), *Psychotherapy with Elderly Patients*. Paper presented at the 24th Annual Meeting of the Gerontological Society, Houston.

────── Ed. (1972), *Sigmund Freud and Lou Andreas-Salomé Letters*. New York: Harcourt, Brace, Jovanovich.

PIAGET, J. (1937), *The Construction of Reality and the Child*. New York: Basic Books, 1954.

POLLOCK, G. H. (1960), The role and responsibilities of the psychoanalytic consultant. *International Journal of Psycho-Analysis*, 41:633-636.

RACKER, H. (1968), *Transference and Countertransference*. New York: International Universities Press.

RADO, S. (1939), Developments in the psychoanalytic conception and treatment of the neuroses. *Psychoanalytic Quarterly*, 8, 427-437.

RAMZY, I. (1974), How the mind of the psychoanalyst works: An essay on psychoanalytic inference. *International Journal of Psycho-Analysis*, 55:543-550.

RANGELL, L. (1954a), Similarities and differences between psychoanalysis and dynamic psychotherapy. *Journal of the American Psychoanalytic Association*, 2:734-744.

────── (1954b), Psychoanalysis and dynamic psychotherapy: Similarities and differences. *Journal of the American Psychoanalytic Association*, 2:152-166.

RAPAPORT, D. & GILL, M. M. (1959), The points of view and assumptions of meta-psychology. *International Journal of Psycho-Analysis*, 40:153-162.

RECHTSCHAFFEN, A. (1959), Psychotherapy with geriatric patients: A review of the literature. *Journal of Gerontology*, 14:73-83.

REDLICH, F. C., HOLLINGSHEAD, A. B., ROBERTS, B. H., ROBINSON, H. A., FREEDMAN, L. Z., & MYERS, J. K. (1953), Social structure and psychiatric disorders. *American Journal of Psychiatry*, 109:729-734.

REICH, W. (1933), *Character Analysis*, T. Wolfe, trans. Rangeley, Maine: Orgone Institute Press.

REID, J. R. & FINESINGER, J. E. (1952), The role of definitions in psychiatry. *American Journal of Psychiatry*, 109:413-420.

RICHFIELD, J. (1954), An analysis of the concept of insight. *Psychoanalytic Quarterly*, 23:390-408.

ROAZEN, P. (1971), *Freud and His Followers*. New York: Alfred A. Knoff.

ROCHLIN, G. (1973), *Man's Aggression: The Defense of the Self*. Boston: Gambit.

ROCKWELL, F. V. (1956), Psychotherapy in the older individual. In: O. J. Kaplan (Ed.), *Mental Disorders in Later Life* (2nd edition). Stanford, Ca.: Stanford University Press.

ROGERS, C. R. (1940), The processes of therapy. *Journal of Consulting Psychology*, 4 (5): 161-164.

—— (1942), *Counseling and Psychotherapy*. Boston: Houghton Mifflin.

—— (1947), Psychotherapy. In: W. Dennis (Ed.), *Current Trends in Psychology*. Pittsburgh: University of Pittsburgh Press.

—— (1957), The necessary and sufficient conditions of therapeutic personality change. *Journal of Consulting Psychology*, 21:95-103.

ROGOW, A. A. (1978), A further note to Freud's "fragment of analysis of a case of hysteria." *Journal of the American Psychoanalytic Association*, 26(2):331-356.

ROSENZWEIG, S. (1936), Some implicit common factors in diverse methods of psychotherapy. *American Journal of Orthopsychiatry*, 6:412-415.

ROWDEN, D., MICHEL, J., & DELLEHAY, R., et al. (1979), Judgments about candidates for psychotherapy: The influence of social class and insight-verbal ability. *Journal of Health and Social Behavior*, 11:51-58.

RUSSELL, B. (1929), *Mysticism and Logic*. New York: W. W. Norton.

RYCROFT, C. (1958), An inquiry into the function of words in the psychoanalytical situation. *International Journal of Psycho-Analysis*, 39:408-415.

SANDLER, A. M. (1978), Problems in psychoanalysis of an aging narcissistic patient. *Journal of Geriatric Psychiatry*, 11(1):5-36.

SANDLER, J., HOLDER, A., KAIVENOKA, M., KENNEDY, H. F., & NEURATH, L. (1969), Notes on some theoretical and clinical aspects of transference. *International Journal of Psycho-Analysis*, 1(4):633-646.

SASHIN, J. I., ELDRED, S. H., & VAN AMERONGEN, S. T. (1975), A search for predictive factors in institute supervised cases: A retrospective study of 183 cases from 1959-1966 at the Boston Psychoanalytic Society and Institute. *International Journal of Psychoanalysis*, 56:343-359.

SCHAFER, R. (1958), Regression in the service of the ego: The relevance of a psychoanalytic concept for personality assessment. In: G. Lindzey (Ed.), *Assessment of Human Motives*. New York: Rinehart & Co., pp. 119-148.

—— (1973), The idea of resistance. *International Journal of Psycho-Analysis*, 54: 259-285.

SCHLESSINGER, N. & ROBBINS, F. (1974), Assessment and follow-up in psychoanalysis. *Journal of the American Psychoanalytic Association*, 22:542-567.

SCHMIDEBERG, M. (1938), Intellectual inhibition and disturbances in eating. *International Journal of Psycho-Analysis*, 19:17-22.

SEGAL, H. (1958), Fear of death. Notes on the analysis of an old man. *International Journal of Psycho-Analysis*, 39:178-181.

SEMRAD, E. (1967), The organization of ego defenses and object loss. In: D. M. Moriarity (Ed.), *The Loss of Loved Ones*. Springfield, IL: Charles Thomas, pp. 126-134.

SHADER, R., BINSTOCK, W., & OHLY, J. et al. (1969), Biasing factors in diagnosis and disposition. *Comprehensive Psychiatry*, 2:81-89.

SHAPIRO, L. N. (1973), Confrontation with the real analyst. In: G. Adler and P. G. Meyerson (Eds.), *Confrontations in Psychotherapy*. New York: Jason Aronson.

SHARPE, E. F. (1947), The psychoanalyst. *International Journal of Psycho-Analysis*, 28:1-11.

SINGER, E. (1965), *Key Concepts in Psychotherapy*. New York: Random House, 338-358.

——— (1970), *Key Concepts in Psychotherapy*. New York/London: Basic Books.

——— (1977), The fiction of analytic anonymity. In: K. Frank (Ed.), *The Human Dimension in Psychoanalytic Practice*. New York: Grune & Stratton.

SILVERBERG, W. V. (1948), The concept of transference. *Psychoanalytic Quarterly*, 17: 303-321.

SJOBACK, H. (1973), *The Psychoanalytic Theory of Defensive Processes*. New York: Halsted Press.

SNYDER, W. (1947), The present status of psychotherapeutic counseling. *Psychological Bulletin*, 44:297-386.

SOBELL, M. B. & SOBELL, L. C. (1973), Alcoholics treated by individualized behavior therapy: One-year treatment outcome. *Behavior Research & Therapy*, 2:599-618.

STEELE, E. as reported by English, O. S. (1953), The essentials of psychotherapy as viewed by the psychoanalyst. *Journal of the American Psychoanalytic Association*, 1:550-561.

STEKEL, W. (1940), *Technique of Analytical Psychotherapy*. New York: W. W. Norton.

STERBA, R. F. (1934), The fate of the ego in analytic therapy. *International Journal of Psycho-Analysis*, 15:117-126.

——— (1940), The dynamics of the dissolution of the transference resistance. *Psychoanalytic Quarterly*, 9:363-379.

——— (1953), Clinical and therapeutic aspects of character resistance. *Psychoanalytic Quarterly*, 22:1-20.

STONE, L. as reported by Chassell, J. O. (1949), Psychoanalysis and psychotherapy. *Bulletin of the American Psychoanalytic Association*, 5:60-64.

——— (1951), Psychoanalysis and brief psychotherapy. *Psychoanalytic Quarterly*, 20:215-236.

——— (1954), The widening scope of indications of psychoanalysis. *Journal of the American Psychoanalytic Association*, 2:567-594.

——— (1961), *The Psychoanalytic Situation*. New York: International Universities Press.

STRACHEY, J. (1934), The nature of the therapeutic action of psychoanalysis. *International Journal of Psycho-Analysis*, 15:127-159.

——— (1953), Editor's footnote. In: S. Freud (1905), Fragment of an analysis of a case of hysteria. *Standard Edition*, 7:118. London: Hogarth Press.

——— (1955), Editor's footnote in J. Breuer & S. Freud (1895), Studies on hysteria. *Standard Edition*, 2:1-310. London: Hogarth Press.

——— (1962), Editor's footnote to S. Freud (1898), Sexuality in the aetiology of the neuroses. *Standard Edition*, 3:259-287. London: Hogarth Press, 273.

———— (1966), Editor's introduction to S. Freud (1888-1892). Papers on hypnotism and suggestion. *Standard Edition*, 1:63-71. London: Hogarth Press.

SULLOWAY, F. F. (1979), *Freud, Biologist of the Mind*. New York: Basic Books.

SZASZ, T. S. (1963), The concept of transference. *International Journal of Psycho-Analysis*, 44:432-443.

TICHO, E. A. (1972), Termination of psychoanalysis: Treatment goals, life goals. *The Psychoanalytic Quarterly*, 41:315-333.

THOMPSON, C. (1938), Notes on the psychoanalytic significance of the choice of analyst. *Psychiatry*, 1:205-216.

TOMLINSON, T. M. (1967), The therapeutic process as related to outcome. In: C. R. Rogers (Ed.), *The Therapeutic Relationship and Its Impact*. Madison: University of Wisconsin Press.

TOMLINSON, T. M. & HART, J. T. (1962), A validation scale. *Journal of Consulting Psychology*, 26:74-78.

TYSON, R. & SANDLER, J. (1971), Problems in the selection of patients for psycho-analysis: Comments on the application of the concepts of "indications," "suitability" and "analyzability." *British Journal of Medical Psychology*, 44:211-228.

VAILLANT, G. E. (1971), Theoretical hierarchy of adaptive ego mechanisms. *Archives of General Psychiatry*, 24:107-118.

———— (1974), Natural history of male psychological health. II. Some antecedents of healthy adult adjustment. *Archives of General Psychiatry*, 31:15-22.

———— (1977), *Adaptation to Life*. Boston: Little, Brown & Co.

WACHTEL, P. L. (1976), *Psychoanalysis and Behavior Therapy: Toward an Integration*. New York: Basic Books.

WAELDER, R. (1956), Introduction to the discussion on problems of transference. *International Journal of Psycho-Analysis*, 37:367-369.

WALDHORN, H. F. (1960), Assessment of analyzability: Technical and theoretical observations. *Psychoanalytic Quarterly*, 29:478-506.

———— (1967), In: *Indications for Psychoanalysis*. (Kris Study Group Monograph II). New York: International Universities Press.

WALKER, A., RABLIN, R. A., & ROGERS, C. R. (1960), Development of a scale to measure process change in psychotherapy. *Journal of Clinical Psychology*, 16:79-85.

WALLERSTEIN, R. S. (1965), The goals of psychoanalysis: A survey of analytic viewpoints. *American Psychoanalytic Association Journal*, 13:748-770.

———— (1969), Psychoanalysis and psychotherapy (The relationships of psychoanalysis to psychotherapy: Current issues). *International Journal of Psycho-Analysis*, 50: 117-126.

WALLERSTEIN, R., ROBBINS, L., SARGENT, H., LUBORSKY, L. (1956), The psychotherapy research project of the Menninger Foundation. Rationale, method and sample use. *Bulletin of the Menninger Clinic*, 20:221-280.

WAYNE, G. J. (1953), Modified psychoanalytic therapy in senescence. *Psychoanalytic Review*, 40:99-116.

Webster's Seventh New Collegiate Dictionary (1967), Springfield, MA: G & C Merriam Company.

WEIGERT, E. (1949), Existentialism and its relation to psychotherapy. *Psychiatry*, 12: 399-412.

———— (1954), The importance of flexibility in psychoanalytic technique. *Journal of the American Psychoanalytic Association*, 2:702-710.

———— (1961), The nature of sympathy in the art of psychotherapy. *Psychiatry*, 24:187-196.

WEINSHEL, E. M. (1971), The transference neurosis: A survey of the literature. *Journal of the American Psychoanalytic Association*, 19:67-88.

WHEELIS, A. (1956), Will and psychoanalysis. *Journal of the American Psychoanalytic Association*, 4:285-303.

WINDHOLZ, E. as reported by Rangell, L. (1954), Similarities and differences between psychoanalysis and dynamic psychotherapy. *Journal of the American Psychoanalytic Association*, 2:732-744.

WINNICOTT, D. W. (1955), Metapsychological and clinical aspects of regression within the psychoanalytical set-up. *International Journal of Psycho-Analysis*, 36:16-26.

WOLSTEIN, B. (1954), *Transference: Its Meaning and Function in Psychoanalytic Therapy*. New York: Grune & Stratton.

——— (1960), Transference: Historical roots and current concepts in psychoanalytic theory and practice. *Psychiatry*, 23:159-72.

WOOLF, L., Ed. (1953), *A Writer's Diary. Extracts from the Diary of Virginia Woolf*. New York: Harcourt, Brace.

YAMAMOTO, J. & GOIN, M. (1966), Social class factors relevant for psychiatric treatment. *Journal of Nervous Mental Diseases*, 142:332-339.

ZARSKY, E. L. & BLAU, D. (1970), The understanding and management of narcissistic regression and dependency in an elderly woman observed over an extended period of time. *Journal of Geriatric Psychiatry*, 3:160-176.

ZETZEL, E. R. (1956), Current concepts of transference. *International Journal of Psycho-Analysis*, 37:369-376.

——— (1965), The theory of therapy in relation to a development model of the psychic apparatus. *International Journal of Psycho-Analysis*, 46:39-52.

——— (1966), Additional notes upon a case of obsessional neurosis: Freud, 1909. *International Journal of Psycho-Analysis*, 47:123-129.

——— (1968), The so-called good hysteric. *International Journal of Psycho-Analysis*, 49:256-260.

——— (1970), *The Capacity for Emotional Growth*. New York: International Universities Press.

ZETZEL, E. R. & MEISSNER, W. W. (1973), Neurotic development and analyzability. In: *Basic Concepts of Psychoanalytic Psychiatry*. New York: Basic Books.

ZILBOORG, G. (1952), Some sidelights on free associations. *International Journal of Psycho-Analysis*, 33:489-495.

ZINBERG, N. E. (1963), Psychiatry: A professional dilemma. *Daedelus*, 92(4):808-823.

INDEX

239